Police Use of Force

Important Issues Facing the Police
and the Communities They Serve

Police Use of Force

Important Issues Facing the Police and the Communities They Serve

Edited by

Michael J. Palmiotto

Wichita State University
School of Community Affairs
Wichita, Kansas, USA

CRC Press
Taylor & Francis Group
Boca Raton London New York

CRC Press is an imprint of the
Taylor & Francis Group, an **informa** business

CRC Press
Taylor & Francis Group
6000 Broken Sound Parkway NW, Suite 300
Boca Raton, FL 33487-2742

Library of Congress Cataloging-in-Publication Data

Names: Palmiotto, Michael, editor.
Title: Police use of force : important issues facing the police and the
communities they serve / Michael J. Palmiotto, editor.
Other titles: Police use of force (CRC Press)
Description: Boca Raton, FL : CRC Press, 2017. | Includes bibliographical
references and index.
Identifiers: LCCN 2016006347 | ISBN 9781498732147
Subjects: LCSH: Police brutality--United States. | Police shootings--United
States. | Police-community relations--United States. | Police
misconduct--United States.
Classification: LCC HV8141 .P59353 2017 | DDC 363.2/32--dc23
LC record available at http://lccn.loc.gov/2016006347

Visit the Taylor & Francis Web site at
http://www.taylorandfrancis.com

and the CRC Press Web site at
http://www.crcpress.com

Printed and bound in the United States of America by Publishers Graphics,
LLC on sustainably sourced paper.

For my wife, Emily, for her unstinting love and support.

CONTENTS

PREFACE

This book on the *Use of Force* fills a void in a major issue facing American society. The use of force takes into consideration the social, criminal, and human rights issues important to a democratic country, such as the United States. The important aspect in dealing with the use of force is that it pits the police against the people they are sworn to protect and serve. It may not be the intent of either the police or the public they deal with to have a confrontation which could lead to deadly force being used.

Deadly force often has been used when an offender or citizen refuses to cooperate with a police request or refuses to listen to an order to perform a specific action. Sometimes, when the citizen refuses to cooperate, the officer, who has the authority to force the issue, may do so, which can lead to serious injury or death. This of course can escalate to demonstrations or riots.

In the early twenty-first century the use of force, especially deadly force, by the police has become a volatile issue that may cost police officers their lives or livelihood. There are activists and organizations that contend that the police are wrong when they use force, especially deadly force. It is generally held at the time of this writing that most police officers consider that they will be considered guilty until proven innocent when using force against a citizen. Along these same lines police officers hold the premise that they will not be supported and that people will do the politically correct thing to maintain the support of politicians and activists. Of course there are those that consider police actions generally wrong and abusive anytime the police resort to the use of force.

Police Use of Force provides a broader perspective than current books on the issue. Books in print include officer involved shooting, self-defense and the use of force, in the kill zone, a cop view of deadly force. A 1992 book published by the Police Executive Research Forum (PERF) on *What WE Know about Deadly Force* and several general books on the use of force all discuss the preceding issues.

The 10 chapters of this book are contributed by authorities in specific areas of the use of force. The contributors consist of those having law enforcement, academic, and research experience. They include technology experts, community psychologists, political scientists, legal scholars, training experts, and criminal justice personnel. With the use of force issue not going away anytime soon, this book should provide a good foundation for understanding the concern.

Chapter 1 by Professor Michael Palmiotto provides a review of social control, crime control, and the use of force from ancient times to modern day. After a look at "kin" police, ancient Roman, Greek, and Egyptian police are briefly examined. Policing in Europe and England is covered. The development of modern policing is discussed. Throughout history the use of force has been used in all societies and cultures and is primarily documented or integrated into the history of a specific society.

Chapter 2 on the "Use of Force" defines brutality and the use of force by the police. There are numerous definitions on what the use of force is when conducted by the police. This chapter addresses the issue when force is "necessary" and "reasonable" as used by the police. Also, covered in this chapter is the "improper" use of force which falls into two categories: "unnecessary" and "excessive." The emerging use of force issues are covered, the use of force continuum is discussed, and examples of excessive use of force by the police are provided, including the Abner Louima case and the Rodney King case, which received national attention.

Chapter 3 on deadly force defines the term and reviews when deadly force may be acceptable. The chapter explains when the police have the authority to use force and when it is not appropriate. For example, police can never use deadly force against someone committing a minor offense. Deadly force can be traced back to the middle ages when felony crimes were punishable by death. If an agent of the state killed someone committing a felony, the agent was considered to be doing the state a favor because the felony was punishable by death anyway. By comparison, in contemporary society, the only felony that can be punishable by death is first degree murder. In the United States, the use of deadly force by government officers can be traced back to colonial times and the Civil War. Most states have laws defining deadly force. When police officers use deadly force against a suspect or offender it usually involves firearms. However, neck holds by the police can also lead to death. The danger they create are discussed and an example is provided. The issue of deadly force acts committed by the police was as much a controversial issue in the last century as it is today.

Chapter 4 on "Nonlethal Weapons and Technology" written by Dr. Szde Yu reviews the controversial issue of nonlethal weapons. The primary concern has been that use of nonlethal weapons can still result in injury to the recipient. This chapter will discuss police use of force, Tasers, and other less lethal weapons.

The historical influence and impact of the police has been carefully reviewed by Dr. Laurence French in the "Militarization of the Police." Professor French traces the militarization of the police to early American history, noting that at times during American history, the military has functioned as the police. Currently, American society gives attention to the police on their strategies and actions that often reflect similar functions the military performs. Dr. French recommends that "law enforcement personnel especially chiefs, sheriffs, et cetera need to lose the military attire that attempts to present themselves as admirals and generals" (p. 78).

"Racism and Profiling" authored by Dr. Michael Birzer reviews theories about whether there is a problem of black crime and how the police relates to minorities. Does racism influence police behavior? If so, how? Do the police profile certain people? Is their profiling based on economic status, race, gender, or ethnic groups? Good profiling versus bad profiling is discussed.

Chapter 7, "Legal Issues," by Alison Brown deals with court decisions involving the use of excessive and deadly force. Court decisions pertinent to the United States Supreme Court, Federal Circuit Courts, and state courts are reviewed. Those uses of force and deadly force cases that have made an impact on police procedures are discussed.

Chapter 8, "Psychological Perspectives," by Jody Beeson reviews the cognitive decision-making process that influences the level of force applied by an officer in specific circumstances. The suspect's demeanor, the officer's personality, prior experience, and cognitive appraisal of the risk for harm to himself/herself and others are key factors that determine the cognitive processes that an officer will utilize in the decision-making process. Understanding this process is essential for preparing officers to make appropriate decisions when under pressure. This chapter discusses those processes.

Chapter 9, "Political Perspective," written by Carolyn Schmidt provides an insight to how activists and politicians view the use of force, specifically deadly force. Dr. Schmidt states that the political impact of police violence being viewed as reasonable or unreasonable depends upon the view of society. Views of police violence may depend upon race, ethnic background, religion, and economic class.

The last chapter, "Training and Prevention," authored by Professors Vladimir Sergevnin and Darrell L. Ross, deals with the important issue of training the police to prevent excessive force, examining when appropriate force can be used and emphasizing prevention of unnecessary use of force. Accordingly, this chapter discusses various prevention and training methods and recommends more than firearms training. Not only do officers need range training in using their firearms; they also need training in situations that teaches them when they may—and may not—use their firearms.

EDITOR

Michael J. Palmiotto, PhD, is a professor of criminal justice and undergraduate coordinator of the Criminal Justice Department at Wichita State University, Wichita, Kansas. He was formerly a police officer in New York, serving in White Plains and Scarsdale. He has experience establishing and operating a police training facility in Western Pennsylvania. Dr. Palmiotto earned a master's degree from John Jay College (CUNY) and a doctorate from the University of Pittsburgh. He has been a faculty member of several universities.

Dr. Palmiotto has published 12 books, 20 book chapters, and numerous articles on criminal justice and law enforcement. He has published in the areas of criminal investigation, community policing, police misconduct, police globalization, and police training among others. He is the recipient of two Fulbright awards.

CONTRIBUTORS

Jodie Beeson
School of Community Affairs
Wichita State University
Wichita, Kansas

Michael L. Birzer
School of Community Affairs
Wichita State University
Wichita, Kansas

Alison Brown
School of Community Affairs
Wichita State University
Wichita, Kansas

Laurence Armand French
Justice Works Institute
University of New Hampshire
Durham, New Hampshire

Michael J. Palmiotto
School of Community Affairs
Wichita State University
Wichita, Kansas

Darrell L. Ross
Department of Sociology,
    Anthropology and Criminal
    Justice
Valdosta State University
Valdosta, Georgia

Carolyn Speer Schmidt
Department of Criminal
    Justice
Wichita State University
Wichita, Kansas

Vladimir A. Sergevnin
Department of Law
    Enforcement
Western Illinois University
Macomb, Illinois

Szde Yu
School of Community Affairs
Wichita State University
Wichita, Kansas

Use of Force Throughout History

Michael J. Palmiotto

☐ Introduction

Human beings establish governments for economic development; to maintain the safety of their citizens; and to control the natural environment. Governments are given or take social control for their state to maintain social order. A government without social order cannot protect its citizens and the country cannot economically prosper. There have been examples of countries in chaos that lack order or economic prosperity. "The idea of social control is often associated with the physical or coercive powers of the police. It is certain that a police force is an important and prominent example of social control" (Chriss, 2013: 36).

Since the early twentieth century social control has come to mean a concept that describes activities that involve the coordination, integration, regulation, or adjustment of individuals or groups to an ideal standard of conduct. Social control has come to mean regulation, either in terms of interpersonal relationships with other people; or regulating human behavior in terms of public safety; or enforcing laws and punishing violators of laws (Chriss, 2013: 23). Social control is often associated with the physical or coercive power of the police. The role of police has a great influence with social control in any culture. However, social norms can influence the behavior of people. For example, specific vocations and professions have specific values which informally control the behavior of fellow workers (Chriss, 2013: 36).

Walter Reckless associates social control as crime control, with the police in modern society having this responsibility. Crime control, according to Reckless, hopes to curb crime and hold it in check, stop it from spreading and provide society with protections from law violators (Reckless, 1955: 655). For decades the police have frequently been placed in situations in which they are given no choice but to use force. Often they are accused of brutality even when they had no other option than to use force to subdue the offender.

Law enforcement with its emphasis on social and criminal control can be traced to ancient times when the family, tribe, or clan assumed the responsibility for the safety of their members. The concept of "kin police" evolved with the idea that an attack against any member of the group was an attack on the entire group. In essence, the enforcers were the people who enforced their laws. Punishment was often inhumane and retaliatory. Branding and mutilation were often used, along with stoning, burning, and crucifixion. Unlike contemporary America, which has a formal process to maintain social control, ancient societies had an informal process to deal with violation against their kin group (Palmiotto, 2013: 11).

As mentioned in the previous paragraph policing can be traced to ancient times. Ancient policing utilized basic features which are still used to this day. This involves the approach of interpersonal mediation. The police were also expected to perform a wide variety of tasks, including firefighting, which had little to do with crime control. The first police organization was created in Egypt in around 3000 BC. Each administrative jurisdiction, there were 42 of them, had an official responsible for justice and security. In ancient Greece, policing duties were assigned to magistrates responsible for municipal upkeep (Britannica, 2014).

Throughout history those in authority have used force against those below them in status, power, and authority. Although specific information is lacking, abuses of authority most likely did occur in ancient societies. In ancient societies individuals addressed these violations themselves. Punishment or retaliation used such inhumane techniques as mutilation and branding. Stoning, burning, and crucifixion were also used as forms of punishment.

The killing of an Egyptian guard for abusing a Hebrew slave provoked Moses to perform the act of murder. This is an ancient example of use of abusive force against an underling. Although there is little information on the abuse of lower status people in ancient times, it seems likely that regular abuse of force took place. Realistically, it would appear that slaves and criminals were recipients of the use of force. It should be mentioned that governments would have to implement laws before law enforcement could be established. The Babylonians, Assyrians, Egyptians, Greeks, and Romans all had a system to maintain order. From the time when some form of government existed, social control was important for governments to function successfully. Governments or those people in authority want to maintain their power and control over the populace and often this requires that force be used.

Similar to ancient Greece, the Roman empire was not peaceful but had crimes committed not only in Italy but also in the provinces of Rome. Threats to the public order frequently occurred. The Roman empire, as in modern society, had similar crimes. There were thefts, riots between sports fans, travel was dangerous, and burglaries occurred. Unlike our modern day, Rome did not have a police force that could compare to twenty-first century police. As with the people of today, the Roman people desired public order. The Romans had four forms of police, with the police coming primarily from the military. The Roman provinces had the authority to maintain order with civilian police who were Roman soldiers in the province under the control of the magistrates and municipal governments. The local magistrates had the authority to use limited force to deter crime, make arrests, and conduct trials for minor offenses (Fuhrmann, 2012: 9).

There were many types of Roman policing. It should be noted that Roman military policing was carried out by soldiers. The types of Roman police were the civilian police which functioned in the provinces. These special troops were under the direct command of the emperor. The emperor was the symbol of public order. The next level of policing was at the provincial or gubernatorial level. Provincial governors were responsible for security and public order and could activate the troops, who functioned as police, under their command. The last level of Roman military policing consisted of out posted soldiers who performed policing among civilians. Out posted soldiers often functioned without supervision (Fuhrmann, 2012: 10). It has been difficult to locate the use of excessive force by the various levels of Roman military police but it seems that excessive force was used by the military police, at least periodically. A good example of excessive force at that time was the scourging of Jesus at the pillar and the crowning with thorns.

Emperor Augustus made a number of contributions to law enforcement. He established the *Praetorian Guard* from the military legions to protect the life and property of the emperor. The *urban cohorts*, units of 500–600 men, were created to keep the peace of Rome. The *praefectus urbi,* the prefect of the city, was given responsibility to maintain order in the city. The *curators urbis* came under the direction of the *praefectus urbi* and were responsible for a specific area of the city. Augustine also established the *vigils of Rome* to assume firefighting duties. Rome was plagued with fires and a unit was needed to spot and fight fires. The *vigils of Rome* also had the responsibility for patrolling the streets (Palmiotto, 2013: 12). Although the literature is weak on the use of force by Roman military police; it would appear that police trained as soldiers would use force or even excessive force to enforce the laws of the Roman empire.

The French police can be traced to the middle ages but this section will only discuss the French police in the nineteenth century. Upon obtaining the leadership of France, Napoleon established law and order to eliminate the havoc caused by the French Revolution. Two police forces were inherited from the French Revolution: the gendarmerie, the model for police organizations in Europe during the nineteenth century and the administrative police, a civilian police unit. The two units were different from each other with the gendarmerie being a paramilitary unit primarily policing the countryside. The gendarmerie came under the control of the minister of war and was not accountable to civilian authorities. The administrative police or civilian police were assigned to policing in towns of over 5000 people and reported to the minister of general police in Paris. During periods of rebellion the gendarmerie proved to be very effective in repression, which has to be considered the use of excessive force to gain law and order (Broers, 1999: 27–35).

The British can trace their concept of policing to the Danish and Anglo-Saxon invaders. Originally citizens were responsible for peace keeping duties. The mutual pledge system was established by Alfred the Great, 870–901 and has been recognized as the initiating of modern policing. Under the mutual pledge system, every man was responsible not only for his own actions but also for the actions of his neighbor. It was every citizen's duty to raise the "hue and cry" when a crime was committed, to collect his neighbors, and to pursue a criminal who fled from the district. History is inundated with individuals who, when given the opportunity to apprehend offenders, would use their authority to abuse individuals arrested. It seems likely that that the conditions under the "hue and cry" made possible the use of excessive force against law violators.

In the thirteenth century, the constable system evolved as a rural form of policing. The constable maintained social order within the parish, the population center of worship. The constable was also a royal officer responsible for keeping the king's peace by the "hue and cry." In the urban area the "watch and ward" system was implemented and the duties of its officers were patrolling the streets, guarding the town's gates, arresting strangers at night, and preventing break-ins.

In 1789 the Gordon riots occurred. This was a Protestant protest against laws passed providing Catholics with special rights. King George ordered that the military be permitted to shoot the rioters at their own discretion. On the king's directive the soldiers killed or fatally wounded 300 persons and ended the riots (Reppetto, 2012: 4) The Gordon riots provide an example of excessive force being used by the British government as well as an example of deadly force.

On August 16, 1819 the Peterloo Massacre took place in Manchester, England when the cavalry charged into a crowd of 50,000 people who were protesting the economic conditions of that period. There was famine and unemployment and a lack of voting opportunities for the lower economic class. The protesters wanted the reform of parliamentary representation. Voting was restricted to adult male owners of land. The number of deaths or injured was not accurately determined. It is estimated that 11–15 people were killed, including women, and about 500 people were injured. The reaction to Peterloo was a crackdown on the reform the demonstrators wanted. A number of Peterloo leaders were tried for sedition. The government supported the cavalry charge. The army's action provides a good example of use of force. Since police forces were not designed to control demonstrations the army functioned in lieu of the police. The action of the army in their cavalry charge indicates a strong case of use of excessive force (Peterloo Massacre, 2016 [Spartacus-Education]).

During the late seventeenth century the policing system began to break down and corruption was rampant and the force unable to deal with social and economic upheaval. Crime in the seventeenth and early eighteenth century began to increase. It should be recognized that where ever corruption exists so does brutality. Corruption and brutality go hand in hand. In 1829, Sir Robert Peel established the Metropolitan Police of London as an answer to incompetence of the police and their corruption. The Metropolitan Police Act and the establishment of the London Police Department became the model for the United States. From the time when some form of government existed social control had to be put into place. Governments or those people in authority want to maintain their power and control over the populace. The putting down of riots forcefully by the police and military provides a good example of governments making every effort to maintain control over the populace.

In 1855, the Sunday Trading Riots lasted for four consecutive Sundays starting the last Sunday in June and continuing on the following three Sundays in July. Working men by the 1850s were allowed to make known their grievances but not allowed to riot. Two reasons for the riots were influenced by religious measures, with the passing of laws: first to close drinking establishments during specific hours on Sundays and second, to prohibit all Sunday trading, except for the selling of meat and fish, newspapers, and cooked meals. These laws created a stir among working people who did their shopping on Sundays, believing goods were cheaper on this day. In addition, many workers were paid on Saturday evening which gave them sufficient funds to shop on a Sunday (Harrison, 1965: 219–222).

On Sunday June 24 a meeting was held in Hyde Park with 200,000 people attending. The police attempted to prevent the public meeting. During the meeting wealthy people were arriving at Hyde Park. The crowd jeered, taunted, shouted, and used improper language for the time. Disorder was created which was condemned by the Monday papers. In the following weeks the Metropolitan Police Commissioner forbade a meeting for Sunday, July 1 in Hyde Park. The order was ignored and approximately 150,000 people gathered in Hyde Park. "The police endured great provocation, but could not restrain themselves when a large eel was removed from the Serpentine and was passed over the heads of the crowd on to a police detachment. In comparison with the previous Sunday, fewer promenading carriages arrived, but the police decided to clear the carriageway. With their truncheons they beat down opposition from the crowd and carried off 72 prisoners to the Vine Street police station" (Harrison, 1965: 223). The police used force on this Sunday and may have used excessive force to control the crowd and make the arrests. Because of the disorder in Hyde Park police brutality had become a preoccupation of the government. The government appointed a commission to look into the events of Sunday July 1 (Harrison, 1965: 224). The accusation of brutality was such a big issue that the government investigated the claim. Several police officers were fired and the incident faded away.

During the fall of 1887 radical demonstrations took place in London despite the government forbidding political meetings. On Sunday, November 13, 14,000 police with special constables and armed soldiers dispersed the crowd. The demonstrators were protesting being unemployed and were attempting to meet in Trafalgar Square. Bloody Sunday, which November 13 has been named, resulted in three fatal injuries, 75 people hospitalized and 50 people arrested (Keller, 2009). As previous writings indicate the police did use force to break-up demonstrations during the nineteenth century, and it could be said that they used excessive force.

☐ English Police: Political and Social History

The development of policing in America has its roots in England. The Eastern coast of the United States was settled predominately by English people who brought the English law enforcement system to the American colonies. As in England, American law enforcement developed slowly. It was not until the 1840s that the United States initiated a modern municipal policing concept. In 1844 the New York legislature provided funds for a night and day watch creating a consolidated police force. The New York model was adopted by other municipalities. With the creation of the modern police force, three issues came to the forefront. The first was the adoption of uniforms, the second arming the police, and third, the appropriate use of force by the police in making arrests. The first issue, the adoption of uniforms, was not highly contested. The second issue of arming the police was somewhat controversial with the talk of militarization of the police. The final issue dealing with the police has remained an issue from the 1840s and 1850s until today, the early decades of the twenty-first century.

The police have been given the authority to use force when necessary to maintain peace and order. The term enforcement actually means that force can be used. It is important to recognize that law enforcement have the legal authority to use force when offenders are threatening them or someone else or refuse to follow police commands. We as citizens have the responsibility to obey police orders. Citizens do not have the legal right to fight the police when requested to perform a specific action by the police.

Skolnick and Fyfe clearly state the important aspect of the issue when they write: As long as some members of society do not comply with law and resist the police, force will remain an inevitable part of policing. Cops, especially, understand that. Indeed, anybody who fails to understand the centrality of force to police work has no business in a police uniform (Skolnick and Fyfe, 1939).

Most rational people will acknowledge that society recognizes that the police have the legal authority to use force to protect themselves or another person who may be in danger. The issue pertaining to the use of force with regard to citizen upheaval occurs when the population believes that inappropriate force or excessive force was used unnecessarily. Of course it is at times difficult to be objective both on the part of the community and police if the use of force was inappropriate. More will be written about this issue in later chapters.

Although the police have authorization to use force, there have been times when an inappropriate use of force has been used in a cruel manner. The slave patrol of the south from colonial days until the mid-1860s provides an example of police brutality. Slave patrols walked into slave quarters and if met with resistance, the slaves would be punished. Slaves were beaten, and there were times when slaves who did not cooperate with slave patrols were beaten to death. At times slave patrollers would beat a slave without cause (Hadden, 2001: 106–114).

During the Civil War riots in New York City the city police used force to curb the riots. One police captain led 80 police officers in dispersing 2000 rioters, and on that same day clubbed a man to death (Reppetto, 2011: 48). Use of force continued in policing after the Civil War. Another captain known for his use of force was Captain Alexander "Clubber" Williams who was known for clubbing individuals. He stated "There is more law at the end of a policeman's nightstick than in a decision of the Supreme Court." He insisted until his death that he never clubbed anyone "that did not deserve it" (Ephemeral, 2009).

Thomas Byrnes who rose from detective to chief inspector, the number two position in the New York City police department, established a rogues' gallery containing pictures of criminals, had a daily lineup of arrested thieves, and required crooks to register at headquarters. He established a zone that forbids criminals from entering on physical punishment. Thomas Byrne was able to support his informal rules with a force not supported by the law. He was a practitioner of the third degree, using physical beatings and psychological torture. For example, he used a sweatbox, a small room where prisoners were kept for days without human contact. Byrnes had the support of political and business leaders and could get as tough as he wanted with criminals (Reppetto, 2011: 55–56).

The use of force or excessive use of force as used by Williams and Byrnes continued into the twentieth century. In 1929 President Herbert Hoover established the National Commission on Law Observance and Enforcement, known as the Wickersham Commission. The Commission submitted their *Report on Lawlessness in Law Enforcement* in 1931. The term "third degree" was defined by the Commission as used by the police to mean "the employment of methods which inflict suffering, physical or mental, upon a person, in order to obtain from that person information about a crime." The Report further states. "The third degree is a secret and illegal practice" (National Commission on Law Observance and Enforcement, 1931: 3). The use of the third degree or inappropriate force is illegal and prohibited by the American constitution. Specifically the following rights are violated: "personal liberty, bail, protection from personal assault and battery, the presumption of innocence until conviction of guilt by due process of law and the right to counsel ...." (National Commission on Law Observance and Enforcement, 1931: 3–4).

The Wickersham Commission found that the police's use of the third degree was widespread and common. Physical brutality, illegal detention, and refusal to allow those arrested access to counsel was common. Brutality and violence in making arrests was common but primarily used by urban police officers and not federal law enforcement personnel. The third degree was primarily used by patrol officers and detectives against arrested persons suspected of committing a crime. However, it is used on other persons suspected of committing a crime. *The Report on Lawlessness in Law Enforcement* came to three conclusions (National Commission on Law Observance and Enforcement, 1931: 7):

First, that they are the type of lawless enforcement of law which is especially liable to create resentment against law and government.

Second, that they may compel an appellate court to reverse the conviction of a guilty man, thus requiring additional trials and sometimes resulting in the escape of a guilty man from conviction.

Third, and perhaps the most seriously, that unfair practices may result in the conviction of the innocent.

The Wickersham Report found the "third degree" unacceptable behavior of the police. They emphasized that social order be controlled within the constitutional and legal framework established by the founding fathers and legislative bodies. The report strongly condemned the use of the "third degree" or police brutality for any reason. It cannot be justified on legal or moral grounds regardless of the seriousness of the offense. The Wickersham Report condemns the "third degree" as evil. The Supreme Court of Illinois has said: "To defend the third degree is to advocate lawlessness—often flagrant and habitual—committed by those who are specifically charged with the enforcement of the law" (National Commission on Law Observance and Enforcement, 1931: 181). The Commission specified four specific evils of the "third degree" (National Commission on Law Observance and Enforcement, 1931: 181–192):

1. The third degree involves the danger of false confessions.

2. The third degree impairs police efficiency.

3. The third degree impairs the efficient administration of criminal justice in the courts.

4. The third degree brutalizes the police, hardens the prisoner against society, and lowers the esteem in which the administration of justice is held by the public.

The "third degree" and police brutality provide the police with a negative image. It also provides the criminal justice process with a poor impression by the public and finally communication between the police and/or other criminal justice agencies lose their credibility with the community and public in general.

This chapter has dealt with the inappropriate use of force from ancient times to recent centuries. The following chapters deal with more specific topics and are relevant to the twenty-first century. These chapters include use of force, deadly force, legal issues pertaining to use of force, a psychological perspective, and training and prevention of excessive use of force.

☐ Summary

The use of force by those individuals representing government, whether the military or those responsible to maintain social order, has been permitted when individuals or groups of individuals have failed to follow the laws of the government. Violence can be traced from ancient times to our present day. Information on the maintaining of order in ancient times is somewhat sketchy and informal. Throughout history those in authority have used force against those below them in status, power, and authority. Although specific information is lacking, abuse of authority most likely occurred in ancient societies. In ancient societies individuals addressed these violations themselves.

Crimes were committed in ancient Egypt, Greece, and the Roman Empire and their provinces. Threats to public order frequently occurred. Unlike our modern day, Rome did not have police that could compare to twenty-first century police. Like the people of today the Roman people wanted public order. Similar to our modern times the Romans had many types of police.

The British began developing the concept of modern policing during the middles ages. Policing was evolving and continues to evolve in the twenty-first century. Modern American policing uses the British model as their policing foundation.

☐ References

Britannica. 2014. Ancient Policing, http://www.britannica.com/EBchecked/topic/46/467289/police/260916/P...

Broers, M. 1999. The Napoleonic police and their legacy, *History Today*, May, 49(5), 22–23.

Chriss, J. J. 2013. *Social Control: An Introduction*, Second Edition, Cambridge, UK: Polity.

Ephemeral New York. 2009. "The NYPD"s infamous 'Clubber' Williams, http://ephemeralnewyork.wordpress.com/2009/11/16/the-nypds-club.

Fuhrmann, C. 2012. *Policing the Roman Empire: Soldiers, Administration, and Public Order*, New York: Oxford University Press.

Hadden, S. E. 2001. Slave Patrols: Law and Violence in Virginia and the Carolinas, *Association for the Study of African American Life and history*.

Harrison, B. 1965. The Sunday Trading Riots of 1855, *The Historical Journal*, 8(2), 219–245.

Keller, L. 2009. Bloody Sunday demonstration, 1887. *The International Encyclopedia of Revolution and Protest*, Immanuel Ness (Ed.), Blackwell Reference Online, http://www.blackwellreference.com/public/tocnode?id=078140518.

National Commission on Law Observance and Enforcement. 1931. *Report on Lawlessness in Law Enforcement*, Washington, DC: U.S. Government.

Palmiotto, M. J. 2013. *Policing: Concepts, Strategies, and Current Issues in American Police Forces*, Kindle Publishing. www. amazon.com.

Peterloo Massacre. 2016. http://spartacus-educational.con/PRpeterloo.htm.

Reckless, W. C. 1955. *The Crime Problem*, Second Edition, New York, New York: Appleton-Century-Crofts.

Reppetto, T. 2011. *American Police: The Blue Parade 1845–1945*, New York: The Free Press.

Reppetto, T. C. 2012. *American Police: 1945–2012*, New York: Enigma Books.

Skolnick, J. H. and J. J. Fyfe. 1939. *Above the Law*, New York: The Free Press.

Police Use of Force

Michael J. Palmiotto

A government, to be successful economically, needs and must maintain an orderly society and protect the safety of its citizens. Only when governments can provide a functional society based on social order can citizens and the country as a whole be productive. The peacekeepers who have been given the responsibility to maintain order in society are the police. Along with society giving the police the authority to maintain social order comes the use of force. Alpert and Smith (1994: 481) stated the following about the police: "The authority of the police to use force represents one of the most misunderstood powers granted to representatives of government. Police officers are authorized to use both psychological and physical force to apprehend criminals and solve crimes."

The authority and power of law enforcement officers is the biggest difference between them and the rest of citizens in society. The United States Civil Rights Commission (1981: 481–482) stated the following about the police: "Police officers possess awesome powers. They perform their duties under conditions with the public eye upon them. Police officers are permitted only a margin of error in judgment under conditions that impose high degrees of physical and mental stress. Their general responsibility to preserve peace and enforce the law carries with it the power to arrest and to use force—even deadly force" (v).

In this chapter we will review the controversial issue connected with the legitimate and illegitimate authority of the police to use force. The illegal, unacceptable, or excessive use of force has often been referred to as *police brutality*. "The lawless exercise of force employed in excess is popularly called police brutality" (Skolnick and Fyfe, 1993: xvi). Modern policing was initiated in the 1840s with the New York City Police Department. Since the beginning of modern policing the use of force, some claim excessive force, by police officers has been a controversial issue periodically receiving a great deal of attention.

The *use of force* by the police can be defined as occurring "any time the police attempt to have citizens act in a certain way" (Roberg et al., 2000: 310). Alpert and Dunham (2004: 20–21) provide definitions of the use of force: "The consensus among law enforcement officials and researchers is that force can be defined as physical action taken to control the movement or freedom of another individual. If there is no resistance to certain police actions, such as handcuffing or the use of firm grips and 'come-along' holds, the use of force may be inconsequential or negligible and no record of the activity need be made."

There are some who consider verbal abuse a form of police brutality while others consider this to consist solely of the excessive use of physical force. However, we begin to be concerned about such use of force used when it is seen as excessive or as an over-reaction to a given situation. For example, a highway patrol officer politely asks to see your driver's license after stopping you on the highway. While there is force involved, that is, you have no recourse but to comply, this is not seen as excessive. How about if the same highway patrol officer asks to see your license while hitting you with a flashlight and yelling obscenities? Here, the force used is definitely going to be seen as excessive, if there is nothing else that indicates violence or resistance on the part of the motorist.

Incidents of police use of excessive force have included beating civil rights protestors, deliberate kicking and choking someone while making arrests, and unprovoked use of deadly force when attempting to control riots and disturbances. Individual officers, a group of officers, or a large number of officers within the police department, thus pervading the culture of an entire police department, may carry out acts of excessive use of force. In the late 1990s in Los Angeles, such excessive force incidents even included officers who robbed banks, shot drug dealers, and then planted weapons on them (Time, March 6, 2000; Newsweek, 2000; Walker, 2000a,b).

It has been recognized that most occupations provide their members with opportunities for misconduct, and police agencies and their officers are no exception. There are three elements to occupational misconduct: "(1) opportunity structure and its accompanying techniques of rule violations, (2) socialization through occupational experiences, (3) reinforcement and encouragement from the occupational peer group, i.e., group support for certain rule violations" (Barker, 1977: 356). The opportunities for police officers to violate laws and departmental policies discouraging the excessive use of force are many. Techniques for accomplishing police operations often go hand in hand with the opportunities for such rule breaking. The socialization of police behavior begins in the recruit-training academy where the police recruit is instructed into the "us" versus "them" mentality. With this attitude the public becomes the enemy and the only friends of a police officer are his fellow police officers. Many cultures, including the United States, encourage group and peer support and police officers should not be considered any different from anyone else in this regard. From the initial day that the recruit enters training he or she quickly learns that the support of fellow police officers is important to his or her career success and future well-being as a police officer. The recruit quickly learns that it is generally best to look the other way when he or she sees fellow officers violating departmental rules and laws by using excessive force. The philosophy of "brother and sister" police officers in which the police subculture becomes a way of life can thus lead to police misconduct.

☐ Use of Excessive Force

Police officers hold a position of legal authority, control, and power over citizens. In our society, it is not unusual for citizens to challenge laws they consider unfair or unjust and thus challenge police authority. Examples of specific situations that police have to deal with which can lead to police misconduct or accusing the police of misconduct include mass demonstrations and sit-down strikes. Civil disobedience and direct confrontation with police authority may be encouraged or may even be a part of the strategy of groups who intentionally want to confront the police. The United States and other democratic countries offer citizens redress when they believe that the police have been involved in police misconduct or perceived misconduct. Citizens in an open society know they have rights and avenues of redress open to them when acts of police misconduct or perceived acts of police misconduct are committed by police officers. The foundations of citizen rights in American society are found in the U.S. Constitution, specifically in the Bill of Rights, which constitutes the first 10 amendments to the Constitution. In 1789, the Bill of Rights was adopted by the founding fathers to protect citizens from governmental abuses from the federal government and their agents. In the twentieth century the U.S. Supreme Court, to protect citizens from governmental abuses from the states and their agents, extended the Bill of Rights to be applicable to the states. The U.S. Supreme Court interpreted the "due process clause" of the Fourteenth Amendment as a protection for citizens against abuses by the state. Currently, the Bill of Rights protects citizens from both federal and state abuses and policing misconduct. It should be remembered that local police officers, city, village, town, and county officers, are agents of the state and the Bill of Rights applies to these police officers in their law enforcement authority.

When citizens directly challenge the authority of the police, it is often perceived by the latter as an attack on them. In confrontations between the police and citizens, the police often find themselves in many "no-win" situations. In such situations, the police are always open to criticism and formal charges of misconduct regardless of how they handled the situation. The police are often attacked for violating the legal rights of citizens in the manner they use in enforcing the law. Frequently police officers are accused of violating the civil rights of citizens under the U.S. Constitution and other relevant laws. Although some of these accusations may be erroneous, the police have the responsibility to use their legal authority within prescribed legal and constitutional restrictions. Further, in any society, the police can be successful in maintaining social order and solving crime only with the cooperation of citizens. When the police lose the confidence of those citizens because they are perceived as brutal or prone to unprovoked violence, the public will cease supporting the police in performing their law enforcement activities. This can include failing to providing information about crimes committed, refusing to serve as witnesses of crimes committed in their presence, or not supporting police when they want salary increase, and other benefits.

☐ Police Use of Excessive Force as Misconduct and Deviance

According to Thomas Barker (1978), the range of police misconduct includes the following activities: perjury, sex on duty, sleeping on duty, drinking and using drugs on duty, and police brutality. When a police officer abuses people physically, this is likely to be lamented and calls from observers for corrective action become loud. This, as we know, coincides neatly with how sociologists have defined the concept of deviance. The meaning of the term *"deviance"* is "conduct which the people of a group consider so dangerous or embarrassing or irritating that they bring special sanctions to bear against the persons who exhibit it," and that "the only way an observer can tell whether or not a given style of behavior is deviant, then, is to learn something about the standards of the audience which is responding to it" (Erikson, 1966: 3). Thus, police brutality can be defined as occurring when a police officer uses force in a way that the usual standards, as understood by the community, for such use are violated. Here are a few examples of police use of force:

- A police officer uses a threatening hand gesture and verbally intimidates a suspect who is being questioned regarding a crime.

- A police officer grabs hold of a motorist and shakes him or her for being slow in responding to a request to participate in a field sobriety test.

- A police officer beats and kicks an individual being interrogated about some discrepant information that he or she provided earlier.

- A number of police officers use pepper spray on an inebriated college student who refuses to obey their command to "move along."

As you can see, these examples run the gamut of possibilities in terms of use of force, from the possibly appropriate to the highly inappropriate. Are they all instances of police brutality? Without considering the situational factors in each of the above decisions to use force and without knowing what happened before each event, we are at a disadvantage in terms of judging whether the legal standards and police polices regarding the appropriate level of force used has been met.

Similar incidents of police use of excessive force in making arrests and in controlling disturbances have occurred throughout history. Such incidents may be carried out by individual officers, a group of officers, or even involve the entire police department or a large number of officers within the police department. Lundman (1980: 140–141) notes that five conditions must be met for police misconduct to be attributed to a dysfunctional police organization, that is, when occupational deviance becomes organizational deviance. Let us apply his ideas to the issue of excessive use of force by the police:

1. It must be contrary to norms or rules maintained by others outside of the police department. Here we should ask if such deviant actions of excessive force are formal violations of existing laws and expectations of police behavior.

2. The deviant action must be supported by internal operating norms that conflict with the police organization's formal goals and rules. To be considered a form of organizational deviance, fellow officers and higher-ups must be perceived as tacitly supporting the excessive use of force even though there may be official rules and policies forbidding it.

3. Compliance with the internal operation norms supportive of police misconduct must be ensured through recruitment and socialization. From this perspective, individuals who are apt to react with force and violence are sought and hired by the department.

4. There must be peer support of the misbehavior of colleagues. Officers are complicit in ignoring inappropriate uses of force by their colleagues and supportive of them when confronted by higher authorities or concerned members of the public.

5. For improper behavior to be organizationally deviant, it must be supported by dominant administrative coalition of the police organization. Those who are in command and those who have influence over the day-to-day operations of the department condone inappropriate or excessive use of force. One major reason for the acceptance of police use of inappropriate force is the "code of silence."

☐ Police Use of Excessive Force and the Code of Silence

As mentioned earlier, the code requires that police officers look the other way when they observe their fellow officers involved in acts of misconduct, in this case, brutality. Skolnick and Fyfe (1993: 110) write that the "code of silence" exists and that it "typically is enforced by the threat of shunning, by fear that informing will lead to exposure of one's own derelictions, and by fear that colleagues' assistance may be withheld in emergencies." Skolnick and Fyfe (1993) believe that, in reality, police officers will not deny assistance to fellow officers, even those who may have informed on fellow officers in emergencies. They suggest that the fear upon which the code of silence appears based is imagined, or that officers are paranoid when they believe that fellow police officers will not come to their aid when they need assistance. According to Skolnick and Fyfe (1993: 112), "The code of silence then, is not one that is enforced by assassins lurking in dark alleys or arranging for drug dealers to terminate cops who inform. The police code of silence is an extreme version of a phenomenon that exists in many human groups. It is exaggerated in some police departments and some police units because cops so closely identify with their departments, their units, and their colleagues, that they cannot even conceive of doing anything else."

☐ Forms of Police Excessive Use of Force

Incidents of the "use of excessive force" by police officers, or "police brutality," can be traced to early times in police history. In 1967, the President's Crime Commission (*Task Force: The Police*: 180) found that abuses in cities studied ranged from discourtesy to physical use of excessive force against people of all ages. The Commission further reported, "While allegations of excessive physical force receive the most attention, verbal abuse and discourtesy were probably greater irritants to community relations" (The President's Commission on Law Enforcement and Administration of Justice, 1967: 180). The same report found that many people, specifically minority groups, believe that the police are often engaged in excessive and unnecessary physical force. Similar to present day efforts, the Commission was unable to determine exactly how serious a problem the excessive use of physical force was in American police departments. However, although the Commission believed police brutality was a major problem, it was deemed to be not "systematic."

Barker (1978: 71) claims that when the public charges the police with excessive use of force, they are referring to any or all of the following actions by the police:

1. Profane and abusive language

2. Commands to move on or go home

3. Field stops and searches

4. Threats

5. Prodding with a nightstick or approaching with a pistol

6. The actual use of "physical force"

Most people would agree that it is inappropriate for police officers to use profanity and abusive language toward the general public. Although abusive language will not be good for police–community relations, should it be considered police brutality? The police have the authority to require people to move along or request they go home often for safety reasons. There are times when groups of individuals block entry into stores or the sidewalk making it difficult for people to pass. The police also have the authority to tell juveniles to go home when communities have curfews.

Third Degree

Some forms of "police brutality" have also been referred to as the *third degree*. The term "third degree" came into vogue during the early decades of the twentieth century and refers to the use of excessive force during the questioning of suspects. Apparently, the term "first degree" presumably means the arrest, the "second degree" the transportation to a place of confinement, and the "third degree" the interrogation, which often means brutality (Skolnick and Fyfe, 1993: 43). In 1930, the American Bar Association's Committee on the Lawless Enforcement of the Law reported, "We can only say that the 'third degree,' in the sense of rigid and severe examination of men under arrest by police officers or prosecuting attorneys or both, is in use almost everywhere if not everywhere in the United States" (Skolnick and Fyfe, 1993: 45). The National Commission on Law Observance and Enforcement (1931) (the Wickersham Commission) appointed by President Herbert Hoover reported, in 1931, that the third degree, which it defined as "the inflicting of pain, physical or mental, to extract confessions or statements" was widespread throughout the United States (Skolnick and Fyfe, 1993: 45). In 1947, the President's Commission on Civil Rights, appointed by President Truman, reported similar findings of excessive physical abuse by the police (181). The United States Civil Rights Commission (1961: 181) concluded, "Police brutality is still a serious problem throughout the United States."

Although it appears that the third degree or police brutality does not occur to the extent that it did in the early decades of the twentieth century, it would be unrealistic to assume that it does not occur at all. Incidents of third degree questioning have occurred not only in poorly administered police departments that lack concern about how their officers treat people, but also in departments that are managed well and concerned about the treatment of citizens they serve.

Major Incidents of Police Use of Excessive Force

The last decade of the twentieth century saw numerous incidents of excessive use of physical force by police officers. Such incidents have continued into the twenty-first century. The first event of excessive use of force that received national and international attention in the 1990s was the Rodney King incident. This event took place on March 3, 1991 in Los Angeles, California. The incident began at approximately 12:40 am when two California Highway Patrol (CHP) officers detected King speeding on the freeway. Apparently King's car passed the CHP car from the rear and passed the officers. The CHP officers paced the King vehicle. The officers activated their emergency equipment and signaled for King to stop. King failed to stop and continued to drive and ran a stop sign and a red traffic light. Later, King explained that he failed to stop because he was afraid of getting a traffic summons, which could result in his probation, for an earlier robbery conviction, being revoked. The CHP officers notified the LAPD (Los Angeles Police Department) that they were pursuing a vehicle at a high rate of speed. King finally stopped his automobile along a curbside where he was ordered out of his car. While this was taking place police officers from other agencies arrived at the scene. There were two passengers in King's vehicle who were ordered to get out of the car. They complied and were taken into police custody. Initially, King refused to leave the automobile and was struck with a Taser. When King finally came out, he was struck in the head with nightsticks and kicked several times by police officers. It appears that King was struck approximately 56 times by police officers. There were somewhere between 21 and 27 police officers who were witnesses or participants to the beating of King. The injuries King sustained consisted of a broken cheekbone, a fractured eye socket, missing teeth, kidney damage, skull fractures, external burns, and permanent brain damage (Christopher Commission, 1991).

What made the King-beating incident significantly different from earlier alleged occasions of police brutality was that a private citizen videotaped this incident. This videotape eventually fell into the hands of Cable News Network, which showed the King beating in the United States and throughout the world. The incident clearly shows excessive use of physical force by police officers at its worst. When brutality is alleged, often a police administrator investigates and takes appropriate actions based upon what is discovered. There is no doubt that the King beating gave the LAPD a black eye. Similar incidents, discussed later in this section that occurred in the 1990s, further damaged the reputation of the LAPD.

Several years after the King incident, another scandalous act of excessive use of force occurred on the eastern coast of the United States. On the morning of August 9, 1997, several New York City police officers responded to a fight taking place outside a club in Brooklyn. When the police officers arrived, one Abner Louima, in attempting to break up the melee, became drawn into the conflict. During the fight, one officer was punched and it was believed that Louima was the culprit. Louima was taken into custody. On the way to the 70th precinct police beat Louima with their fists in their patrol vehicle. While at the precinct, Louima, who was handcuffed, was taken to a restroom where a police officer rammed a 2–3 ft stick into Louima's rectum. Within a short period of time an ambulance was called and Louima was hospitalized. A nurse reported the incident to the Police Internal Affairs Unit. Within hours of the report, the Louima incident became a local and national sensation. Similar to the Rodney King incident, which affected the credibility of the LAPD negatively, the Abner Louima incident discredited the public image of the NYPD (New York City Police Department).

There are parallels and differences between the Rodney King beating and the Abner Louima case. Rodney King had a criminal history and failed to stop his vehicle when told to do so by police officers. The beating of King was a classic example of excessive use of physical force. The assault on Louima was bizarre; the lawyer of a codefendant of the officer who placed the stick up Louima's rectum condemned the act as defying "humanity" and labeled the officer who performed it as a "monster." Both the King and Louima cases were tried in federal court eventually and the police officers responsible were convicted of crimes.

King and Louima were both African American men who were brutalized by white police officers. The acts of brutality by white police officers against black men cannot fail to raise the question of racism. The LAPD chief and the NYPD commissioner both characterized these acts of police brutality as aberrations and denied that racism played a part in these incidents. Police critics agree that these acts were aberrations, but only in that white police officers used excessive physical force against blacks, which received wide publicity, and then were punished.

What We Know About Police Use of Force[*]

Bayley and Garofalo (1989) observed that it was quite rare in police–citizen encounters for police to be involved in use of force and injury.

---

[*] Taken from Use of Force, Kenneth Adams Chapter 1, U.S. Department of Justice 1999.

The International Chiefs of Police (IACP) in their study on the use of force found that force is used in less than one-half of 1% of dispatched calls for service (Adams, 1999: 3). The Bureau of Justice Statistics found the nearly 45,000 people had contact with the police during a 12-month period and that about 1% were subjected to the use of force or threat of force (Adam, 1999). The data indicate that the police rarely use force and the following information (1999) was recorded:

- Police use of force occurs at the lower end of the force spectrum, involving grabbing, pushing, or shoving. Relatively minor types of force dominate statistics on police use of force.

- Use of force typically occurs when police are to make arrest and the suspect is resisting. Research indicates that the police are most likely to use force when pursuing a suspect and attempting to exercise their arrest powers.

- A small number of studies suggests that use of force appears to be unrelated to an officer's personal characteristics, such as age, gender, and ethnicity.

- Police use of force is more likely to occur when police are dealing with persons under the influence of alcohol or drugs or with mentally ill individuals. More research needs to be done in this area. Police deal with a wide variety of situations in their work. They encounter minor to serious potentially dangerous deadly incidents.

- A small proportion of officers are disproportionally involved in use of force incidents. More research is needed.

- The incidence of wrongful use of force by police is unknown. Research is critically needed to determine reliability, validity, and precisely how often transgressions of use of force powers occur. We do not know how often police use force in ways that can be judged as wrongful.

- The impact of differences in police organizations, including administrative policies, hiring, training, discipline, and use of technology, on excessive and illegal force is unknown.

- Influences of situational characteristics on police use of force and the transnational nature of these events are largely unknown. Research on police–citizen encounters reveals that use of force by police is situational and transactional.

Use of Force Factors

Before a police officer decides to use force many factors should be considered which include a number of important factors. For instance is the use of force justified, did the officer receive proper training when legally appropriate to use force, and what liability will the police department be accountable for if force is used? The justification of the use of force must be considered the most important decision-making tool before the use of force takes place. Generally, the use of force can be justified when it is necessary to make an arrest, detain a suspect, or to protect the officer or a third party (Wittie, 2013).

The appropriate extent that the use of force can be considered reasonable is the degree necessary to obtain the compliance of a citizen. The determination of reasonable use of force is not an exact science since how and why the force was used against a citizen must be determined, and this is most difficult to evaluate after the fact. According to Wittie, a general definition of "reasonable in relation to the use of force" is any action that is reasonable in relation to the use of force and that a prudent person would believe to be necessary to complete the required task. "According to most experienced officers, reasonableness can be easily determined. However, in a civil or criminal case, the officer is not the one that has to determine if the force was reasonable, but rather, the citizens sitting on the jury will be tasked with determining the reasonableness of the force used by the officer" (Wittie, 2013: 17–18). Studies have indicated that police officers have often arrested people because of their demeanor and at times verbal confrontations have led to police using force against a person. O.W. Wilson, the renowned police administrator and innovator of the twentieth century had this advice to police officers:

> The officer ... must remember that there is no law against making a policeman angry and that he cannot charge a man with offending him. Until the citizen act overtly in violation of the law, he should take no action against him, least of all lower himself to the level of the citizen by berating and demeaning him in a loud and angry voice. The officer who withstands angry verbal assaults builds his own character and raises the standard of the department. (The President's Commission on Law Enforcement and Administration of Justice, 1967: 181)

Use of Force Continuum

The use of force continuum was initiated to provide guidelines to police officers (Hampton, 2009). The guidelines were established to provide officers with information regarding the amount of force may be used against a subject resisting the commands of a police officer in a specific situation. The hope of the guidelines was to clarify for the officer and citizens the appropriate amount of force that an officer could legitimately use in a specific situation. It appears the use of force continuum that evolved in the 1980s and 1990s did not have one specific model for all police agencies. Police agencies established their own approach on a use of force continuum. The National Institute of Justice, in their outline of the use of force continuum, indicated that police agencies have policies to guide police officers to resolve use of force issues (The Use-of-Force Continuum 2009). The use of force continuum has several levels with officers instructed to respond to the level of resistance given to the officer. An example of the National Institute of Justice use of force continuum follows:

- *Officer presence*—No force used. Considered the best way to resolve a situation.

  - The mere presence of a law enforcement officer works to deter crime or diffuse a situation.

  - Officers' attitudes are professional and nonthreatening.

- *Verbalization*—Force is not physical.

  - Officer issues calm, nonthreatening commands, such as "Let me see your identification and registration."

  - Officers may increase their volume and shorten commands in an attempt to gain compliance. Short commands might include "Stop," or "Don't move."

- *Empty-hand control*—Officers use bodily force to gain control of a situation.

  - Soft technique. Officers' use grabs, holds, and joint locks to restrain an individual.

  - Hard technique. Officer's use punches and kicks to restrain an individual.

- *Less lethal methods*—Officers use less lethal technologies to gain control of a situation.

- Blunt impact. Officers may use a baton or projectile to immobilize a combative person.

- Chemical. Officers may use chemical sprays or projectiles embedded with chemicals to restrain an individual (e.g., pepper spray).

- Conducted energy devices (CEDs). Officers may use CEDs to immobilize an individual. CEDs discharge a high-voltage, low-amperage jolt of electricity at a distance.

- *Lethal force*—Officers use lethal weapons to gain control of a situation. Should only be used if a suspect poses a serious threat to the officer or another person.

  - Officers use deadly weapons such as firearms to stop an individual's actions.

It should be noted that there are various articulation of force continuum. According to Ken Wallentine (2009), the typical continuum generally progresses from "officer presence" to "deadly force" in specific steps. Wallentine's illustration follows:

Officer to	→	**Verbal to**	→	**Hand to**	→	**Impact to**	→	**Deadly**
Presence		**Command**		**Control**		**Weapon**		**Force**

Wellentine provides a common sense approach to police officers in their use of force. He recommends the best approach for police use-of-force decision making is a solid understanding of the law of force, linked with sound threat assessment skills. Wellentine recommends obtaining the advice of the department's legal counsel who can provide police officers with the legal understanding, risks of decision making, deficiencies in departmental policies, and in training pertaining to the use of force.

In a study of self-reported data by the Phoenix Police Department on the use of force continuum, Garner et al. found interesting information on the use of force. The authors of the study state, "This research emphasizes that force is a continuum and that understanding the use of force by and against the police requires systematically collected representative samples of incidents where different amount of force—including no force at all—are used" (Garner et al., 1995: 165). The authors provide an excellent recommendation on a use of force study by police officers. Several interesting points were reported by Gardner et al., for instance that the department and news media do not appear to appreciate the common absence of force by police officers. Their study also brings out that there are times when force may be used with no arrest being made. Another interesting point brought out by Gardner et al. is that arrests involving physical force are higher than reported in police–citizen encounters studies (Garner et al., 1995: 165).

In 1989 the *Graham v. Connor* case established guidelines on the use of force stating the "Fourth Amendment jurisprudence has long recognized that coercion or threat thereof effect it. Because the test of reasonableness under the Fourth Amendment is not capable of precise definition or mechanical application, however, its proper application requires careful attention to the facts and circumstances of each particular case, including the severity of the crime at issue, whether the suspect poses an immediate threat to the safety of officers or others, and whether he is actively resisting arrest or attempting to evade arrest by flight." The parameters of the *Graham v. Connor* require police officers to use reasonable force and inform officers when they can use force as the U.S. Supreme Court finds acceptable. To put it simply the courts evaluate the constitutional limits on the use of force on the Fourth Amendment of the U.S. Constitution.

After the *Garner v. Connor* decision, questions were raised as to the necessity of the use of force continuum. Defense attorneys, police trainers, and administrators became concerned that police officers, trainers, and administrators would be exposed to liability and this would be detrimental to police officers accused of using excessive force. Detractors of the use of force continuum claim that it confuses jurors and judges about the legal standard pertaining to excessive force. Additional complaints against the use of force continuum argue that some judges interpret the use of force continuum to equate to the Fourth Amendment's constitutional standard. Police unions report that officers have received inappropriate discipline, including being terminated when the use of force standard was inappropriately used as legal standards (Peters and Brave, 2006).

Many police departments have abandoned their use of force continuum (there are about 50) in favor of a "force option" model. In 2000, the San Jose Police Department became one of the largest police departments to move away from a continuum and toward a "force option" model. The "force options" are not ranked like the use of force continuum. The model considers that the "force options" provide the officers with more flexibility and discretion based on the total facts available to the officer. Use of force continuum models were developed several decades ago to provide officers guidance since the court system did not provide such direction. Detractors of use of force models claim that the continuum models were not based on law but in actuality many are in conflict with laws (Flosi, 2012).

A police officer may only use force when it is reasonable and necessary to make an arrest or detain someone. Anything beyond this guideline is excessive (*Payne v. Pauley*, 2003). The courts will consider the *Graham v. Connor* test and also the need to use force, the relationship between the need and amount of force used, and the extent of the injury on the suspect that the police officer inflicted. The previous sentence supports the "just be reasonable standard" in which advocates of this standard make arguments that the use of force continuum is dying. Fridell et al. argue that police departments should have the use-of-force continuum in departmental policies and officer training. The authors further claim that in the "just be reasonable" departments that police officers are trained that their use of force must be reasonable concerning the totality of the circumstances. Departments using the use of force continuum considers training in reasonableness that includes references to the continuum of several categories or levels of resistance of subjects (Fridell et al., 2015).

Fridell et al. do not support the "just be reasonable" standard and claim that critical analysis has not been conducted to validate the standard. Nevertheless, there are pros and cons.

Arguments for the "just be reasonable" standard (or against continuums) are presented below followed by Fridell et al.'s assessment.

- Continuums do not reflect the constitutional standard of reasonableness.

- Continuums are subjective and the "just reasonable" standard is objective.

- Continuums do not allow for consideration of the "totality of the circumstances."

- The profession will be well served by the added flexibility that "just be reasonable" provides to officers on the streets.

- The continuum is detrimental to quick decision making.

- Jurors cannot understand the nuances of continuums.

- Continuums must be eliminated because common definitions do not exist for the levels of resistance and force.

Fridell et al. counter the claims of the "just be reasonable" standard with the following:

- Continuums are designed to facilitate an officer's understanding of what "reasonable" means and represent the appropriate middle ground between (1) the impossible-to-achieve precise definition and mechanical application of reasonableness and (2) the very imprecise, ambiguous direction to "just be reasonable."

In May 2011 the IACP in cooperation with the Office of Community-Oriented Policing Services (COPS) sponsored a use of force symposium. The purpose of the symposium recognized by the organizations were the importance of research, the inquiry of use of force issues, and the findings of model policies and procedures for policing. Any findings from the study and findings on the use of force issues can assist police administrators to make decisions based upon facts pertaining to the use of force policy and provide a means of improving communications with the public (*Emerging Use of Force Issues*, 2012: 12). "It was suggested that the everyday attitude of officers during the course of their routine activities has as great an influence on perception as the actual use of force" (*Emerging Use of Force Issues*, 2012: 18). This symposium put forward several worthwhile recommendations. The following recommendations are found in the *Emerging Use of Force Issues* in 2012:

- Develop a model communications strategy for law enforcement on the topic on the use of force.

- Develop a national media guide to inform the public regarding the dangers of policing and the necessity to use appropriate force in furtherance of public safety.

- Develop a sustainable online resource library detailing programs and summaries of approaches that have proven to build better relationships between police and their communities (*Emerging Use of Force Issues* 2012: 18).

The symposium participants suggested that behavioral scientists should explore police responses to deadly encounters. The participants further mentioned that neither the police profession nor public understand the hundreds of factors that contribute to use of force incidents. It was brought out that the complexities involved in the decision of an officer to use force is not appreciated or understood. The IACP/COPS symposium made further recommendations as suggested by the participants of the symposium. The recommendations are:

- Propose national use of force reporting standards.

- Collect data and conduct annual national use of force analysis.

- Conduct evaluation of use of force issues for mid-size and small police agencies.

- Charge a single government-sponsored entity with responsibility for collection, analysis, and dissemination of real-time data describing violence directed at the police (*Emerging Use of Force Issues*, 2012: 20).

Police chiefs, according to symposium participants, need to be prepared for use of force issues. They need specialized training in maintaining the confidence of their police officers while communicating with the public. Planning has to be accomplished in advance before addressing an incident and not during an emotionally charged event. The IACP/COP symposium has the following recommendations for police leaders:

- Develop use of force management institute for police leaders.

- Develop use of force management publication for city officials.

Symposium participants indicated they were concerned with the training that officers were receiving in the use of force. Some participants wondered if training was ineffective since it was based on what officers could not do, and not on what they could do. The symposium recommended the following for training:

- Survey to determine nationally the current spectrum of use of force training.

- Develop model in-service use of force training.

- Validate use of force in-service training in pilot departments.

Participants of the symposium wanted access to actual violence used against the police. This information is important to police administrators. If police are subject to a large amount of violence then the use of force can be more readily justified. Also, what is the mindset of the police officers dealing with the public on a daily basis? Police administrators wanted information on the actual threat of violence toward officers and the state of mind of their officers. The recommendation on these questions is as follows:

- Survey to evaluate the use of force mindset of police officers.

- Support efforts such as LEOKA (law enforcement officers killed and assaulted) and the National Center for Prevention of Violence Against Police to collect, evaluate, and publish in real time, data that speaks of trends in violence against the police.

The IACP/COPS symposium provided excellent recommendations that need to be carried out but so far little or no action has taken place to put these recommendations in place. The use of force as an issue has been with American policing since the 1840s when the New York City Police Department was established. Over the decades the use of force has had high and low points as an issue. The IACP/COPS symposium has provided an excellent starting point to solve the use of force issue.

☐ Summary

Generally, a government to be successful must maintain social order and protect its citizens' safety. Governments to maintain social order provide for a peacekeeping force known as the police or law enforcement. The authority and power of the police are the biggest difference between them and the rest of citizens in society. The powers of the police have with it the responsibility to preserve peace and enforce the laws with the power to arrest and use force—even deadly force.

In this chapter controversial issues related to the legitimate and illegitimate authority of the police use of force was covered. The illegal, unacceptable, or excessive use of force often has been referred to as *police brutality*. According to Roberg et al. the use of force can be considered as any time a police officer attempts to force a citizen to behave in a specific way. Basically, a police officer uses force to control the free movement of an individual. The use of force has a broad definition from verbal abuse to excessive physical force being used.

There are numerous methods explaining police use of excessive force from beating civil rights protestors, deliberately kicking someone being arrested, and unprovoked use of deadly force while attempting to control disturbances. It has been recognized that most occupations provide workers with opportunities for misconduct and police departments and police officers are no different. The opportunities for police officers to violate laws and departmental police encouraging the excessive use of force are many.

The range of police misconduct includes activities such as perjury, sex on duty, drinking and using drugs on duty, and police brutality. When a police officer abuses people a call for corrective action can become loud. The use of force runs the gamut from the possibly appropriate to the highly inappropriate. There exists the claim that the police have a code of silence which means they look the other way when they observe their fellow officers involved in an act of misconduct.

Incidents of the "use of excessive force" by police officers or "police brutality" can be traced to early times in police history. In the 1930s the Wickersham Commission discovered that the "third degree," which can be considered police brutality, was commonly used by police officers during this period. The President's Crime Commission in the 1960s found that brutality still existed but not to the extent that occurred in the 1930s. Police brutality that occurred in the 1990s in the Rodney King incident was videotaped and shown worldwide. Approximately some 20 Los Angeles police officers gave King a broken cheekbone, fractured eye socket, missing teeth, skull fractures, external burns, and permanent brain damage. On the other coast, a case that parallels King's is the Abner Louima case. The assault on Louima was bizarre with a police officer placing a stick up Louima's rectum. Both of these cases were tried in federal court and the officers responsible for these incidents were convicted of crimes and sent to prison.

An officer must take into consideration many factors before he decides to use force. He must decide if the force is justified. Generally, the use of force can be justified when it is necessary to make an arrest, detain a suspect, or to protect the officer or a third party. To assist police officers when to use the appropriate amount of force a "use of force continuum" has been developed as a guide for police officers. The continuum functions as a guide as to the appropriate extent of force to be used by a police officer. During the last decade the "use of force continuum" has been challenged. With the Supreme Court *Garner v. Connor* decision of 1989 advocates against the continuum claim the guidelines should be the standards established by the Garner decision. At the time of this chapter's writing the final conclusion has not been reached.

☐ References

Adams, K. 1999. What we know about use of force, in *Use of Force by Police*, Washington, DC: National Institute of Police, p. 1.

Alpert, G. P. and R. G. Dunham 2004. *Understanding Police Use of Force*, New York, New York: University of Cambridge.

Alpert, G. P. and W. C. Smith 1994. How reasonable is the reasonable man? Police and excessive force, *Journal of Criminal Law and Criminology*, Volume 85, 481–501.

Barker, T. 1977. Peer group support for police occupational deviance, *Criminology*, Volume 15, No. 2, 356.

Barker, T. 1978. An empirical study of police deviance other than corruption. *Journal of Police Science and Administration*, Volume 6, No. 3, 264–272.

Bayley, D. and J. Garafolo 1989. The management of violence by patrol officers, *Criminology*, February, Volume 27, No. 1, 1–25.

Christopher, W. 1991. *A Report of the Independent Commission on the Los Angeles Police Department*, Los Angeles: City of Los Angeles.

Cukan, A. 2000. Jurors: The Only Issue Was the Law: Say Race Had No Part in Diallo Verdict? *APBnews.com*. May 18.

Emerging Use of Force Issues: Balancing Public and Officer Safety. 2012. Washington, DC: IACP/COPS.

Erikson, K. T. 1966. *Wayward Puritans: A Study in the Sociology of Deviance*, New York, New York: Allyn and Bacon.

Fielding, N. 2005. *The Police and Social Conflict*, Second Edition, Portland, Oregon: Cavendish.

Flosi, E. D. 2012. Use of force: Downfalls of the continuum, http://www.policeone.com/use-of-force/articles/5643926.

Fridell, L., S. Ijames and M. Bekow, 2015. Taking the straw man to the ground: Arguments in support of the linear use-of-force continuum, *Police Chief*, http:// www.policechiefmagineazine.org/magazine/index.cfm?fuseaction=dispay_arch&article_2548&issue_id=12201.

Fyfe, J. J. 1981. Observations on police deadly force, *Crime and Delinquency*, Volume 27, No. 3, 376–389.

Garner, J. H., T. Schade, J. Hepburn and J. Buchanan 1995. Measuring the continuum of force used by and against the police, *Criminal Justice Review*, Volume 20, No. 2, 146–168. Retrieved from: https://www.ncjrs.gov/App/Publications/abstract.aspx?ID=167543.

Geller, W. A. and M. S. Scott 1992. *Deadly Force: What We Know*, Washington, DC: Police Executive Research Forum.

Hampton, R. E. 2009. *Use of Force Continuum: A Debate*, National Black Police Association.

Herzog, S. 2001. Deviant organizational messages among suspect police officers in Israel, *Policing*, Volume 23, No. 4, 416–438.

Herzog, S. 2002. Police violence in Israel: Has the establishment of a civilian complaints board made a difference? *Police Practice and Research*, Volume 3, No. 2, 119–133.

Kolber, E. 1999. The Peril of Safety: Did Crime-Fighting Tactics put Amadou Diallo at Risk? *The New Yorker*, p. 50 (March issue). Retrieved from http://www.newyorker.com/magazine/1999/03/22/the-perils-of-safety.

Lundman, R. J. 1980. *Police and Policing: An Introduction*, New York, New York: Holt, Rinehart, and Winston.

National Commission on Law Observance and Enforcement. 1931. *Report on Police*, Washington, DC: U.S. Government Printing Office.

Newsweek. 2000. L.A's bandits in blue: A shocked city investigates charges that its cops lied, stolen and shot suspects for sport, *Newsweek*, Volume 155, No. 18, 48.

Palmiotto, M. J. 1997. *Policing: Concepts, Strategies, and Current Issues in American Police Forces*, Durham, North Carolina: Carolina Academic Press.

Peters, J. and M. A. Brave 2006. Force continuums: Are they still needed? *P and S Police and Security News*, Volume 22, No. 1, 2.

Roberg, R., J. Crank and J. Kuykendall 2000. *Police and Society*, Second Edition, Los Angeles, California: Roxbury.

Skolnick, J. H. and J. J. Fyfe 1993. *Above the Law*, New York, New York: The Free Press.

Terrill, R. J. 1990. Alternative perceptions of independence in civilian oversight, *Journal of Police Science and Administration*, Volume 17, No. 2, 77–83.

The President's Commission on Law Enforcement and Administration of Justice. 1967. *Task Force Report: The Police*, Washington, DC: U.S. Government Printing Office, p. 181.

The Use-of-Force Continuum. 2009, August 4. Retrieved 2015, from http://www.nij.gov/topics/law-enforcement/officer-safety/use-of-force/pages/continuum.aspx.

Time. 2000. Time and again, I stepped over the line: If Rafael Perez is telling the truth, an L.A. Cop Scandal will the city millions and more," *Time*, March 6, Volume 135, No. 110, 25.

United States Civil Rights Commission. 1947. *To Secure These Rights*, Washington, DC: U.S. Government Printing Office.

United States Civil Rights Commission. 1961. *The 50 States Report*. Washington, DC: U.S. Government Printing Office.

United States Civil Rights Commission. 1981. *Who Is Guarding the Guardians?* Washington, DC: U.S. Government Printing Office.

Vaughn, M. S., T. W. Cooper and R. V. del Carmen 2001. Assessing legal liabilities in law enforcement: Police chiefs' views. *Crime and Delinquency*, Volume 47, No. 1, 3–27.

Wallentine, K. 2009. The risky continuum: Abandoning the use of force continuum to enhance risk management. *International Municipal Lawyers Association Journal*, 1–2. Retrieved 2015, from http://imla.org.

Walker, J. 2000a. Gangsta cops, *Reason*, January, Volume 31, No. 18, 13.

Walker, J. 2000b. Gangster cops, *Reason*, Volume 31, No. 119, 13.

Wilson, O. W. 1967. In The President's Commission on Law Enforcement and Administration of Justice. 1967. *Task Force Report: The Police*, Washington, DC: U.S. Government Printing Office.

Wittie, M. C. 2013. Police use of force, *PB and J*, Vol. 2, No. 1, 17.

Use of Deadly Force

Michael J. Palmiotto

"Deadly force can best be described as a force capable of causing serious bodily injury or death. Generally, the police have the authority to use deadly force to save their lives or the lives of others." (Palmiotto, 2001: 27). The police use of deadly force can be traced back to the common law of England, the historical foundation of American law. In our contemporary society the police legal right to use deadly force no longer comes from common law, it comes from statutory law. Statutory law is legislative law that has its foundation in common law.

Generally, police officers have the authority to use deadly force, to cause death of another human being, when their life or the life of another person is jeopardized. The police can trace their legal authority to use deadly force to the common law of England, which was developed during the middle ages.

Under common law the police have the authority to use deadly force against someone who was suspected of committing a felony, which was and is still considered a serious crime. Law enforcement under English common law had few felonies compared to our modern law which has too many felonies to count. The police never could use deadly force against a suspect committing a misdemeanor, a less serious crime than a felony. Felonies under the common law legal system were punishable by death. The police could use deadly force against a suspect absconding from the scene of a crime. The rationale for this was simply that since felonies committed were punishable by death, the police in a sense were doing the state a favor if he killed the suspect.

Since the nineteenth century and the passing of statutory laws only first-degree murder is a capital offense, punishable by death. Felonies are no longer a capital offense, except for first-degree murder, under the statutory laws passed by the legislative branch. The police who use deadly force against a felony suspect while apprehending them are exercising more authority and power than a judge or jury.

There are various methods in which physical force by a police officer could result in deadly force. The most common deadly force method used by police is firearms. Another method that can cause death is neck holds that can cut off circulation and/or blood flow. An unusual method of using deadly force was used by the Philadelphia Police in 1985, when they dropped an incendiary bomb from a police helicopter onto a house killing 11 members of a militant group.

Most states would have laws describing deadly force. Kansas is one such state which states the "Use of deadly force means the application of any physical force which is likely to cause death or great bodily harm to a person. Any threat to cause death or great bodily harm, including but not limited to, by the display or production of a weapon, shall not constitute use of deadly force, so long as the actor's purpose is limited to creating an apprehension that the actor will if necessary, use deadly force in defense of such actor or to affect a lawful arrest" (Kansas Statute Annotated, Article 32, Chapter 21, supp.·21-5221).

The Model Penal Code specifies when the use of deadly force can and cannot be used. First, the arrest is for a felony, the person making the arrest is a peace officer or assisting the peace officer, the force used by the officers causes no risk to innocent people, the officer believes the arrest involved includes the use or threatened use of deadly force and the person being arrested may cause substantial risk of serious bodily injury or death if apprehension is delayed (Model Penal Code 3.07(2) (b)).

☐ Reason for Firearms

In the United States in the 1840s there was an increase in the use of firearms in individual disputes. In the late 1840s and 1850s, police officers were occasionally shot in the line of duty. In the 1850s, it was a matter of personal choice for an officer to carry firearms for protection. Eventually, carrying firearms became an acceptable practice for police officers. Generally, many Americans felt that law enforcement was for others and not for them, and so during periods of social turmoil when violence was acceptable behavior for a specific segment of society, the establishment found the use of force acceptable police behavior (Johnson, 1981: 28–31).

During the 1840s New York City initiated the modern municipal police concept in America. New York City combined its day and night force into one department. By the 1860s the New York model had been accepted by many cites with some modification. While the basic principles of the New York model were largely acceptable, the new police system confronted three issues:

1. A controversy over the adoption of the uniform

2. A concern about arming the police, and

3. The issue of appropriate force in making arrest (Johnson, 1981: 28).

The purpose of the uniform was to make police officers readily visible to the public and for them to avoid hiding. The uniform issue is nonexistent today. The other two issues, firearms and force, especially deadly force, have been controversial since the police have carried firearms and were given legal authority to make arrest. The use of firearms and deadly force has led to violence in American streets. In the second decade of the twenty-first century violent mobs still take to the streets protesting police use of deadly force, usually with the use of a firearm. It appears that police using deadly force may be an issue that will never go away. The comments made by Anthony Bouza, former Minneapolis police chief in 1992 are as valid today as they were when he made them:

> The importance of police-involved shootings stems not so much from their frequency (they are rare compared with the hundreds of thousands of encounters each year between police and persons suspected of violating the law) but from their potential consequences. Any experienced police officer knows the potentially devastating effects of even justified shootings by police—loss of life and bereavement, risks to an officer's career, the government liability to civil suits, strained police–community relations, rioting and all the economic and social crisis that attend major civil disturbances (Geller and Scott, 1992: 1).

The Police Foundation is in agreement with Chief Bouza when it reports that with the United States having more than 750,000 police officers and with the police contacting millions of citizens each year, shootings by police are of a low frequency. They provide the reason that police officers are limited to specific circumstances as to when they can use deadly force (Klinger, 2005). Fyfe agrees with Bouza and the Police Foundation that the frequency of the use of deadly force is quite small. He indicates that most shooting occurs in large cities (Fyfe, 1982: 8).

The following studies reveal that the issue of deadly force and firearms use by the police began from the time the police became armed in the mid-nineteenth century up to our present day. Our first study of police shootings from the years 1875–1920 indicates that the police have had a long history of violent behavior. This violent behavior can be traced when police were nicknamed "clubbers" when they used their nightsticks against citizens until now when they have used deadly force, usually with firearms against unarmed citizens. Between 1875 and 1920, Chicago police officers killed 307 people (Adler, 2007: 233–237). From 1910 to 1920, African Americans made up only 3% of the population but comprised 21% of deaths by the police. These figures seems to parallel our modern day. More African Americans are killed by police than any other racial or ethnic group. During the period of this study death by police officers accounted for 85% to either defend themselves or arrest fleeing felons (Adler, 2007: 246). Police shootings in the twentieth century have fueled social unrest in the United States and were the cause of major race riots including Detroit (1943), Harlem (1943), Miami (1980, 1982, 1984), Washington, D.C. (1991), and New York City (1992) (Adler, 2007: 233). Demonstrations, if not riots, are continuing into the first decades of the twenty-first century because of police shooting. Ferguson, Missouri, a suburb of St. Louis had demonstrations and looting after a Ferguson police officer shot an unarmed black teenager.

☐ Fleeing-Felon Rule

Historically, police officers could use deadly force when a suspect was fleeing from a crime. A Tennessee statute provided that if a police officer has given notice of an intent to arrest a criminal suspect and the suspect flees or forcibly resists, "the officer may use all the necessary means to make an arrest." On October 3, 1974 at 10:45 p.m. Memphis police officers Elton Hymon and Leslie Wright responded to a prowler call. Upon arriving on the scene the officers observed a woman pointing to an adjacent house stating that someone was breaking in next door. While Wright was notifying the dispatcher that they had arrived at the scene, Hymon went to the back of the house. Hymon heard a door slam and observed someone run across the backyard. The runner, later discovered to be Edward Garner, stopped at a 6′ link fence. Hymon had his flashlight on and was able to see Garner's face and hands. There was no sign of a weapon and Hymon thought Garner was unarmed. Garner, according to Hymon, was about 17 or 18 and about 5′5″–5′7 ″ tall. Hymon told Garner to halt but he began climbing the fence. If Garner got over the fence he would not be apprehended. Hymon shot Garner who eventually died in hospital. Hymon's actions were reviewed by the Memphis Firearms Review Board and presented to the grand jury with neither body taking any action. Gardner's father brought a civil suit in the Federal District of the Western District of Tennessee, seeking damage under 42 U.S.C. 1983 for violating Edward Gardner's constitutional rights. The complaint alleged that the shooting violated the Fourth, Fifth, Sixth, Eighth, and Fourteenth Amendments of the U.S. Constitution. The district judge held that Hymon's actions were authorized by the Tennessee statute, which was constitutional. The judge held Hymon's actions were reasonable and a practical means of preventing Gardner's escape. Gardner had recklessly attempted to vault over the fence to escape and thereby assumed the risk of being fired upon.

In 1983 the Court of Appeals reversed the District Court's decision. The Court of Appeals held that the killing of a fleeing suspect is "seizure" under the Fourth Amendment and is constitutional only if reasonable. The court further held that the facts did not justify the use of deadly force under the Fourth Amendment and is constitutional only if reasonable. Police officers cannot resort to deadly force unless they have probable cause to believe the suspect poses a risk to the safety of police officers or the community. The U.S. Supreme Court in 1985 affirmed the judgment of the Court of Appeals *Tennessee v. Garner et al.* (1985).

The impact of the Gardner decision influenced police homicides. The number of police homicides decreased substantially. The Gardner decision not only reduced the number of police shootings of fleeing felons but all shootings. As a result of the Gardner decisions all police shootings not related to protecting life seems to be decreasing (Tennenbaum, 1994: 258–259).

The Gardner case is limited to deadly force, and only in the context of the fleeing felon. Longo writes that the *Graham v. Connor* case pertains to all use of force, including deadly force. The Graham decision, according to Longo, established a loose framework that can be used to determine reasonableness of force (Longo, 2011: 267). Longo writes that the courts consider three fundamental questions in assessing use-of-force scenarios:

1. What is the nature or severity of the offense?

2. Did the suspect pose an immediate threat to the officer or others?

3. Is the suspect actively resisting or attempting to escape? (Longo, 2011: 267).

As mentioned in Chapter 2 there seems to be disagreement between the use of force continuum and "just be reasonable" standard as set forth in the U.S. Supreme Court in *Graham v. Connor* (1989). The U.S. Supreme Court stated that an arrest by using force has to be "objectively reasonable in view of all the facts and circumstances of each particular case, including the severity of the crime at issue, whether the suspect poses an immediate threat to the safety of officers or others, and whether he is actively resisting arrest or attempting to evade arrest by flight" (Alpert and Dunham, 2004: 21).

Fyfe (1981: 376), a recognized scholar on police use of deadly force, asserts that a hullabaloo over deadly force can be attributed to "Presidential Commissions, police practitioners, radical criminologists, traditional academics, social activists, law reviews and popular writers." As previously mentioned in this chapter there are a variety of ways the police can use deadly force against an individual.

The decision as to when police officers should draw their weapons has never been clearly defined nor has the question of when they should fire them. While both actions depend upon the discretion of the officer, there exists a difference between drawing and firing their firearms. Police officers who are well trained draw their firearm only when circumstances present a reasonable expectation that they will encounter life-threatening violence. Police officers working in busy police stations will draw their weapons more frequently than officers from slow police stations, since they have a greater chance of being fired upon. At times, police officers draw their firearm whey they respond to a violent crime. Officers who make arrests for serious crimes may have their weapons drawn to obtain quick response from suspects. Competent officers understand that it may be unwise to have their weapons visible to the mentally disturbed or those individuals acting in an illogical manner. It has not been determined as to whether the display of an officer's weapon may stimulate violence rather than discourage it. The police officer and the general public should be aware that every year there are officers who are shot with their own weapon (Skolnick and Fyfe, 1993: 41–42).

At times, shootings by police officers results in major unrest in the community they serve. On February 4, 1999, in the Soundview section of the Bronx, four New York City police officers, who were members of the Street Crime Unit, shot and killed Amadou Diallo, an immigrant from Africa. Forty-one rounds were fired, while 19 struck Diallo. Diallo was unarmed and standing by himself in the lobby of his apartment building. The victim was only 20 ft away from the officers who shot him. The death of Diallo became an outrage with racism as an outcry because four white police officers killed an African man. Following Diallo's death the building became a memorial, with messages of condolence and flowers lining the hallway (Kolber, 1999: 50). The four police officers on February 25, 2000 were found not guilty of second-degree murder, reckless endangerment, and manslaughter and criminal negligence in the death of Diallo by a mixed-race jury of seven men and five women. The jury concluded that the four officers feared for their life and acted in self-defense (Cukan, 2000: 2–4). The jury's verdict was poorly accepted and for several days, demonstrations occurred in New York City. The parents of Diallo petitioned the U.S. Justice Department to investigate the shooting for potential civil rights violations. The Justice Department decided in 2001 that the civil rights of Diallo were not violated and that federal charges would not be brought against the police officers.

There have been demonstrations and rioting in America for decades, even going back to the Civil War and colonial America. Some of the incidents that set off demonstrations and riots in earlier decades are mirrors for some of the demonstrations and rioting in the early decades of the twenty-first century.

The 1964 Harlem riots were initiated like so many violent incidents over a minor situation. You might say they were initiated when a white superintendent of an apartment building turned a water hose on some young black men who were loitering on the front steps of the apartment building and refused to move. Fifteen-year old James Powell chased him into the building. An off duty police lieutenant heard the commotion and was confronted by Powell who had a knife. Powell slashed the lieutenant on his forearm. The lieutenant drew his revolver and warned Powell who again lunged at him. The officer shot Powell and killed him. Some members of the community could not understand why the lieutenant could not have disarmed the young man without shooting him. Community activists motivated the crowd to march on the 123rd police precinct and make demands. The police were waiting for the crowd which was a hostile mob. The police informed the crowd that the shooting incident was being investigated by the district attorney's office. The crowd would not accept this information and the police soon had bricks and bottles coming from the roof at them. The riot police went after the crowd with their nightsticks and voices in the crowd called out "killer cops" and "murders." The angry mob went down the street breaking windows and looting. They began throwing Molotov cocktails at the police. Rioting spread to Bedford-Stuyvesant across the river in Brooklyn then to Rochester, New York. On July 22, there were 1000 people attacking the police (*Harlem—The Backlash Begins*). The 6 days of rioting left a large number of people arrested and injured. During the 1960s there were many riots in American cities and the reasons are for the most part similar today as in the 1960s. There exists a lack of respect toward the police by minorities. Also, Afro-Americans believe the police are abusive toward them and that they are treated in an inferior manner when compared to whites.

The use of deadly force appears to be an issue in many cities and states throughout the United States. One such state which has a history of deadly force, racially tinted police confrontations is Florida. Many of the police confrontations have involved unarmed men, which resulted in protests, riots, and hostility between minorities and the police. No police officer in the last 20 years has been charged with using deadly force improperly. Even getting a decision in Florida to seek charges is problematic. An example of such a case is a 2011 memorial day weekend shooting in South Beach, when 12 officers fired 110 rounds at a 22-year old young man whose car was stopped. In addition, four bystanders received wounds. This shooting was one of 42 cases involving the use of deadly force by the police (Alvarez, 2014: 1).

Another area of the country that overlooks police shooting is Clark County, specifically Las Vegas, Nevada. One 31-year-old, 8-year veteran Las Vegas police officer had shot two men in 21 months and was disciplined for dating a prostitute while off duty. He shot a third man; all three under peculiar circumstances and not one had a witness. The police officer was exonerated by the coroner's inquest and the department's internal Use of Force Review Board. The officer had several weeks off and returned to work cleared of any wrongdoing. In the last 20 years, the Las Vegas police had 310 shootings. Since 2000 the Las Vegas police on an average fired their weapons 17 times (Mower et al., 2011: 1–6).

A knife-wielding man was killed in Times Square, New York by two police officers who fired 12 shots at the man. The man was waving a kitchen knife scaring tourists. Experts on police procedures said the police did what they were trained to do. The New York City Police Commissioner and Mayor both said the police officers acted appropriately (McGeehan, 2012: 1).

Shooting by the Philadelphia police increased in 2012 while violent crimes decreased. The 2012 shootings by police was at the highest level in 10 years. The Philadelphia police shot 52 suspects with 15 of those being shot dying in 2012. Similar to Florida and Las Vegas, the Police Internal Affairs investigators and the district attorney's office had no concerns about the shootings (Wood, 2013: 1).

On Sunday morning on April 1, 2012, the Wichita Police shot an unarmed 24-year old black man, named Troy Lanning Jr., after a car chase. The police reported that after the car chase Lanning reached into a bag of belongings and the police reported he appeared to aim it against an officer in a threatening manner. Lanning was told by the police officer to stop looking into the bag but Lanning continued to reach into the bag. The officer claims Lanning continued pointing the bag at him. After several warnings the officer shot Lanning killing him. No weapon was found in the bag or in the vehicle Lanning was driving. Lanning's father believes the Wichita Police could have used a Taser on his son or a K-9 dog to catch him, rather than shooting him (Wenzl, 2012: 1).

Lanning's shooting led to demonstrations and a march on the police department. The demonstrators mentioned that since October 2011 five people were killed by the police under dubious circumstances with the Wichita police not being transparent and being disrespectful toward families of the victims (Stephenson and Shatz, 2012: 1). Stephenson and Shatz state, "Police killings are not an anomaly. In the United States, police kill over 7000 citizens each year. Activists from Anaheim and Baltimore announced through social media that their police force have killed their citizens unjustly, and their police departments continue to defend the actions of their police forces" (Stephenson and Shatz, 2012: 2). The authors quote Wichita police chief Norman Williams who stated in a press conference on July 11, "When you look at each one of these situations, the police gave commands for people to obey, to drop their weapon, to comply with what's going on, and they choose not to" (Stephenson and Shatz, 2012: 2). Stephenson and Shatz respond "In other words: blame the victim" (Stephenson and Shatz, 2012: 2).

On August 9, 2014 an incident occurred in Ferguson, Missouri which has occurred often in America: A police officer shoots a citizen. As history has shown more often than not the citizen being shot is a black man. The shooting of blacks by specifically white police officers have led to a lack of trust of Afro-Americans toward the police. Evidence indicates that throughout American's history blacks have been treated poorly and in an unjust manner. History reveals that they have been treated more unjustly than any other racial or ethnic group. It seems realistic to expect that Afro-Americans have a distrust of the police. The police have functioned at times as an "occupational army" rather than protectors of the community they police. The night of August 9, 2014 in Ferguson, Missouri was a night which led to looting, rioting, and demonstrations. This night lead to confrontation between the police and citizens. A scene not considered uncommon in the United States. You may say generations matured watching confrontation between police and citizens on television. It may have come to the point that the police may never be considered justified in shooting a black man regardless of the circumstances or evidence.

The fatal shooting by Ferguson, Missouri police officer Darren Wilson of 18-old Michael Brown, a black man, created attention not only in America but also throughout the world. The hullabaloo resulted from a simple incident of Michael Brown walking down the middle of the street with Dorian Johnson when Officer Wilson drove up to them and ordered them to walk on the sidewalk. Reports indicate a struggle occurred between Officer Wilson and Brown through the car window and somehow Wilson's revolver was fired. It is undermined whether the weapon was fired accidentally or intentionally. Brown and Johnson fled from Wilson in different directions with Wilson in pursuit of Brown. Officer Wilson fired his weapon 6 times killing Brown. A controversy exists as to whether Brown had his hands up or was approaching Wilson when he was shot.

St. Louis County police chief made the following comment about the incident. "When the officer tried to exit his vehicle, Chief Belmar said one of the two pushed the officer back into the cruiser. The suspect allegedly assaulted the officer in the car and the two struggled over his gun. At least one shot was fired inside the vehicle. A few moments later, Chief Belmar said, the officer allegedly fired multiple shots outside the vehicle that killed the suspect, about 35 feet from the cruiser" (Kesling et al., 2014).

When the news of Michael Brown's death reached the community, peaceful protests took place but eventually escalated to looting, vandalism, and confrontations with police officers that lasted for several days. With the police having difficulty maintaining order a curfew was established. Not only was the community of Ferguson and St. Louis County involved in the Brown shooting, but also the state and federal government became involved. For example, President Obama offered his condolences to the Brown family, Attorney General Holder made a visit to Ferguson and ordered a civil rights investigation of the Ferguson police department. The Governor of Missouri placed a Missouri State Highway Patrol captain in charge of maintaining order in Ferguson. Even the Secretary-General of the United Nations got into the act. He requested that all protestors' rights to peaceful assembly and freedom of expression be ensured (McAllister and Carey, 2014; U.N. Chief, 2014).

Several months after the interview, Darren Wilson, the police officer who shot Michael Brown, gave his account of the incident to federal civil rights investigators who were assigned by the Department of Justice. Officer Wilson said he was pinned in his vehicle and was fearful for his well-being. Wilson reported he struggled with Brown over his gun. He informed the investigators that Brown reached for his gun which was fired twice in the car as verified by forensic tests conducted by the Federal Bureau of Investigation. Michael Brown was struck in the arm by the first bullet while the second bullet missed. Forensic tests revealed Brown's blood was on the gun, the interior door panel, and on Officer Wilson's uniform. Officer Wilson informed investigators that Brown had punched and scratched him repeatedly leaving cuts on his neck and swelling on his face. This first account of Officer Wilson does not explain why he emerged from the car and fired several shots at Brown. Darren Wilson's account of the incident contradicts several witness accounts. The information provided by Wilson will not calm those who want to know why an unarmed man was shot 6 times (Schmidt et al., 2014).

On August 22, 2014 the St. Louis Post Dispatch published the autopsy report of the St. Louis Medical Examiner's Office. The report stated the following: "The deceased body sustained multiple gunshot wounds; three (3) wounds to his head, one was to the top of his head, right eye and right central forehead area. There were two (2) wounds to his chest, one wound to his upper right chest near his neck and the other was just right to his breast. Three (3) wounds to his right arm, one wound in his upper right arm, one wound in his upper right arm, middle of the arm and one to his forearm. One (1) wound to the inside of his right hand near his thumb and palm." The report further stated "The deceased had abrasions to his right side of his face and on his left hand. The deceased hands were bagged with paper bags to save any trace evidence." The medical examiner found marijuana in Brown's body (St. Louis County Health, 2014).

The forensic pathologists hired by the family of Michael Brown questioned the St. Louis County medical examiner's finding. The medical examiner concluded that Brown had gunshot residue on him after he had been fatally shot. Michael Baden, the forensic pathologist, hired by the Brown family in August, claims that the teen could have been shot from a distance of 30 ft. A leaked copy of the medical examiner's report, by the *St. Louis Post Dispatch* reported that microscopic particles of gunshot residue were found in a deep layer of skin, revealing that the teen was shot once in his thumb at close range. Baden claims he want to testify before the grand jury. He further reported that dirt can appear similar to gunshot residue. Further, Baden stated he wanted copies of the microscopic slides that show what the medical examiner claims is gunshot residue (Alcindor, 2014: 3A).

Traditionally, when a police officer is involved in a shooting, including the killing of a person, the investigation is sent to the grand jury by the district attorney. The police officer either has to be indicted and the case goes to trial or the officer is exonerated. Police officer Wilson's shooting of Michael Brown was sent to the St. Louis County grand jury. On November 21, the grand jury of St. Louis County after months of deliberation exonerated Officer Wilson from any wrongdoing in the death of Michael Brown.

The U.S. Government, through the Department of Justice, conducted an investigation of Officer Wilson's shooting of Michael Brown (Darren Wilson resigned November 30, 2014 from the Ferguson Police Department prior to the Justice Department's findings). The Justice Department's investigation of the shooting incident of Michael Brown was made public by the Attorney General Eric Holder on March 5, 2015. The law provides the government the authority to investigate the Brown shooting, or for that matter any shooting by a law enforcement officer. The investigative powers fall under the criminal statute that enforces the constitutional limitations that pertains to the use of force by police officers. The Federal law 18 U.S.C. 242 states the following "Whoever under color of any law,...willfully subjects any person...to the deprivation of any rights, privileges, or immunities secured or protected by the Constitution or laws of the United States [shall be guilty of a crime]." This law allows federal investigators to determine if a police officer had violated an arrested person or deceased person's civil rights. The Justice Department's investigation concluded that Darren Wilson shot and killed Michael Brown as a defensive act to save his life (Memorandum, 2015).

Approximately 2 months after the Ferguson shooting, another shooting occurred a short distance away. On October 8, 2014 an off duty St. Louis police officer in uniform working as a security guard shot an 18-year old black man. The black man fired three shots at the police officer before his weapon jammed. The officer returned fire with 17 shots at the black man and killed him. The parents of the man claimed their son was carrying a sandwich and not a weapon. The police found a weapon at the scene and three projectiles found at the scene of the incident (Muskal, 2014: 7A).

On Monday, October 13, 2014 demonstrators attempted to shut down a street in front of Emerson Electric in St. Louis holding signs reading, "Black lives do matter." Other demonstrators marched on City Hall, while attempting to hang a banner reading "What side are you on?" Nineteen people were arrested by St. Louis police according to a St. Louis County spokesman (Fiona, 2014). Since the Ferguson incident there have been numerous incidents of police shootings of black males usually followed by demonstrations. These shootings followed by demonstrations have occurred during the writing of this book and are expected to continue long after this book is published.

Delroy Burton, chairman of the Washington DC police union said the following, "People want to make generalizations that cops get away with stuff most of the time. No they don't. Most of the time their use of force is appropriate. But now, every single case of deadly use of force, particularly where race is a factor, it automatically becomes racism, and that's just not true.... The fact that officers are now guilty until proven innocent, or the force is inappropriate until an investigation is done—I think that sends a message to police officers, and I think it's a waste of resources for society in general" (Drehle, 2015: 27).

☐ Summary

The use of force and specifically deadly force had been an issue since the police began arming themselves in the 1840s. It has become a major issue in the second decade of the twenty-first Century. The use of deadly force by the police can be traced back to the middle ages when common law was the law of England. During the middle ages deadly force could be used by law enforcers against anyone committing a felony. Since, during this period of time, felonies were punishable by death a law enforcer killing a felon was considered doing the state a favor.

Unlike the middle ages, our modern society has many crimes considered a felony and only one punishable by death. First-degree murder is the only crime punishable by death. The police who use deadly force against a felony suspect while apprehending them are exercising more authority and power than a judge and jury.

Most states have laws describing deadly force. The Model Penal Code specifies when the use of deadly force can and cannot be used. Since the police are armed and have the authority to use deadly force to protect their lives or another person they will resort to deadly force when they consider it appropriate. Often, deadly force is used against an offender who refuses to cooperate with the police. If the offender is unarmed this can create a major issue for the police officer. The shooting of an unarmed offender can lead to demonstrations and rioting. Family members of offenders and those not police supporters often claim that the police could or should have subdued the offender without using deadly force. They make this claim even when the offender is bigger than the officer or has a weapon, such as a knife.

Demonstrations and rioting can be traced to colonial times and the Civil War. It has continued into the first decades of the twenty-first century. Riots were serious in the 1940s and 1960s and have been somewhat severe this second decade of the twenty-first century. However, as long as police shoot offenders it should be expected that demonstrations and rioting may be the outcome.

☐ References

Adler, J. 2007. Shoot to kill: The use of deadly force by the Chicago police, 1875–1920, *Journal of Interdisciplinary History*, Autumn, XXXVIII(2), 38(2), 233–254.

Alcindor, Y. 2014. Brown family's pathologist wants to testify, *USA Today*, October 31, 3A.

Alpert, G. P. and R. G. Dunham 2004. *Understanding Police Use of Force*, New York: Cambridge University Press.

Alvarez, L. 2014. Florida prosecutors face long odds when police use lethal force, *International New York Times*, September 3, www.nyti.ms/1r2UkzJ

Bouza, A. 1992. Introduction, In: Geller, W. and M. Scott (Eds.), *Deadly Force, What We Know*, Washington, DC: PERF, p. 1.

Cukan, W. 2000. Jurors: The only issue was the law: Say race had no part in Diallo verdict? *APBNews.com*, May 18.

Drehle, D. V. 2015. Line of fire, *Time*, April 20, 24–28.

Fiona, O. 2014. Protesters demonstrate in St. Louis area over police shooting of blacks, *Reuters*, http:://www.reuters.com/article/2013/10/13/us-usa-missouri-shooting-idUSKCN01201520141013

Fyfe, J. J. 1981. Observations on police deadly force, *Crime and Delinquency*, 27(3), 376–389.

Fyfe, J. J. 1982. *Readings on police use of deadly force*, Washington, D.C.: Police Foundation.

Geller, W. A. and M. S. Scott 1992. *Deadly Force: What We Know*, Washington, DC: Police Executive Forum.

Harlem, R. 1964. (n.d.) *Harlem—The Backlash Begins*, www.detroits-great-rebellion.com/harlem-riot.html

Johnson, D. R. 1981. *American Law Enforcement: A History*, St. Louis: Forum Press.

Kansas Statute Annotated Article 32, Chapter 21, supp. 21-5221.

Kesling, B., M. Peters and D. Barrett 2014. FBI probes Missouri teen's shooting, *The Wall Street Journal*, (August 12) http://online.wsj.com/articles/missouri-teenager-killed-by-police-after-fight-1407698036

Klinger, D. 2005. Special theory and the street cop: The case of deadly force, *Ideas in American Policing*, Number 7, Police Foundation.

Kolber, E. 1999. The perils of safety: Did crime-fighting tactics put Amadou Diallou at risk, *New York Times*, May 22, p. 50.

Longo, T. 2011. Defining instrumentalities of deadly force, *Touro Law Review*, 27(2), 261.

McAllister, E. and N. Carey. 2014. Michael Brown remembered in Missouri with calls for peace, justice. *Reuters*, (August 26). Retrieved 2015, http://www.reuters.com/article/usa-missouri-shooting-idUSL1N0QV0Q220140826

McGeehan, P. 2012. Officials defend fatal shooting of a knife-wielding man near times Sq., *New York Times*, August 12, www.nytimes/2012/08/nyregion/police-fire-12-shots-in-killing-near-times-square.html-square.html

Memorandum 2015. Department of Justice Report Regarding the Criminal Investigation into the Shooting Death of Michael Brown by Ferguson, Missouri Police Officer Darren Wilson, March 4.

Mower, L., A. Maimon and B. Hayes 2011. Analysis: Many Las Vegas police shootings could have been avoided, *Las Vegas Review Journal*, November 27, www.reviewjournal.com/news/deadly-force/always-justified/analysis-many

Muskal, M. 2014. St. Louis braces for weekend of protests over Michael Brown killing. *Reuters*, (October 9). Retrieved 2015, http://www.reuters.com/article/us-usa-missouri-shooting-idUSKCN0HY08H20141009

Palmiotto, M.J. (eds.) 2001. Police misconduct: What is it? In: *Police Misconduct: A reader for the 21st century*, Upper Saddle River, N.J.: Prentice-Hall, p. 27.

Schmidt, M. S., M. Apuzzo and J. Bosman 2014. Police officer in Ferguson is said to recount a struggle, *New York News*, October 17. http://nyti.ms/1qtLBnC8

Skolnick, J. H. and J. J. Fyfe 1993. *Above the Law*, New York, New York: The Free Press.

Stephenson, R. and M. Shatz 2012. Wichitans take a stand against police shooting, August 13, http://www.occupy.com/article/wichitans-take-stand-against-police-shootings

St. Louis County Health. 2014. Narrative report of investigation, Exam case 2014–5143, Office of Medical Examiner, August 8.

Tennenbaum, A. 1994. The influence on the Gardner decision on police use of deadly force, *Criminology*, 6(1), 241–260.

Tennessee v. Garner et al. 1985. Supreme Court of the United States, 471 U.S 1; 105 S.Ct. 1694; 85 L.Ed2d 1; 1985 U.S. LEXIS 195; 53 U.S.L.W.4410.

U.N. Chief calls for protection of Rights in Missouri protests, *Reuters*, August 18. http://www.reuters.com/article/2014/08/usa-missouri-shooting-un-idSKBN0D11MF20140818

Wenzl, R. 2012. Wichita police give details of weekend shooting, April 2, http://www.kansas.com/news

Wood, S. 2013. Exclusive shootings by Philly police soar as violent crime plummets, *Philly Com*, May 14, www.philly.com/philly/news/Police_shootings_soar_as_violent_crime_falls.html

CHAPTER 4

Nonlethal Weapons and Technology

Szde Yu

☐ Introduction: Police Use of Force

Police use of force has always been a controversial subject. Ideology aside, the reality is the police must be allowed to use force when necessary and they must be allowed to exercise discretion in deciding what force is necessary under the circumstances. The controversy stems from such discretion for the most part. Admittedly, some people simply make bad decisions, and wearing a police uniform does not guarantee better decision making. When the police make a decision to use force, especially deadly force, the consequences are often irrevocable even when it turns out to be a bad decision. A simple search for "police brutality" on You Tube can bring up a variety of examples. We will not dwell on that in this chapter. Instead, the focus is on how the use of nonlethal weapons may or may not help reduce controversies surrounding police use of force.

☐ Nonlethal Weapons

Police officers have to deal with dangerous criminals on a daily basis. When they are under attack, they need to subdue the attackers by any means necessary not only to save their own lives but also to ensure the public's safety. Using a gun should be fairly reasonable in a situation like this, considering how many criminals have firearms. The use of lethal weapons is justified by the police even if the criminal does not have a firearm, as long as the threat is imminent. So, why do the police need nonlethal weapons? This is because at their discretion sometimes the officers do not feel the need to kill but they do need some leverage to control the situation. Firing a gun at someone could easily result in death even without the intention to kill.

There are many factors that influence police discretion, such as departmental policy, personal belief, experience, politics, and so on. The availability of alternative means is another factor. When the situation calls for the use of force but it is not really life threatening, less than lethal options should be available as an alternative to guns. Without such options, officers might be compelled to use lethal weapons, or they might be hesitant to use lethal weapons and in turn endanger themselves. Hence, while most people automatically think of guns when it comes to police force, nonlethal weapons actually play a crucial role in police work as well. To be exact, nonlethal weapons do not mean they cannot be used to inflict fatal wounds. Rather, the term "nonlethal" simply suggests the weapon is not designed to end a life. Just like a car is not designed to kill, but it is not incapable of killing.

There are a variety of nonlethal weapons that have been invented, and quite a few of them have been widely adopted in the police force. Generally, weapons other than firearms can all be considered nonlethal. Oleoresin capsicum (aka pepper spray), stun guns, tear gas, beanbag guns, rubber bullets, and plastic bullets are the commonly seen nonlethal weapons or less-than-lethal weapons. Some nonlethal weapons are not aimed at stopping people. Instead, they are designed to stop vehicles such as caltrops. Impact weapons, such as batons, are not usually included in the discussion of nonlethal weapons, but essentially they are not designed to kill, either. Regardless of the variety, the concept of nonlethal weapons is simple, that is, demobilizing the target without directly inflicting fatal wounds. Indirectly, however, as mentioned the use of nonlethal weapons could still result in a fatal outcome.

Although sufficient evidence is not yet in place to prove that nonlethal weapons can reduce justifiable citizen killings by the police (Bailey, 1996), the use of nonlethal weapons seems to have reduced death rates in suicide-by-cop incidents (Homant and Kennedy, 2000). Further, research has found that the use of nonlethal weapons lowers the likelihood of the suspect sustaining an injury (MacDonald et al., 2009). Likewise, the odds of injury to police officers are also significantly lower when nonlethal weapons are used, compared to the use of other physical force (MacDonald et al., 2009). On July 17, 2014, the death of Eric Garner in Staten Island, New York stirred controversies when Garner was ruled to have died from a chokehold put on him by a New York City Police Department officer. In that event, which was video recorded by eyewitnesses, Garner appeared to be resisting arrest although he did not attack the officer trying to handcuff him. In response, the officer used his arms to place a headlock which resulted in a chokehold on Garner's neck, according to the medical examiner. Although the officer was not indicted by a grand jury, which implies a crime was not committed, there is definitely room for discussion regarding how the situation could have been handled differently. For starters, it might have not been necessary for the officer to engage in such physical restraint, when Garner's physical resistance was minimal. Besides, there were multiple other officers on the scene, so there was no need for that one officer to overpower the suspect in such a manner. If force was needed in that situation, the use of nonlethal weapons or even batons would have been more appropriate to restrain Garner's movement, compared to choking him with bare hands. It would have been safer for the officers as well. Hence, it is important to note that the availability of nonlethal weapons is supposed to be beneficial to both the suspect and the officer involved in an incident where the use of force is warranted but death is unnecessary.

Another scenario where nonlethal weapons such as caltrops are preferred is when the suspect is fleeing in a vehicle but there are other people in the vehicle. In this case, shooting at the vehicle greatly endangers the innocent passengers, and therefore using caltrops, if available, to stop the vehicle is a less lethal option and thus preferable. In a riot or a protest, the police also often resort to nonlethal weapons, such as plastic bullets or beanbag guns, to quell the unrest or to compel protesters to move away. Certainly when violence escalates and becomes a threat to the safety of the police and the public, sometimes firearms are necessary to control the situation. Nevertheless, nonlethal weapons first used in these situations could signify a gesture that suggests the police have no intention to really hurt the people while maintaining order. A less hostile gesture may often prevent the need for further use of force when the crowd was not seeking violence in the first place. On the contrary, the display of deadly force prematurely in a peaceful protest could easily instigate violent reactions.

☐ Controversies

Although nonlethal weapons are meant to reduce unnecessary injuries and deaths, they have had their fair share of criticism regarding injuries and deaths caused by their use. Oleoresin capsicum (OC) spray and conducted energy devices (CEDs) are the most widely used nonlethal weapons nowadays, so they are at the center of these controversies. CEDs such as a stun gun or Taser are generally safe when they are tested in experiments because most people in the experiments are healthy people and the experiments are usually conducted in controlled environments. However, when they are used on the street in the line of duty, there are more variables that are unknown and uncontrollable to the officer. For instance, the subject's heath condition is a big risk factor. Strong electric currency could trigger a heart attack on a person with preexisting heart conditions (Zipes, 2014). It could also exacerbate existing injuries especially head injuries. Some drug use factors might also come into play and cause damages that would not be otherwise seen in a healthy person. As for OC spray, in theory it could cause asphyxia if the recipient had respiratory conditions, such as asthma. Although these are plausible claims, currently empirical data are rather limited in proving them (Sheridan, 2014), in part because it is highly unethical to intentionally test these weapons on people who are known to have these risk factors. It is also because current studies in this regard usually failed to control for circumstantial variables, such as the level of resistance from the suspect and the involvement of illicit drug use (MacDonald et al., 2009). However, tentative evidence does suggest that the likelihood of severe injuries resulting from these common nonlethal weapons is pretty small. Moreover, using CEDs could reduce the rate of injury to officers (Alpert et al., 2011), and therefore they are generally seen as a favorable addition to police weaponry.

Nonetheless, the low rates of injury are actually another cause for concern. Some police officers may feel too comfortable using these nonlethal weapons since they are less likely to result in severe injuries. On November 18, 2011, some demonstrators in an Occupy Wall Street movement at the University of California, Davis were pepper sprayed by a campus police officer John Pike, while they were peacefully sitting on a paved path on campus. UC Davis Chancellor later apologized for this incident and said the police were acting against her orders. This incident spawned heated debate on the propriety of using pepper spray on a peaceful demonstration, a right that many believe is protected by the First Amendment to the U.S. Constitution. In December 2014, a Texas police officer used a Taser on a 76-year-old man in a traffic stop regarding driving a car with an expired inspection sticker. As the incident was video recorded, it soon became clear that such use of force, albeit non-lethal, was uncalled for because the old man did not initiate any physical resistance that would warrant this level of police force. In 2015, this officer was fired. These incidents show that sometimes the use of nonlethal weapons can be controversial even when they do not cause permanent injury physically. Accordingly the police should be mindful that the availability of nonlethal weapons is not to be misconstrued as a loosened standard for police use of force. In other words, the police should not feel they can use nonlethal weapons any time they want because probably no one will die from it. On the New Year's Day in 2009, Oscar Grant III was shot by a police officer working for Bay Area Rapid Transit in Oakland, California. Grant was lying face down and handcuffed when he was shot by Officer Johannes Mehserle, who was convicted of involuntary manslaughter later in 2010. Mehserle claimed he was intending to use his Taser on Grant but mistakenly withdrew his pistol instead. The incident was video recorded and the video suggests there was no reason for the officer to either shoot or tase a man who was already handcuffed on the ground face down. Had the officer used Taser correctly, it would still have been excessive force. Oscar Grant died the next day.

☐ Body Cameras

The Eric Garner incident, the UC Davis incident, the Texas officer Taser incident, and Oscar Grant's death mentioned above all had one thing in common, that is, the incident was video recorded. When there is a recording, the truth is usually easier to be revealed even though different people may interpret the moral of it differently as some people would believe the police are simply doing their job and justify the use of force, while others assert that there is abuse of power. Nonetheless, we will know what happened and draw our own conclusion accordingly. In contrast, some events involving police use of force are not accompanied by a video or the video fails to record the full context of the event. In these cases, the truth becomes elusive as a 'he says she says' situation tends to produce many versions of story. Worse yet, in some events the participants could be dead and have no say in the revelation of the truth. Without a video showing what really happened, it is especially difficult for an agreement on accountability to be formed. As society does not typically have much trust in the police's ability to admit their wrongdoing, visual evidence becomes more crucial than ever for the public to expose police misconduct. On the other hand, the police need visual evidence to free themselves from wrongful or malicious accusations.

On August 9, 2014, in Ferguson, Missouri, Michael Brown, an 18-year-old black man, was fatally shot by Darren Wilson, a white police officer. Darren Wilson was responding to a police dispatch's call for the search for a robbery suspect. When he encountered Michael Brown and another black man, he believed they matched the description of the robbery suspect. An initial confrontation occurred on the street and led to an altercation in which Michael Brown allegedly engaged in physical struggle with the officer through the window of the police vehicle until Wilson's gun was fired. Brown and his friend then fled. Darren Wilson's pursuit of Michael Brown ended in the fatal shooting that later became the center of national controversies. One version of the story suggests Brown was moving toward the officer and hence was perceived as a threat even though he was unarmed. Another version of the story depicts Brown as surrendering himself with both hands raised. Due to the lack of a video recording the entire happening and the different eyewitness accounts, naturally people in the nation chose whatever they were inclined to believe as the truth. Fueled by a longstanding racial tension in the area, this equivocal event involving a dead black man and a white police officer quickly ignited social unrest in Ferguson as well as in other cities across the country. The way the Ferguson Police Department responded to the protests and riots entailed more criticisms. The militarized response suggests the police were not only willing to use deadly force but also employing lethal weapons that are deemed excessive by critics. The debate on militarization of the police force is ongoing, but it is beyond the scope of this chapter.

The truth about the shooting of Michael Brown remains open to discussion. To avoid such incidents, many police agencies responded by requiring their officers to wear a body camera on duty so as to record their interaction with citizens. The concept is similar to the one behind dashboard cameras installed on police vehicles. In the 1990s, allegations about racial profiling in traffic stops were rampant. A dashboard camera thus became a solution as it records the car being stopped and the interaction between the officer and the driver. One benefit of dashboard cameras is increasing officer safety, because officers could review the recordings and learn from others' mistakes, such as turning back on a potentially dangerous situation. These videos could also reduce civilian complaints, and most of time they can prove the officer was not at fault in the complaint. Early studies found that 96.2% of the time, the recording from a dashcam exonerates the officer (Westphal, 2004; IACP, 2004). Moreover, they can have a positive impact on public perception of the police, and the videos can be used as crucial evidence in a trial or sources of information on homeland security issues. With funding provided by the Department of Justice's Office of Community-Oriented

Policing Services (COPS), the majority of major police agencies in the United States now have this type of camera installed on their police vehicles. Ironically, the Ferguson Police Department did not install dashboard cameras on their vehicles (CNN.com, 2014).

Despite the benefits of dashboard cameras, most police–citizen interactions actually take place outside the view of a dashboard camera. Hence, the call for body cameras gains a louder voice in the wake of recent police shooting incidents. The belief is wearing body cameras can be useful for documenting evidence, preventing complaints from the public, resolving complaints, and strengthening police transparency and accountability (COPS, 2014). Basically the benefits of this implementation are expected to be similar to those of dashboard cameras, but it is believed body cameras can offer a more complete perspective on the interaction in question, assuming the cameras are being used properly.

The concern, however, is with respect to privacy and trust. When recording an event, participants may be captured by the camera unwillingly. For example, the victims of an incident may not want to have their identity revealed on a video, or they may not want the event to be recorded and become a permanent trauma that could be revisited anytime in the future especially when such videos end up on the Internet. The people in the video may have very little control over who can view the video and under what circumstances the video will be used. Police officers may also perceive this as a sign of distrust because they may feel the purpose of the body camera is to monitor their every move. To be fair, these concerns are not really new, nor are they specific to body cameras. In modern days, cameras are already prevalent in one's daily life, such as traffic cameras, surveillance cameras, or a random person's cell phone. Nevertheless, to officially adopt this implementation in the police force requires a thorough evaluation of its pros and cons. The storage and management of such videos produced by police body cameras need comprehensive planning. Otherwise, it could result in a waste of taxpayers' money when it fails to resolve the issues of public trust, and it could bring about more controversies about the use of digital evidence. For example, why should the public trust the police-generated video if the video does not fully show the officer's action because the camera is worn on the officer's body? When the police claim the footage is not available, how do the public know if the camera was not functioning or the police are simply trying to hide the evidence? Can the video be digitally altered? Should the videos follow the chain of custody as a form of digital evidence? Should these videos be used for any purposes other than resolving a citizen complaint? Should these videos be released to the press without all participants' permission? All these potential issues need to be given some forethought before implementation, instead of waiting for incidents where we realize these cameras do not really help strengthen a better relationship between the public and the police.

Some research endeavors funded by the federal government have been underway to address some of these issues in an attempt to offer evidence for the presumed benefits of police body cameras. For instance, the National Institute of Justice in 2014 has announced a few grants dedicated to the study of police body cameras. It is too soon now to draw conclusions. A policy of this scale should not be based on anecdotal evidence, and scientific evaluation takes time. However, police departments should still proceed to enact sensible policies regulating the use of these cameras since implementation is already underway. Some additional benefits or drawbacks may be less straightforward and require more exploration. In the meantime, both the public and the police ought to be more patient and give each other some time to get used to this new implementation. The police should be mindful of the concerns the public might have especially when they are not yet familiar with body cameras, whereas the public should understand the success of this implementation lies in sound policies and the police may need to go through some trial and error before perfect policies, if existent, can be reached.

☐ Technology

The implementation of body cameras in police work is a salient example that shows how technology is expected to improve police performance. The concept of using a camera to garner visual evidence has been long-standing. Besides dashboard cameras and body cameras, some agencies now have installed a camera on Taser guns, so as to evaluate how police officers use these nonlethal weapons and their effect on controlling a potentially dangerous situation. These videos can work both ways. They can protect officers from false complaints or they can expose inappropriate use of such weapons. As technology advances, most of the videos produced from these various types of cameras can offer high-resolution recording and clear audio. Many of them allow for filming in lowlight. Some manufacturers have developed software to help manage and analyze the videos, such as adding GPS stamps to connect the videos to a map. Some cameras even have the capacity to offer live stream so that a real-time visual can be provided for people who are not on the scene. This can be seen as a useful weapon at the police's disposal that not only generates solid forensic evidence but also keeps officers safer. Hence, it is not too far-fetched to imagine that one day perhaps a camera on lethal as well as nonlethal weapons will become a common standard in the police force.

Certainly technology utilized by the police is not limited to cameras. Other technologies, such as thermal imaging, drones, lasers, language translators, crime mapping, license plate recognition, global positioning systems, and record databases that provide instant comparison, can all be contributive to police work. Technically they may not be categorized as weapons, but there is no doubt they can greatly enhance efficiency in crime fighting when used properly. The downside is often related to the cost. Before police agencies purchase these technologies, a cost-benefit analysis is warranted. Such analysis should be aimed at determining whether the money spent on these technologies is worthwhile. To this end, police agencies must clearly define their goals first. Without knowing what to accomplish and without clear measurement of this accomplishment, there is no way to know if it is worth spending taxpayers' money on new technologies that may or may not improve police work in spite of the sales pitch. Moreover, ethical issues regarding civil rights also need to be addressed in case these technologies are misused for ulterior purposes.

☐ Policy Implications

As mentioned earlier, the police must be allowed to use weapons in the line of duty. It is equally critical, however, that the police use of force is under control and guidance. The delicate balance depends on two main factors: discretion and policy. This is true for both lethal and nonlethal weapons.

First, police discretion is inevitable. It refers to the officer's decision making given the circumstances. It is impossible to train police officers like a computer which reacts to a situation in the exact same way by following a set protocol. Although the police do have many protocols regarding what procedures should be taken in a given situation, there are still many factors that cannot be fully covered in the protocol. We call these factors variables, because they vary from case to case. When faced with variables, police officers must exercise discretion to decide the best action needed to be taken. When it comes to discretion, it means different officers could make very different decisions in the same situation. For instance, when an officer perceives a threat, the officer must make a quick decision to eliminate the threat. Personal discretion will dictate exactly what action is taken by the officer, because personal discretion also affects how the threat is perceived in terms of severity and urgency. Thus, when an encounter between the police and the public turns into a confrontation, police discretion will determine what force is used. With nonlethal weapons being a viable alternative, the officer can afford to exercise discretion more liberally. On the other hand, without these alternatives, police discretion could be trapped between two extremes, that is, no force or deadly force. Hence, to say the least, police officers should be equipped with these nonlethal alternatives, and training should be in place to guide officers about the proper use of these nonlethal weapons. As mentioned, the use of nonlethal weapons can be excessive and controversial as well. Besides, in some situations lethal weapons are actually more suitable than nonlethal weapons. Either way, better decisions result from better discretion. Education and training are the two main methods to ensure better discretion. Contrary to what is often portrayed in movies, the quality of police work is usually defined by the decisions officers make (i.e., discretion), instead of their physical strength or the speed of their bullets.

Second, departmental policies help guide police discretion. Research found that the type of police use of force is associated with departmental policies in that less restrictive policies on the use of nonlethal weapons could reduce the number of fatal shootings by police (Ferdik et al., 2014). This is to say police officers are more likely to adopt less than lethal options when the agency policies allow them more room to do so. On the other hand, no evidence suggests that adopting nonlethal weapons will expose the officer to more danger because research supports that the police use of the Taser is closely related to the resistance presented more than other situational factors (Crow and Adrion, 2011). This follows that most police officers would not put themselves in harm's way for the sake of using nonlethal weapons.

Nevertheless, less restrictive policies on the use of nonlethal weapons may cause abuse of such weapons. One salient concern is that some officers might resort to the use of nonlethal weapons, such as the Taser, too quickly instead of trying to defuse tension with personal skills (Ready and White, 2011). Hence, it seems departmental policies ought to put some restrictions so as to avoid such abuse. Research found that the level of Taser usage is largely affected by departmental policies (Crow and Adrion, 2011), which means if the department's policy aims to reduce Taser use, it generally would be effective in achieving this goal. Given existing research findings, there seems to be two somewhat contradictory implications. On the one hand, the officers should be allowed more leeway to use nonlethal weapons because by doing so it reduces fatal shootings by police. In turn, it reduces controversies surrounding situations in which deadly force may not be called for. On the other hand, the officers ought to be restricted in their use of nonlethal weapons to avoid excessive use. Is there a way to enact perfect policies that can accomplish both ends? Perhaps there is but the solution certainly is not obvious, considering all the controversies regarding police use of force in these years.

There are few universal policies that can adequately apply to every agency. Each police agency needs to create policies that serve the agency's needs in line with the agency's mission, while the agency's mission must reflect public interest within the jurisdiction. Many controversies arise from the discrepancy between the public's anticipation and the police's self-image. Sometimes the public and the police are actually aiming for the same goal, but public perception somehow suggests otherwise. In this regard, police agencies need to be more transparent in policy making by putting more effort into explaining the rationale behind their policies to the public. The public need to know the police policies about use of force, and understand why such policies are in place. The public need to know that some policies are necessary to ensure the safety of police officers, even though it means that with hindsight, the use of force may seem unnecessary. When the public is more informed, the benefit is twofold. First, it is less likely the public would overreact to a situation in which police use of force is involved. Second, police officers are less likely to find excuses to abuse power and engage in excessive force. Mutual understanding is the key. The public understand the police must use force under some circumstances according to departmental polices so that there is no need to respond to an incident emotionally before all facts are clear, whereas the police understand the public are aware of what action is just and what action is unjust according to the policies so that officers would be less likely to resort to excessive force for the sake of intimidation or manipulation.

Certainly, police agencies cannot expect that the public will actively seek to understand policies. Just because you make something public record, it does not mean most people would pay attention to it. This is why more proactive effort is warranted. Similar to the concept of community policing, police agencies may look for or even create opportunities to communicate with the public about their policies, especially the policies regarding police use of force. When should the public expect to see the police use deadly force? When should the public expect to see nonlethal weapons be employed? To what extent should the officers use such force? Why are they using such force? What should the public do in these situations, either as a participant or a bystander? What are the consequences when officers abuse power or misuse weapons? How will unjust police use of force be determined? Who is overseeing these issues? All these questions ought to be clearly addressed in departmental policies, and then they should be clearly conveyed to the public. An open discussion should be welcome when necessary. Listening to the public does not mean police agencies must give in to every demand from the public. It is always beneficial to know what the public's expectation is even if sometimes the expectation is unrealistic.

Besides written policies, police agencies need to constantly explore better training and screening methods in terms of strengthening police officers' discretion. As mentioned, policies cannot cover all possible scenarios. On a daily basis, officers are making decisions based on personal discretion. Policies not only should guide police discretion but also need to define how poor discretion will be judged and penalized. When it comes to the use of nonlethal weapons, in addition to regulating the timing of using these weapons, policies should encourage officers to exercise better discretion in assessing the manner of using these weapons, since nonlethal weapons are supposed to be used in a non-life-threatening situation in which there is usually more room for different approaches to work.

In addition to nonlethal weapons, the use of technology also needs to be guided by sound policies. Almost every new technology applicable to police work comes with privacy issues. To dispel public doubts on the application of these new technologies, police agencies need clear policies that illustrate the purpose, the procedure, and the safeguard. For instance, a secretive police technique has recently been brought to light, namely, StingRay. It is a device that is intended to track a suspect's cell phone activities, such as texts, emails, phone calls, and location, by functioning like a cell phone tower (Business Insider, 2015). Supposedly this technology should be of great help to the police in tracking criminals and terrorists. The problem is this device may capture data from not only the target but also everyone around the target. Hence, the privacy issue is in question, to say the least. In the absence of public polices, no one knows exactly how the data captured from this device would be used. In fact, no one knows for sure how many agencies have adopted this device in their daily practice. When there is no policy explaining the purpose, the procedure, and the safeguard with respect to the use of such technologies, it is only fair for the public to have doubts on the propriety of applying these spy technologies to police work. Doubt is not something beneficial to police agencies as it further weakens the mutual trust that is essential to a healthy public–police relations.

☐ Summary

In this chapter, we discuss the use of nonlethal weapons and technology in police work. As stressed, the police need to be allowed to use force, so there is no need to automatically assume that the police are in the wrong every time police use of force occurs. The real issue lies in the timing and extent of force. Nonlethal weapons provide an alternative to deadly force when the situation does not involve imminent threat to life. This is not to say nonlethal weapons are not capable of resulting in death. It simply means these weapons are not designed to kill, but they might still induce a fatal outcome. Hence, some people prefer to call them less-lethal weapons instead. Nevertheless, what we call them is nothing more than a label. The important thing to consider is how to make sure these weapons can be used properly. They not only should be helpful in reducing unnecessary killing by the police, but also should provide officers sufficient protection.

The abuse of nonlethal weapons is a distinct possibility, especially since they are perceived as less likely to inflict fatal injuries. Some controversial cases are discussed in this chapter. Even if in some of those cases the officers might not have done anything wrong technically, there definitely is room to examine how the situation could have been handled differently to avoid controversies. Certainly, the police should not be doing their job in fear of controversy all the time. Officers must do what is necessary in response to a situation, without worrying about how their actions may be misinterpreted in the aftermath. There are two factors that may alleviate such worries: discretion and policy. First, police officers need to be trained and encouraged to exercise better discretion. In other words, they need to possess the capacity to make proper decisions that can be effective in resolving a conflict and can be justified under scrutiny. The importance of training needs no further explanation, but simply knowing what they should do is not enough. Officers must be encouraged to make better decisions, rather than doing whatever is more convenient. For instance, losing your temper is more convenient than maintaining patience; using a Taser on someone verbally belligerent is more convenient than talking them down. The convenient solutions may not be the most appropriate. This is where policy comes in as the second factor. Agency policies need to aim not only at regulating police conduct but they should also aim at emphasizing the individual ability to make a better decision when policies do not offer detailed instructions. Moreover, agency policies need to be transparent from the public perspective. The public should be made aware of how policies are in place to regulate police use of force and what the public should anticipate to avoid unrealistic expectations.

This is also true for the police use of technologies. These technologies are often costly, and a lot of them have not been comprehensively tested for their benefits and potential downsides. Evaluation is warranted before spending tax dollars on expensive new gadgets. Agency policies ought to proactively provide safeguards against misuse and dispel public doubts. Because technology is advancing rapidly and can be new to everyone, both the police and public should give each other time to adjust. More importantly, the implementation of such new technologies should not be seen or used as a political stunt. It is not just about looking good or sounding good. If it works, the accomplishment should be clearly defined and publicized, whereas changes need to be made if it does not work. Scientific evidence should be constantly solicited so as to make sure whatever the police are doing with tax dollars actually benefit both the police and the public in the most cost-effective way.

☐ References

Alpert, G.P., Smith, M.R., Kaminski, R.J., Fridell, L.A., MacDonald, J., and Kubu, B. 2011. Police use of force, Tasers and other less-lethal weapons. *National Institute of Justice Research in Brief.* Retrieved on February 12, 2015 from https://www.ncjrs.gov/pdffiles1/nij/232215.pdf

Bailey, W.C. 1996. Less-than-lethal weapons and police-citizen killings in US urban areas. *Criminology & Penology,* 42(4), 535–552.

Business Insider. 2015. Police are using a secret gadget that can track your phone, and they can't talk about it. Retrieved March 16, 2015 from http://www.businessinsider.com/stingray-phone-tracker-used-by-police-2015-3

CNN.com. 2014. No dashcams in Ferguson: One less tool in Michael Brown shooting investigation. Retrieved on February 19, 2015 from http://www.cnn.com/2014/08/14/us/ferguson-dashcams/

COPS. 2014. Implementing a body-worn camera program: Recommendations and lessons learned. Retrieved on February 19, 2015 from http://www.justice.gov/iso/opa/resources/472014912134715246869.pdf

Crow, M.S. and Adrion, B. 2011. Focal concerns and police use of force: Examining the factors associated with Taser use. *Police Quarterly,* 14(4), 366–387.

Ferdik, F.V., Kaminski, R.J., Cooney, M.D., and Sevigny, E.L. 2014. The influence of agency policies on conducted energy device use and police use of lethal force. *Police Quarterly,* 17(4), 328–358.

Homant, R.J. and Kennedy, D.B. 2000. Effectiveness of less than lethal force in suicide-by-cop incidents. *Police Quarterly,* 3(2), 153–171.

IACP. 2004. The impact of video evidence on modern policing. Retrieved on February 19, 2015 from http://www.theiacp.org/Portals/0/pdfs/WhatsNew/IACP%20In-Car%20Camera%20Report%202004.pdf

MacDonald, J.M., Kaminski, R.J., and Smith, M.R. 2009. The effect of less-lethal weapons on injuries in police use-of-force events. *American Journal of Public Health,* 99(12), 2268–2274.

Ready, J.T. and White, M. 2011. Exploring patterns of Taser use by the police: An officer-level analysis. *Journal of Crime and Justice,* 34(3), 190–204.

Sheridan, R.D. 2014. Letter by Sheridan regarding articles, "Taser electronic control devices can cause cardiac arrest in humans" and "TASER electronic control devices and cardiac arrests: Coincidental or causal?" *Circulation,* 130, 167.

Westphal, L.J. 2004. The in-car camera: Value and impact. Retrieved on February 19, 2015 from http://www.policeone.com/police-products/police-technology/articles/93475-The-in-car-camera-Value-and-impact/

Zipes, D.P. 2014. TASER electronic control devices can cause cardiac arrest in humans. *Circulation,* 29, 101–111.

Militarization of the Police

Laurence Armand French

☐ Introduction

There is much concern and consternation within America today concerning what many perceive to be the excessive use of force by law enforcement personnel especially when encountering threatening, yet unarmed, suspects, usually minority males. Part of this problem can be traced to the type of equipment available to law enforcement agencies, notably the increased firepower of modern military-style weapons. Also pertinent to this discussion is the continued undercurrent of racial/ethnic, sectarian, and class biases that are inherent in a complex multicultural environment such as the United States. Add to this the proliferation of high-capacity handguns and assault rifles within the general population, a situation worsened within the twenty-first century by *Second Amendment advocates* such as the National Rifle Association. While better training in the use of nonlethal weapons is a desired outcome for the prevention of the advent of deadly force, the disharmonious relations existing between law enforcement and those perceived by the police to be "troublemakers" also need to be addressed. A common social-psychological principle is that reciprocal antagonism involving members of polarized groups tends to fuel mutual antipathy. Georg Simmel explained this phenomenon as such: "Out-group hostility increases in-group cohesion."[1] Consequently, in divided societies where there this sense of polarized antagonism prevails, such as between white police officer and minority young-adult males, an otherwise minor incident can mushroom into a serious crisis. These situations often lead to elevated emotional states among those involved in the altercation, kicking in the participant's autonomic reactions of the sympathetic nervous system. This results in an increased adrenal response that, at this stage, is difficult to regulate with a rational override, hence resulting in mutual "fight or flight" responses where the better-armed party usually prevails—such as a police officer emptying his/her weapon at the "perceived" threat. This phenomenon is clearly illustrated with the November 29, 2012 Cleveland, Ohio case in which more than 100 police officers in 60 cruisers chased two unarmed blacks, because their car backfiring was mistaken for gunfire, for 22 miles ending when the car stopped and 12 officers on the scene fired 137 shots into the vehicle with one officer, Michael Brelo, firing 49 of those bullets, 15 while standing on the car's hood firing directly at the black male and female through the windshield. Brelo was subsequently charged with voluntary manslaughter but acquitted by a judge at his trial in May 2015. Although the United States now is known for its highly decentralized law enforcement apparatus, there is a long history of the symbiotic relationship between the military and police in enforcing U.S. laws. In addressing these issues we need to look at the interactions between the military and police in American society from its colonial roots to the present day situation.

☐ A Brief History of Police–Military Connection

British common laws prevailed in the 13 colonies along with the concept of county sheriffs and justices-of-the-peace. The sheriff and his deputies were considered to be "officers of the court," a system that continued after independence, making the county sheriff a constitutional law enforcement officer. This system, along with state militias, continued following independence. It is important to recognize the nature of the legal system during this time. Laws did not apply to all members of society but instead were made to protect the privileged class. Even the *Bill of Rights,* notably the first 12 amendments to the U.S. Constitution, pertained only to franchised white males. Women and children held no legal standing and had to rely on church officials for any redress for serious abuse. Blacks and American Indians, on the other hand, were not even considered to be "people" under the Constitution's preamble, "We the people of the United States... ." Indeed, the new U.S. republic's laws were based on the concept of *Divine Rights* under the term, *Manifest Destiny*. Hence, these laws were based on the concept of white supremacy, a political philosophy that encouraged the widespread practice of *ethnic cleansing* in addressing the *Indian Problem*. The new U.S. republic, like many nations at the time, relied on the military as the major national police force giving it overall jurisdiction over state militias and county sheriff's departments.[2]

American Indian tribes posed the greatest obstacle to whites reaping the riches of America and considerable efforts were made to reduce their influence mainly through their removal from lands and resources desired by whites. Colonial militias were organized as a form of local *homeland security* force within each colony with the original function of providing protection from Indian raids or retaliation. This model carried over to the new republic following independence. Hence, the earliest form of policing in American involved a paramilitary organization that had a solid link with the U.S. military. In 1803, the United States not only doubled its size and eliminated French colonial influence; the Louisiana Purchase also provided a dumping ground for unwanted Indian tribes with the creation of *Indian Territory* (Oklahoma). This set the stage for legal, forceful, removal of Indian tribes, a job initiated by the U.S. Army. Clearly, the major law enforcement task of the nineteenth century was policing American Indians. In addition to aiding the militias in fighting Indian flare-ups, the U.S. Army first played a significant policing role in the forceful removal of Indian tribes from the original 13 states west of the Mississippi River to *Indian Territory*. This action is best illustrated by the removal of the Five Civilized Tribes, notably the Cherokees in 1838, known as the *Trail of Tears*. This police action began in May 1838 under Congressional authorization via the 1830 *Indian Removal Act* and was conducted under the direction of the head of the U.S. Army, Major General Winfield Scott. Cherokees were forced at gunpoint and bayonets to leave their homes and placed into makeshift military stockades. By the end of June Scott's men had detained more than 10,000 Cherokees. In all some 20,000 Cherokees were rounded up and forced west to Indian Territory under army guard. More than 4000 died due to this police action, some while in the stockades and many more along the forced march to Oklahoma. Hundreds more died upon arrival in Indian Territory as a result of illnesses, and exposure during the 1000 mile forced march.[2]

The U.S. Army played a significant role in policing states and territories throughout the nineteenth century, mainly policing American

Indians that incidentally involved the United States longest war—the *Indian Wars* (1860s to the 1890s). The long military police action against American Indians in the west coincided with the advent of the U.S. Civil War. The war effort served to mitigate deplorable conditions on the Indian reservations leading to outbreaks by Sioux, Navajo, and Apache, among others. The Great Sioux Uprising, for example, occurred in the fall of 1862 whereby the Santee Sioux, on the verge of starvation, was led by Little Crow in attacks on white settlers occupying their former tribal lands. In June 1863, the U.S. Army, under the command of Colonel Kit Carson, began a punitive expedition against the Navajo resulting in their forceful removal known as the *Long Walk.* As with the removal of the Five Civilized Tribes 25 years earlier, herds, crops, and villages were destroyed and those who refused to be removed were hunted down and killed by the U.S. Army. Eight thousand Navajo were eventually removed to Fort Sumner in New Mexico where many more died due to the poor living conditions in the military concentration camp. Only in 1868 were the Navajo allowed back to their greatly reduced tribal lands.[3]

These police actions using the U.S. Army as the primary law enforcement backup to the U.S. marshals changed dramatically following the end of the U.S. Civil War. Now the Indian campaign became the main focus of the U.S. Army where the west was divided into military regions. Those battles fought from 1865 until 1891 qualified servicemen, both white and black (Buffalo Soldiers) with the *Indian Campaign Medal* thus making the Indian Wars the longest U.S. military campaign, longer than the current war on terrorism in Afghanistan. The *Indian Campaign Medal* provided the forerunner for the *Silver Star* given that a silver citation star was attached to the medal for meritorious or heroic conduct. The highest U.S. military award, the *Congressional Medal of Honor,* established during the Civil War, was also awarded during the Indian campaigns.[4]

Interestingly, the current contentious argument surrounding the Second Amendment has its roots in the British colonial era. The *right to bear arms* was actually a colonial requirement for local policing. During the colonial era, the 13 British colonies maintained militias (Provincial Defense Forces, the forerunner of both the current National Guard system and state police agencies) mainly for protection from the French and Indian forces. The Provincial Defense Force consisted of all able-bodied, Protestant males between the ages of 16 and 60. They were required to own their own musket, a bayonet, knapsack, and cartridge box, with 1 lb of black powder, 20 bullets, and 20 flints. They mustered 4 times yearly and were on-call the remainder of the time. Each regiment was headed by a colonel (commanding officer), and a lieutenant colonel (executive officer), with majors heading battalions and captains in charge of companies. A New England colonial militia captain (later major) Robert

Rogers, created a "commando unit patterned after the Indian fighters, living off the land and making hit-and-run strikes into enemy territory. More companies were added forming a ranger battalion with major Rogers in charge. Rogers "28 Rules of Ranging" provided the foundation for both the Queen's York Rangers of the Canadian Army and the U.S. Army Rangers.[5] Other local protection included night watchmen until the advent of municipal police in the mid-1800s. State police forces came about with the advent of automobiles and state highways that transcended county lines. Again they based their organizational structure on the British colonial "Provincial Defense Force" with a colonel in charge and barracks (companies) headed by captains distributed throughout the state jurisdiction.

Federal law enforcement agencies in the United States, on the other hand, trace their origin to 1789 when Congress authorized the Revenue Cutter Service, now the U.S. Coast Guard, and the U.S. federal marshals. The U.S. marshal is the federal counterpart to the county sheriff, both being officers of the court. The new U.S. republic was now divided into a two-tier law enforcement system based on state/local jurisdictions and the federal jurisdiction. Much of the federal legal system dealt with international relations, including interaction with Indian tribes that initially held the status of independent nations which were dealt with via treaties. George Washington appointed the first 13 U.S. marshals on September 24, 1779, one for each of the states, making them the first "officers of the court" with the responsibility of carrying out the death sentence imposed by the federal courts. The U.S. marshal was also responsible for taking the census in his jurisdiction (state) every 10 years for the annual tally.

The U.S. marshal's office was the civilian federal law enforcement for Indian Country beginning with the Louisiana Purchase. On July 1, 1870, the U.S. Congress created the Department of Justice giving it authority over federal law enforcement, including the U.S. marshals making them the first police agency authorized to enforce federal laws in the states and territories. Given this authority, the U.S. marshals and their deputies played a significant role in Indian Territory during the Indian Wars up until the beginning of the twentieth century. That is why the U.S. marshal and not the FBI is portrayed in western lore, movies, and television shows. Later, in 1908, U.S. Attorney General Bonaparte created the Bureau of Investigation as the investigative arm of his office. In 1932, it was renamed the U.S. Bureau of Investigation, and, finally, in 1935, the Federal Bureau of Investigation or the FBI. Hence, the FBI emerges at about the same time as state police agencies. The "Bureau," however, had its influence in federal Indian Country beginning in 1908 primarily due to passage of the Major Crimes Act of 1885, now sharing these responsibilities with the long-established U.S. marshal's office.

Today the FBI, perhaps best known worldwide, is but one of many federal law enforcement agencies that have emerged over the past century, each with its own special jurisdictional authority established by Congress. All four major branches of the U.S. military (Army, Navy, Air Force, Marines) have their own law enforcement agencies under the Department of Defense (DOD) while the U.S. Coast Guard acts as a law enforcement agent under the newly created Department of Homeland Security (DHS) following the September 11, 2001 terrorists attacks along with numerous other law enforcement agencies including Customs and Border Protection (CBP); Office of Border Patrol (OBP); United States Secret Service (USSS); and the Transportation Security Administration (TSA). Other federal agencies with law enforcement authority include the U.S. Department of Agriculture (USDA); Department of Commerce (DOC); Department of Education; Department of Energy (DOE); Department of Health and Human Services; U.S. Department of the Interior (USDI) with the Bureau of Indian Police (BIA Police) and Bureau of Land Management and U.S Park Rangers; Department of Justice (USDOJ) which includes the U.S. Marshals Service (USMS); the FBI; the Bureau of Prisons (BOP); Bureau of Alcohol, Tobacco, Firearms, and Explosives (ATF); U.S. Drug Enforcement Administration (DEA); and Office of Inspector General (DOJOIG); Department of State (DoS); Department of Labor; Department of the Treasury; and the Department of Veteran Affairs.

☐ The Evolution of Firearms and Deadly Force

During the colonial era and the time of the Second Amendment (1791), muzzle-loader, flintlock firearms prevailed, notably the musket which had a smoothbore like that of shotguns today. This limited the effective range of these weapons often requiring close combat involving bayonets. The advent of the Kentucky rifle during the early 1800s now made the muzzle-loader more accurate and at a greater range. The addition of "lands and groves" in the barrel of rifles and pistols along with a firing cap replacing the flintlock provided greater accuracy but still limited these to a single-shot action. The bow and arrow used by most American Indian tribes provided greater firepower and equal accuracy as the early muzzle-loaders. It was the advent of the rapid-fire revolver, and later the rifle–carbine, that transformed both the U.S. military and law enforcement. Samuel Colt developed a muzzle-loader, black powder, single-action revolver in the 1830s, but its widespread fame came from the Texas Rangers.

The Texas Rangers emerged as the militia for the breakaway Republic of Texas following the disbandment of both the regular army and navy. And the Texas Rangers are closely linked to the Colt revolver. Indeed, the Republic of Texas became the proving grounds for this innovative weapon. Texas was Colt's first customer, ordering 180 .36-caliber holster-model, five-shot, Paterson Colt revolvers for its navy in August 1839. The Texas Rangers, on the other hand, had been ordering them individually since they first became available in 1837. Once President Sam Houston disbanded the Texas navy, these Colts were reassigned to the Texas Rangers. The Texas Rangers often carried three or more revolvers with loaded extra cylinders, greatly increasing their firepower thus enhancing the Texas Rangers' image as a deadly force. Once Texas was annexed to the United States in 1845 as a slave state, the Texas Rangers became one of the most deadly forces during the Mexican War (1846–1848). With modifications suggested by the Texas Ranger (trigger guard, six-shot capacity…), the United States adopted the revolver now called the Colt 1851 Navy Revolver. As such, it became a popular sidearm for both Union and Confederate forces during the U.S Civil War (1861–1865).[6]

The development of the self-contained (integrated) cartridge (bullet) further enhanced the firepower of repeating weapons, both rifles and pistols, and allowed for more rapid firing breech-loading single-shot rifles such as the Sharps Military Carbine, widely used during the Indian Wars. Prior to the self-contained cartridge, both long guns (smoothbore or rifles) and handguns (including the revolver) required the additional step of activating the "cap-and-ball" sequence whereby black powder had to be packed into each cylinder (muzzle loading) along with the installation of a firing cap at the hammer. The early cartridges had the powder held together in a cardboard bullet that was either rim- or center-fired by a firing pin that ignited the percussion cap. The French were the first to invent the cartridge which soon evolved from a cardboard to a metallic shell (shotgun shells still use the cardboard format). Indeed, the .22 caliber percussion cap soon became a bullet in itself with the .22 LR (long rifle) one of the most popular calibers today.

The advent of the bullet led to new adaptations to the revolver, notably the Colt Single Action Army Revolver introduced in 1873. The civilian model of this .45 caliber six-shooter was commonly known as the *Peacemaker.* It was used by both the military during the Indian Wars and by law enforcement, notably U.S. Marshals and county sheriffs, as well as being popular with outlaws. The .45 Colt saw action in all military actions from 1873 including World War I. It was replaced with the semiautomatic, single-action .45 caliber M1911, 7-shot pistol which itself served the U.S. military through three wars (World War II, Korea, and Viet Nam). It fired a shorter ACP (automatic Colt pistol) round than the Colt revolver that was also in submachine guns like the Thompson and its various adaptations. The M1911 semiautomatic pistol was unique in that it was gas-operated so that the slide extracted the spent round and cocked the hammer on the back stroke while chambering another round from the magazine on its return. The M1911 was single-action in that the initial round needed to be manually fed which, in turn, cocked the hammer. It replaced the double-action .38 caliber military revolver that proved ineffective against the Moros during the Philippine resurrection early in the twentieth century. Later modified to double-action, the .45 automatic continues to be popular with military (USMC, Navy, Delta Force) units and with federal (FBI, etc.), state (New Mexico, etc.) and local police (LAPD, SWAT, etc.) in the United States as well as in other countries. The M1911 was the prototype for later semiautomatic pistols, foreign and domestic, that now come in a variety of calibers. When the U.S. military replaced the .45 pistol with the M.9 mm Beretta, many local law enforcement agencies followed suit but the trend in both law enforcement and the military is to go back to the more powerful .45 caliber pistol.

The cartridge (bullet) was used by the U.S. military in its Sharps rifles which eventually led to the popular .45–70 caliber. The single-shot, breech loaded, falling block design provided a rate of fire of 8–10 shots per minute. The carbine model was used by both Union and Confederate cavalry troops during the Civil War and was used throughout the Indian Wars. During this same era, Christopher Spencer created the lever-action repeating rifle that was also used during the Civil War and throughout the Indian Wars. It used copper rim-fire bullets stored in a removable 7-round tube magazine. The bullet (aka cartridge, round) led to the development of repeating rifles and carbines with lever, bolt, or pump actions. Winchester lever-action rifles and carbines were built on this model and became even more popular in the U.S. west following the Civil War up into the early twentieth century. Indeed, the Winchester Model 1873 became known as "the gun that won the west." Models 1873 and 1876 (centennial model) were widely used during the Indian Wars and the Spanish-American War as well as by the Texas Rangers and the Canadian North-West Mounted Police. The 1876 model also introduced smokeless powder that replaced the black powder round. Lever-action .30–30s remains a popular hunting rifle to this day.

The introduction of a rapid-fire weapon, the *machine gun* also has its origin with the Civil War with the *Gatlin Gun*. The Gatlin gun was used by Union forces during the Civil War and during the Indian Wars, the Spanish-American War, Philippine-American War, Boxer Rebellion, and the Russo-Japanese War, and other conflicts. The Gatlin gun used a cyclic multibarrel design that synchronized the firing-reloading sequence keeping the barrels from overheating. Just as the U.S. Civil

War provided the incentive for better military firearms, World War I provided the testing ground for submachine guns, two American models that saw action in both military and civilian operations. The M1918 Browning Automatic Rifle (BAR) was designed in 1917 and saw limited action during the World War I, yet remained the light machine gun for both the U.S. Army and the U.S. Marine Corps up through the Viet Nam War where it was replaced by the M60 machine gun. The BAR used the powerful 30–06 caliber bullet and came with 20-round magazines and a bi-pod for prone firing. The M1928A1 Thompson submachine gun (Tommy gun) was developed at the end of the World War I (1921) and chambered the .45 ACP round that the military 1911-model .45 pistol used. It came with a variety of magazines holding from 30 to 100 rounds. It was widely used during World War II, Korea, and Vietnam. It was widely used by law enforcement agencies in both the United States and Israel and by U.S. gangsters and the Irish Republican Army (IRA) during the 1969–1998 conflict known as *The Troubles*. The BAR was good up to 500-yards making it a versatile military weapon and was issued as the automatic weapon among USMC squads. The Thompson, on the other hand, had a limited effective range like its .45 pistol of about 50–60 yards.[7] Indeed, these two weapons were often stolen from National Guard Armories and used by criminals like Pretty Boy Floyd, the Barrow Gang, the Barker-Karpis Gang, the Baby Face Nelson Gang, the Dillinger Gang, and Bonnie and Clyde during America's *Great Crime Wave* during the Depression Era. This use of deadly force by these gangs armed with Thompsons and BARs provided J. Edgar Hoover the incentive he needed to petition the U.S. Congress to finally arm the FBI which up to that time remained unarmed and had to rely on either local law enforcement agencies or the U.S. Marshals for backup.[8]

The .30 caliber M1 carbine was also one of the first gas-operated assault weapons with the M2 having the option for semiautomatic or fully automatic fire. The M1 carbine was widely used in World War II, Korea, and Vietnam as well as by British forces in Northern Ireland during *The Troubles*. It remains a popular weapon among law enforcement agencies in both the United States and abroad. The more powerful M1 rifle (Garand) is a gas-operated, semiautomatic rifle using the 30–06 caliber round like its BAR counterpart. It was widely used during the World War II and in Korea. It was replaced by the M14 which was of a similar design as the M1 Garand but instead of using an 8-round clip, it used a magazine like the BAR and M1/M2 carbine and had the capacity for fully automatic fire. It also used the 7.62 NATO round (US 308 caliber) which was similar to the 30–06 round. The M14 is still the NATO preferred long-distance rifle. However, the jungle warfare in Vietnam required another type of weapon hence the M16 rifle in caliber 5.56 mm.

Used selectively by the U.S. Army beginning in 1963, it became the standard service rifle for the U.S. military in 1969 and was later modified to fire 3-round burst per trigger pull. The smaller version, M4 carbine, is used as well.[9] The M16 rifle/M4 carbine played a significant role in the militarization of U.S. law enforcement in that they coincided with the advent of Special Weapons and Tactics (SWAT) teams devised during the 1960s in Los Angeles for riot control, and with the creation of the Law Enforcement Assistance Administration (LEAA) each state began creating its own SWAT teams for potential riot control as well as to participate in the national *war on drugs*. An even more intense militarization effort followed the 9/11/01 terrorist attacks and the new *war on terrorism*. Clearly, a major factor in the militarization of law enforcement in the United States was the creation of SWAT teams and their federal support through programs such as LEAA and Homeland Security.[10]

☐ The Contemporary Scene

Federal training of police included law enforcement agencies within the United States and beyond, began in earnest in an effort to curtail the influx of illicit drugs into America. The focus turned to Mexico following the successes in Colombia, resulting in the recent militarization of the U.S./Mexico border. The *war on terrorism* that began following the 9/11/01 attacks in New York and DC led to another round of federal funding for state and local law enforcement through grants made available through the newly created DHS. Here, the Border Patrol, National Guard units, state, country, and local law enforcement act in unison against perceived threats against the United States. Granted these coordinated efforts are needed and the end result has contributed toward better law enforcement coordination and standards, nonetheless, some feel that these achievements have been at the expense of traditional community policing. The effectiveness of these coordinated efforts was clearly demonstrated with the manhunt subsequent to the 2013 Boston Marathon terrorist attack on April 15 which included both federal and state (Massachusetts and New Hampshire) law enforcement personnel.

Police: The Civilian Military—Authority and Status

An interesting outcome of the militarization of law enforcement is the corresponding rank/status phenomenon. Anthropologists and sociologists have long recognized that authority and privilege are associated with a person's status within the society. In this sense, all organized societies define the status hierarchy. Ralph Linton noted that cultures usually subscribe to two types of status, *ascribed* based mainly on sex, age, and family/clan affiliation; and *achieved,* based on individual accomplishments or elective processes such as occupation, marriage, and the like. I would add two subcategories to the latter—*enhanced* and *fabricated* status. Enhanced status is when an obviously legitimate status is elevated to something higher while fabricated status is when someone creates a status far removed from their actual position.

In societies like the United States where there are no inherited titles, military status ranks high. The military is based on a caste system that divides commissioned officers from enlisted personnel. The officer ranks (O-1to O-10), in turn, are divided into two echelons with "field-grade" ranks, that is major and above, being the most prestigious. Within this system, a captain (O-3) is the commanding officer (CO) of a company or battery while a battalion has a lieutenant colonel (O-5) as the CO and a major (O-4) as the executive officer (XO). Colonels generally head regiments, while brigadier generals are CO's of brigades and major generals lead divisions and so on. Thus, a field-grade officer can command anywhere from 1,000 to 10,000 military personnel, including entire armies or navies. The United States did not have a permanent four-star general until 1866 when this status was awarded to U.S. Grant. The Confederate Army, however, created the four-star rank during the Civil War. When U.S. Grant became president, the sole four-star rank was passed on to William T. Sherman and then to Philip H. Sheridan who led the Indian Wars in the west. This permanent rank was not allocated again until 1919 when it was given to John (Black Jack) Pershing. World War II not only saw the proliferation of four-star generals and admirals but also the creation of the five-star generals; even then, only nine men held this rank; four admirals and five generals. This was a lifelong position and was retired in 1981 with the death of General Omar Bradley. George Washington was added to the list posthumously on July 4, 1976. Today, the head of the Joint Chiefs-of-Staff, the heads of the four military services (Army, Navy, Air Force, and Marines), and the head of NATO forces, are four-star generals or admirals, albeit superior to other four-star officers serving under their command.

Civilian superiors, such as the Secretary of the Army, Navy, and Air Force, do not hold military rank. Yet, the use of military rank predominates within U.S. society especially within the paramilitary police organizations. The military structure at the state level, on the other hand, occurs with the National Guard which follows the regular military rank structure with the governor appointing the commanding general. Using

New Hampshire as an example, the commanding general until recently was a brigadier general. However, the prolonged *war on terrorism* in Iraq and Afghanistan, with greater reliance on the federalized National Guard, resulted in an upgrade to the rank with a major general in command of the overall National Guard and brigadier generals as heads of the two components, the Army National Guard and the Air National Guard. This inflation at the higher echelon of military rank has also afflicted the U.S. military in general.

Within the civilian criminal justice systems, both federal and state, the top law enforcement officer is the Attorney "General." Within the state system, the state police is the law enforcement agency assigned to the attorney general's office with statewide jurisdiction. At the federal level, the U.S. Marshal's office was designed in 1789 to act as the law enforcement for U.S. Courts with a high marshal appointed to each state and territory. State police agencies, on the other hand, usually follow the military rank structure with the director using holding the rank of O-6 colonel acting under the direction of the AG (attorney general). State police forces often have "troops" located throughout the state's jurisdiction, again using the military rank model with a captain heading the troop.

When looking at the largest municipal police department in the United States, New York City with a population of over 8 million and covering 468.9 square miles in five boroughs, it becomes evident that a well-organized police force is justified. In the New York Police Department (NYPD) we again see the five-star rank, this time for the police commissioner who supervises up to 40,000 personnel. Clearly, this falls under the enhanced status category while the basic rank hierarchy below the commissioner's office clearly follows a reasonable paramilitary format: chief of department holds four stars; bureau chief, three stars; assistant chief, two stars; and deputy chief, one star. Inspectors are full-bird colonels; deputy inspectors, lieutenant colonels; while captains head precincts. Below captains are lieutenant, sergeant, and patrolmen. Captains head the 76 precincts. The Los Angeles Police Department (LAPD) has jurisdiction for a similar geographic area as the NYPD but with half the population. The LAPD's (third largest U.S. police agency—Chicago is second largest), rank structure has the politically appointed (by the mayor) chief of police holding four-star general status with the assistant chief (Deputy Chief II) holding three-star general rank while the Deputy Chief I is a two-star general, and police commanders hold one-star status. The intermediate field-grade military ranks (O-4 major/lieutenant commander; O-5 lieutenant colonel/commander; and O-6 colonel/captain) are omitted with the next highest rank being that of captain and then lieutenant, police sergeant II/police detective III (staff sergeants), police sergeant I/police detective II (buck sergeants); police detective I/ police officer III (corporals) with police officers I and II having no military insignia.

Other police departments soon picked up on this military-style ranking, assigning themselves the rank of general regardless of the size or jurisdiction of their department. The proliferation of this fabricated status was soon demonstrated with heads of departments putting on general's stars (including four or five stars) regardless if their legal status was high sheriff or chief of police. This practice clearly speaks of the "arrogance of position" raising serious questions concerning their commitment as public servants, who are licensed to use lethal force, in their role in securing public safety. Law enforcement represents a public service agency, one licensed to use deadly force in protecting the public at large. Enhanced and inflated status has little to do with carrying out law enforcement functions. Instead, it can lead to a self-fulfilling prophecy whereby the chief or high sheriff comes to believe that they are, in fact, far superior to their fellow officers, an image conveyed to the public as well. Law enforcement was not intended to be a high-status occupation. All that is necessary to convey their authority to the public is the uniform and shield or badge. The standard for any state should be the state police force which has the broadest jurisdiction.

☐ Conclusions

The issue of policing is not a simple matter where a single solution can solve all the issues confronting America and other societies. All societies have rules and enforcement agents whether they are a secular or sectarian dictatorship, or some form of representative government (parliament, legislature, executive committee, etc.). Indeed, law enforcement, by its definition, compels police to enforce the laws/rules promulgated by societal leaders. Unfortunately, given human nature, these rules are often biased to favor the majority or the group in control. Consequently, discrimination needs to be addressed at the leadership level (U.S. Supreme Court, federal–state legislative levels) first before we can adequately train and better regulate enforcement agencies such as the police. These issues are more complex within multiethnic, multisectarian societies including contemporary, developed societies such as the United States.

Good, viable solutions were offered by the numerous Presidential Blue Ribbon commissions/committees that followed the riots of the 1960s and 1970s. They included such concepts as hiring police officers with a minimum of a 4-year liberal arts college degree. Instead, police academies morphed into military-style boot camps (cop shops) providing the mind-set of an occupation force ready to face the perceived "enemies" of society. This was the antithesis of the concept of "community policing" whereby law enforcement is an integral component of the community within its jurisdiction (its patch/beat). Ideally, the police would be trained to be available to all members of the community regardless of race, ethnic origin, gender, or religion. And for this to be effective, the police would have to be attired for easy recognition without looking like a military occupational force.

Another recommendation at the time of the Omnibus Crime Control and Safe Streets Act was for civilian oversight in the form of "police commissions." Unfortunately in many instances these positions became politicized with civilian commissions, like the prosecution, often automatically siding with law enforcement when issues of excessive force or blatant discrimination surfaced. Toward this end, the states and federal government need to provide professionally trained omnibus personnel that are independent of any political or ideological influence. And as stated earlier, law enforcement personnel, especially chiefs, sheriffs, et cetera, need to lose the military attire that attempts to present themselves as admirals and generals. Law enforcement personnel also need to align with their community and not with the *Blue Brotherhood* (aka *Bubbahood)*. Clearly, this is a profession where unions should be exempt if only because they instill a sense of "us versus them" within society, and yet another factor is the polarization of police and segments of the public.

Another critical factor is the screening process. Psychological scales can determine, to a fair accuracy, not only mental suitability (*mad cop)* but also problematic character logic flaws including serious personality disorders (*bad cop)*. The machismo/macho image also needs to be addressed, especially if steroids are involved. At minimum, psychological reassessments need to be administered if a clique of officers falls into this group. This can be seen as a form of intimidation among members of society, notably minority members of the community. Moreover, training needs to focus on the use of nonlethal approaches to crisis situations where the subject does not have a viable weapon (firearm, machete, etc.). Psychological protocols can train officers to control their level of adrenal response to crisis situations (those situations where officers empty their clip of 15–17 rounds in their response to a perceived threat). These options have been available for over 40 years, yet seldom employed. Law enforcement is an integral part of any viable society, how it is used is often a political factor and as long as divisions are allowed and fostered within a society, so will police abuses.

☐ References

1. See, G. Simmel, *Conflict* (K.A. Wolff, trans.). New York, New York: The Free Press, 1955; L. Coser, *The Functions of Social Conflict*. New York, New York: The Free Press, 1956.

2. See, L.A. French, *Winds of Injustice: American Indians and the U.S. Government*. New York, New York: Garland Publishing, 1994; L.A. French, *Legislating Indian Country: Significant Milestones in Transforming Tribalism*. New York, New York: Peter Land, 2007; *Indian Removal Act* (May 28, 1830). U.S. Statutes at Large, 4:411–412.

3. *Op cited* #2; and C. Kluckhohn and D. Leighton, *The Navajo*. Cambridge, Massachusetts: Harvard University Press, 1946; G. Bailey and R.G. Bailey, *A History of the Navajo*. Santa Fe, New Mexico: School of American Indian Research Press, 1986; L.R. Baily, *The Long Walk*. Los Angeles, California: Westernlore Press, 1964.

4. See, F.N. Schubert, *Black Valor: Buffalo Soldiers and Medal of Honor, 1870–1898*. Wilmington, Delaware: Scholarly Resources, Inc. 1997; R.W. Stewart (ed.). Winning the West: The Army in the Indian Wars, 1865–1890 (Chapter 14). *The Unites States Army and the Forging of a Nation, 1775–1917, Vol. I* (*Army Historical Series*). Washington, DC: U.S. Government Printing Office, 2001.

5. See, J.R, Cuneo, *Robert Rodgers of the Rangers*. New York, New York: Oxford University Press, 1959; J.F. Ross, *War on the Run: The Epic Story of Robert Rogers and the Conquest of America's First Frontier*. New York, New York: Bantam Books, 2009.

6. See, L.A. French, *Running the Border Gauntlet: The Mexican Migrant Controversy*. Santa Barbara, California: Praeger, 2010; C.H. Harris, III and L.R. Sadler, *The Texas Rangers and the Mexican Revolution: The Bloodiest Decade, 1910–1920*. Albuquerque, New Mexico: University of New Mexico Press, 2004; C.T. Haven and F.A. Belden, *A History of the Colt Revolver*. New York, New York: Morrow, 1940; J.E. Parsons, *The Peacemaker and Its Rivals: An Account of the Single-Action Colt*. New York, New York: Morrow, 1985.

7. See, C. Bishop, *The Encyclopedia of Weapons of World War II*. New York, New York: Sterling Publishing, 2002; FM23–15, *Basic Field Manual—Browning Automatic Rifle, Caliber 30, M1918A2*. Washington, DC: U.S. Department of Defense, 1940; *M1 Thompson (Tommy Gun)—Submachine Gun, History, Specs and Pictures, Military Security and Civilian Guns and Equipment*, www.militaryfactory.com/smallarms/detail.asp?

8. See, B. Burrough, *Public Enemies: America's Greatest Crime Wave and the Birth of the FBI, 1933–34*. New York, New York: Penguin Books (2004).

9. See, E.D. Ezell, *The Great Rifle Controversy: Search for the Ultimate Infantry Weapon from World War II through Vietnam and Beyond*. Harrisburg, Pennsylvania: Halstead Press, 1984; D.R. Hughes, *The History and Development of the M16 Rifle and its Cartridge*. Oceanside, California: Armory Publications, 1990.

10. See, P.B. Kraska and V.E. Kaeppler, Militarizing American police: The rise and normalization of paramilitary units, *Social Problems*, 44(1):1–18, 1997.

Racial Profiling: The Intersection of Race and Policing

Michael L. Birzer

☐ Introduction

On August 9, 2014, Officer Darren Wilson of the Ferguson, Missouri Police Department was on patrol when he observed Michael Brown, an 18-year-old African American male walking in the middle of the street. Officer Wilson pulled up beside Brown and requested that he get out of the middle of the street. Facts later reveal that Brown had robbed a convenience store minutes earlier. Brown allegedly took a package of cigarillos. What happened next is sketchy but witness reports say that Brown reached into Officer Wilson's police cruiser and which point an altercation occurred between him and Officer Wilson. A single gunshot was then heard. Within seconds, witnesses saw Brown running from the police cruiser with Officer Wilson chasing after Brown and yelling for him to stop. Brown turned around and charged at Officer Wilson. Officer Wilson fired several rounds with his handgun killing Brown.

The shooting prompted rumors throughout Ferguson, albeit inaccurate and largely fueled by the media that Officer Wilson executed Brown as he had his hands up and was attempting to surrender. A St. Louis area prosecutor announced that a grand jury had decided not to indict Officer Wilson and that no charges would be brought against Officer Wilson. A Department of Justice investigation also cleared Officer Wilson of wrongdoing in the shooting of Brown (United States Department of Justice, 2015a).

The shooting of Michael Brown and the decision not to indict Officer Wilson sparked several days of protests and riots resulting in millions of dollars of property damages to Ferguson's businesses. Since the Ferguson riots, unrest has erupted in many other cities across the United States as the result of what many perceive to be police abuse of African American citizens. More recently in Baltimore, following the death of Freddie Gray, an African American man who died while in police custody, large-scale rioting and unrest occurred. Six police officers were charged with crimes ranging from second-degree murder to unlawful arrest of Freddie Gray. The rioting in Baltimore resulted in property damages to businesses totaling nearly 10 million dollars.

Community activist groups such as Black Lives Matter contend that the recent shootings and other abuses of African Americans at the hands of the police are merely the tipping point of what they view as biased police practices and a criminal justice system in which they more often than not are treated unfairly. In Ferguson this appears to be the case. After the Michael Brown shooting incident the Department of Justice investigated the practices of the Ferguson Police Department in light of reports of biased practices against racial minority citizens (United States Department of Justice, 2015b). The investigation uncovered a systemic pattern of biased practices against African Americans by police authorities in Ferguson. Specifically, the Department of Justice found that the police department engaged a pattern or practice of

- Conducting stops without reasonable suspicion and arrests without probable cause in violation of the Fourth Amendment

- Interfering with the right to free expression in violation of the First Amendment

- Using unreasonable force in violation of the Fourth Amendment

The Department of Justice found that Ferguson Municipal Court has a pattern or practice of

- Focusing on revenue over public safety, leading to court practices that violate the 14th Amendment's due process and equal protection requirements.

- Court practices exacerbating the harm of Ferguson's unconstitutional police practices and imposing particular hardship upon Ferguson's most vulnerable residents, especially upon those living in or near poverty. Minor offenses can generate crippling debts, result in jail time because of an inability to pay and result in the loss of a driver's license, employment, or housing.

The Department of Justice found a pattern or practice of racial bias in both the Ferguson Police Department and the municipal court.

- The harms of Ferguson's police and court practices are borne disproportionately by African Americans and that this disproportionate impact is avoidable.

- Ferguson's harmful court and police practices are due, at least in part, to intentional discrimination, as demonstrated by direct evidence of racial bias and stereotyping about African Americans by certain Ferguson police and municipal court officials.

This chapter examines the intersection of race and the police through what many believe is racial profiling or bias-based policing. The chapter has three primary objectives. First, an examination of past abuses by the police on racial minorities will be discussed, providing the important context into why so many racial minority citizens have distrust of the police and equate the practice of racial profiling as a continuation of past injustices. Second, the chapter examines how racial minority citizens experience what they believe to be racial profiling. The chapter concludes with a discussion on strategies that the police and community can engage together in an attempt to begin to resolve racial profiling.

☐ A Fractured History

Racial minorities, particularly African Americans, have had a long and troubled history of disparate treatment by United States Criminal Justice Authorities. Some argue that the police, the law, the courts, and the correctional system, have all been used as instruments of oppression based on race, and if the nation is to complete the processes eliminating this subjugation, we "must move to eliminate all vestiges of racial bias" from the criminal justice system (Moss, 1990, p. 88).

The perceptions of racial profiling by the police of minority citizens may exist, in part, because of the long history of disparate treatment by the criminal justice system. Consequently, there is a race coding of sorts that takes place and which culminates in stereotyping that associates race to crime (Quillian and Pager, 2001, 2010). The symbolic criminal figure is often portrayed as a black male who is in turn subjected to increased surveillance, profiled, policed, adjudicated, and incarcerated disproportionately. Therefore, racially biased policing in law enforcement is merely a symptom of a more serious problem that afflicts the entire criminal justice system. Moreover, it represents one of the single most pressing issues that face fundamental criminal justice policy and practice which to date has only been addressed in a superficial manner.

Underpinning of Race

Race and policing, and for that matter, criminal justice are inextricably linked. To dismiss this fact is somewhat naïve. Consider that more than 60% of the individuals in prison are racial and ethnic minorities. In the case of black males the data are more alarming. One out of eight black males in their 20s are in prison or jail on any given day. While Black Americans represent between 13% and 14% of the general population, "they are disproportionally represented in every aspect of the criminal justice system, as victims, offenders, prisoners and arrestees" (Ogletree et al. 1995, p. 13). In federal prisons alone, blacks represent nearly 38% of inmates serving time. Similarly, over half the inmates incarcerated in our nation's jails is either black or Hispanic (United States Census Bureau, 2012).

The intersection of race and the criminal justice system from a historical lens reveals a pattern of the disparate treatment of racial minorities, especially of blacks. This includes of a legacy of Jim Crow laws and other injudicious acts. From the inception of the American police they were charged with upholding the status quo, a status quo that in some cases legally mandated inequality (Barlow and Hickman-Barlow, 2000). The following is a telling description of this legacy:

> The fact that the legal order not only countenanced but sustained slavery, segregation, and discrimination for most of our nation's history, and the fact that the police were bound to uphold that order, set a pattern for

police behavior and attitudes toward minority communities that has persisted until the present day. That pattern includes the idea that minorities have fewer civil rights, and the police have little responsibility for protecting them from crime within their communities. (Williams and Murphy, 1990, p. 2)

During slavery in the United States, slave catchers acting with police authority in many southern states were charged with the duties of returning runaway slaves to their masters. Every slave-owning state had active, established slave patrols, and though they had many functions within the community, their primary objective was to act as the first line of defense against a slave rebellion. Slave patrols caught runaway slaves, enforced slave codes, discouraged any large gathering of blacks, and generally perpetuated the atmosphere of fear that kept the slaves in line (Hadden, 2001).

Slave patrols were a unique form of policing. They worked closely with the militia and were virtually given free rein to stop, search, and when necessary, beat slaves all under the protection of the legal system. It is an uncomfortable fact that police forces in the south actively pursued slaves. Slave patrols proved to be an integral step in the development of southern police organizations (Wadman and Allison, 2004). Professor Samuel Walker referred to slave patrols as "a distinctly American form of law enforcement," and he went on to say that they were probably the first modern police forces in this United States (Walker, 1999, p. 22).

Slave patrols were made up of mostly poor whites that frequently brutalized slaves caught without passes after curfew (Genovese, 1976). The influence of slave patrols in the southern states is the cornerstone to what some contend is the institutional racism mentality that continues to plague some American police departments (Wadman and Allison, 2004).

At the conclusion of the radical reconstruction (the year 1877) in the south, the criminal justice system represented one of the major instruments of white supremacy (Walker, 1980). Some police agencies in the south maintained white supremacy through their brutal and discriminatory practices toward African Americans (Barlow and Hickman-Barlow, 2000). Slavery was officially abolished in 1865 but its dark shadow would continue to impact African Americans for many years to come (Patterson, 1998). Southern whites found ways to defy reconstruction, preserve their social order which subsequently limited economic growth (Lynch, 1968). The humiliation and subjugation of African Americans continued through the enforcement of Jim Crow laws, economic and educational segregation, and the acceptance of lynching as means of social control (Wadman and Allison, 2004).

If an African American found himself on the wrong side of the criminal justice system he had a mark even going into a trial. If he did go to trial, the deck was stacked against him.

The standards of evidence in most court trials were so low, the means of obtaining damaging testimony so dubious, the importance of constituted authority so evident, that insurrection prosecutions at law must be seen as a religious more than a normal criminal process. By such means individual slaves, and sometimes the whites affiliated with them, were made sacrifices to a sacred concept of white supremacy. (Wyatt-Brown, 1982, p. 402)

Jim Crow laws (roughly 1880s through the 1960s) were passed throughout the south as a way to keep African Americans in inferior positions segregated from whites. Under Jim Crow laws it was permissible in Mississippi to require African Americans to pass literacy tests in order to vote. Other states throughout the south in unison fashion passed similar Jim Crow laws that mandated separate bathrooms for African Americans, forbade interracial marriage, prohibited African Americans from eating in the same room as white customers in restaurants, forbade black barbers from cutting a white man or woman's hair, and made it unlawful to bury African Americans in the same cemeteries as deceased whites.

In September 1962 a federal court ordered the University of Mississippi to accept James Meredith, a 28-year-old African American, much to the vehement opposition of segregationists. The Mississippi governor at the time said he would never allow the school to be integrated with African Americans. This outraged whites and set off several days of violence and rioting in Oxford, Mississippi. Meredith, accompanied by federal law enforcement officials enrolled on October 1, 1962. The point that is important here is that James Meredith was escorted into the University of Mississippi by U.S. marshals, with minimal or no protection by state or local police authorities (Hendrickson, 2003).

There are many cases throughout the 1960s, where police authorities refused to protect racial minorities. In her book *Mississippi Challenge*, Mildred Pitts Walter describes police practices in the State of Mississippi during the 1960s.

Good citizens averted their eyes. Law-enforcement officers, if not actually involved, did nothing to prevent the seizure of jailed suspects, and no mob leader is known to have been punished. Police officials refused to launch investigations when ordered to do so. Some victims were seized in daylight hours and blowtorched immediately after their trials for murder. Yet no one was able to identify the mob leaders. (Pitts Walter, 1992, p. 79)

Law enforcement's refusal to protect citizens is further exemplified by the many civil rights protesters in the 1960s that were regularly pelted with rocks and bottles from hostile white crowds while police authorities offered minimal or no protection (Pitts Walter, 1992). In some cases the police were the aggressors. One such case occurred in Canton, Mississippi in the late 1960s. In this case the police used tear gas to disrupt a peaceful civil rights march (Katz, 1995). Images such as Birmingham, Alabama's public safety commissioner Eugene "Bull" Connor further exemplify how law enforcement was used by the power structure to maintain deplorable practices by any standards. Commissioner Connor was an outspoken proponent against racial integration and without hesitation ordered the brutal use of police dogs and fire hoses to disperse civil rights demonstrators in Birmingham (Nunnelley, 1991).

What follows is another example of law enforcement's tactics used against African Americans in the southern United States. This event took place in 1967. Neshoba County Mississippi's sheriff Lawrence Rainy and his deputy sheriff Cecil Ray Price were two of the 18 Mississippians convicted in 1967 of conspiring to violate the civil rights of three civil rights workers who were murdered in 1964. It was determined that the murders were carried out with the help of Neshoba County sheriff's officials and the Ku Klux Klan (Huie, 2000).

Let's examine a few more fairly recent cases. One incident occurred early one spring morning on March 3, 1991, in Los Angeles. That is when Rodney King, an African American man was pulled over for a traffic violation. He had been speeding and took police on about a 15-min car chase. According to police, King emerged from his automobile in an aggressive manner that suggested he might have been high on drugs. Numerous officers confronted King and before handcuffing him, they delivered over 50 blows with their batons, numerous kicks, and two 50,000 shock volts from a Taser stun gun. Twenty other police officers stood by and watched the beating. Here is how King (2012) described the beating in his official memoir:

> Suddenly I was being hit with multiple baton blows to every part of my body—my knees, ankles, wrists, and head. The beatings continued to rain down on me. (King 2012, p. 45)
>
> How many bones did they have to break, how many quarts of blood did I have to lose before their fear died down? After 40 plus baton blows, after a dozen kicks to the head, neck, and testicles, after not one but two Taser electrocutions, how could they possibly justify continuing to mutilate me because they were still afraid of me? (King, 2012, p. 95)
>
> Each baton hit and boot kick, each word I remembered the officers screaming at me, "you better run. We're going to kill you, nigger, run!" (King, 2012, p. 102)

A man named George Holliday, standing on the balcony of a nearby building, videotaped the incident. The next day, he gave his 81-s tape to Los Angeles TV channel 5. By the end of the day, the video was being broadcast by TV stations around the world. Four days later, all the charges were dropped on King and four officers were charged with felony assault and other beating-related charges.

The Independent Commission on the Los Angeles Police Department came out 3 months later documenting the "systematic use of excessive force and racial harassment in the LAPD." It also noted management problems and condemned the department's emphasis on crime control rather than crime prevention which served to isolate the police from the public (Christopher Commission, 1991).

On April 29, 1992, the four police officers were found not guilty of committing any crimes against Rodney King. After the announcement of the verdict, the local police were caught fleeing several south central Los Angeles neighborhoods where large-scale riots had erupted. The National Guard was called in and the riots ended 6 days after they began. The collateral damage was the deaths of 42 people, the burning of 700 structures, the arrest of nearly 5000 people, and almost $1 billion in property damage.

Almost a year after the riots, LAPD (Los Angeles Police Department) Sergeant Stacey Koon and Officer Laurence Powell were convicted by a federal jury for violating the civil rights of Rodney King. The other two officers involved in the incident were acquitted. The 1991 *Report of the Independent Commission on the Los Angeles Police Department* (also called the Christopher Commission Report) was published in the aftermath of the notorious beating of Rodney King. The report stated:

> Within minority communities of Los Angeles, there is a widely held view that police misconduct is commonplace. The King beating refocused public attention to long-standing complaints by African Americans, Latinos, and Asians that Los Angeles Police Department officers frequently treat minorities differently from whites, more often using disrespectful and abusive language, employing unnecessarily intrusive practices such as the "prone-out" (prone-out refers to the police practice of placing individuals who are being questioned on the street face down on the pavement), and engaging in the use of excessive force when dealing with minorities. (Report of the Independent Commission on the LAPD, 1991, p. 70)

An incident involving Malice Green and the Detroit police in 1992 is another case to consider. In this case four Detroit police officers beat to death a black motorist named Malice Green. Green was reportedly struck in the head numerous times by one of the officers with a heavy flashlight which resulted in his death. Four Detroit police officers were charged in Green's death.

One other case of police abuse occurred in New York City in 1997. This case involved Abner Louima, a Haitian immigrant who was brutalized by New York City police officers. Louima suffered a torn bladder and intestine which required several surgeries to repair the damage after New York police officers beat him and rammed the handle of a toilet plunger into his rectum and mouth at a Brooklyn police station. Several officers plead guilty or were convicted in federal court for violating Louima's civil rights.

In November 2011, Kenneth Chamberlain, Sr., an unarmed 67-year-old African American was shot to death by White Plains, New York, police officers. Mr. Chamberlain, a retired veteran of the U.S. Marine Corps, who suffered from a chronic heart condition and wore a pendant to signal Life Aid, had mistakenly triggered his medical alert, and although he told police he was OK and did not need assistance, he ended up in an hour-long standoff with the police. Witnesses report hearing the officers using the "N" word and screaming at Mr. Chamberlain to open the door. Police eventually broke in to Chamberlain's apartment and shot him with a stun gun and a beanbag shotgun. The police said they were acting in self-defense because Chamberlain was emotionally disturbed and pulled a knife on them. Only recently did the Westchester District Attorney's Office announce that they will present the case to a grand jury.

On July 17, 2014 New York City police officers investigated Eric Garner, a 43-year-old African American man who was suspected of selling single cigarettes on the street corner without a tax stamp. There were some words exchanged between Garner and the investigating officers and a physical confrontation ensued. One of the police officers placed a choke hold on Garner while pulling him to the ground in an attempt to handcuff him. Garner reportedly yelled that he could not breathe as several officers plummeted on him. During the altercation Garner lost consciousness. Police officers called for an ambulance and Garner was transported to a hospital where he later died. At no time did the officers attempt to administer CPR (cardiopulmonary resuscitation) or other lifesaving procedures. An autopsy by the medical examiner determined that Garner had died from the choke hold along with compression of the chest and positioning by the police officers while being arrested. A grand jury failed to indict the police officers involved in the incident. Once again, like many others, Garner's death at the hands of police authorities sparked national outrage.

You may question how these incidents, especially those occurring many years ago, are relevant to a discussion of racial profiling. The past injudicious treatment of minorities by the police is very relevant to the contemporary discourse centering on racial profiling. For many racial minority citizens, especially African Americans, the police represent a troubled part of their history. The police in many states enforced oppressive laws that resulted in devastation for many racial minorities. The not-so-glamorous portrait of history can help foster a better understanding of the perceptions and experiences of racial minority citizens with racial biased policing along with other concerns about the police by the minority community.

☐ Racial Profiling

Racial profiling represents one of the most pressing issues of our time. American Presidents have spoken about it and denounced it. Police authorities are trained not to engage in it. Laws have been passed criminalizing it, and reported cases have been the subject of endless hours of media stories. In spite of the considerable attention centering on racial profiling, a great many racial minority citizens say it happens frequently in their communities.

When black and white Americans are surveyed about the prevalence of racial profiling, they both believe it is a widespread phenomenon in the United States (Police Executive Research Forum, 2014). A 2004 Gallup poll of citizens found a substantial proportion of Americans believe racial profiling is widespread. Fifty-three percent of those polled think the practice of stopping motorists because of their race or ethnicity is widespread (Carlson, 2004). One other analysis of public opinion of racial profiling found 90% of blacks that were polled believed that profiling was widespread, followed by 83% of Hispanics, and 70% of whites (Weitzer and Tuch, 2005).

Experiencing Racial Profiling

A few years ago the author spent nearly two years interviewing racial minority citizens who believed that they had been racially profiled by the police. Fifty-three African American citizens, 33 Hispanic citizens, and one Asian citizen living in the midwestern United States were interviewed after they reported that they had been profiled because of their race and subsequently stopped while driving their automobiles. There were six common themes that appeared to weave through each of their stories of racial profiling. Because racial profiling is arguably one of the more contentious issues impacting the relationship between racial minority communities and police authorities, a summary of these themes are presented in the following pages. For a more detailed discussion of this study see Birzer (2013).

Theme 1: Emotional and Affective

In this theme, citizens talked about their emotional experiences as a result of being stopped by the police for what they believe to be based solely on their race. For many, these emotions had a lasting impact. This theme carried with it several subthemes such as embarrassment, heightened alertness upon seeing police, increased anxiety, anticipation of being stopped, frustration, anger, a sense of helplessness, and lasting emotional trauma.

Racial minority citizens spoke of the embarrassment of being stopped by the police. They told stories of being made to stand alongside the street while their vehicles were being searched. They spoke of the humiliation of having other motorists staring as they drove past. Finally, they felt a sense of embarrassment because they firmly believed that they did not do anything wrong, and that the sole reason they were stopped was for driving while being black or brown. This seemed to be exacerbated by the reason for the stop (e.g., cracked windshield, failure to use a turn signal within 100 ft of an intersection, cracked brake light, tinted windows, etc.). There was a pervasive feeling among participants that the police use, for example, a pretext such as a cracked windshield as a reason to stop them, when the real underlying motive may be that they suspect other criminality, which, according to participants, is perpetuated by race, appearance, type of car, and/or geographical area. In order to cope, many participants said they purposively avoid driving in areas where there is a high probability that the police will be present. Read how some of the citizens describe the feeling of embarrassment and humiliation when stopped by the police.

Sharla, a black female in her early 40s with a graduate degree and employed as a parole officer, recalls one memorable encounter that she and her family had with the police. Sharla and her family were stopped one summer morning at about 12:30 a.m. They had been playing cards at a friend's home and as they were driving back to their home they were stopped by the police. During the encounter, she questions the treatment her family received by the police. Sharla's husband was driving a 1987 Cadillac which he takes great pride in keeping in pristine condition. Sharla was sitting in the front passenger seat, and two of their friends along with their toddler grandson were sitting in the backseat. All were black with the exception of the grandson who Sharla described as biracial. Listen to Sharla tell the story.

My husband was driving and we noticed the police were following us for a long time. The police officer signaled his red lights and we heard the siren and we pulled over. He walked up to the car and asked for my husband's driver's license. My husband gave him the license. He [the officer] then asked where we were headed to. My husband said, well why do you need to know, why did you pull me over? Then the officer said do you have your registration? So my husband pulls it out and gives it to him. My husband asked the officer again why we were being stopped. And then my husband asked, "What did I do wrong?" The officer was like just stay right here, as if we were going to go somewhere. So he goes back to his car and he never told us what he stopped us for. Finally he walked back to our car and we noticed two other police cars drive up and I was like what the hell, what's going on? So he comes back to the car. Now I begin to question him and was asking like what is the problem? He says well your car is reported stolen. We were like what! What are you talking about! So then he tells us we need to get out of the car, first he tells my husband to step out of the car. So my husband steps out of the car and he [the police officer] says well I'm going to have everybody step out of the car.

By this time there were five other police cars that had driven up, so there were a total of like seven police officers. So he asks my husband to step back, does his procedure, and asks him if he can search the vehicle. I started talking then and said no, why do you need to search our vehicle? If it was reported stolen why are you searching the vehicle? And I want to know who made the report? So then he says, well ma'am, I'm not addressing you and you need to be quiet. I said No, I will not be quiet. This car is registered to us—you see who it is registered to, my husband. The owner is driving the car so how can it be stolen. The officer got really upset with me because I was arguing with him and asking him questions. He said that I was being argumentative and that if I did not shut up he was going to put me in the back of the police car. So now my husband is angry because he [the officer] just threatened to put me in the police car for trying to find out what's going on. My husband started yelling that you just pulled us over because we are Black. After several more minutes it was over, all of sudden the officer said we could get back in our car and were free to leave. We did not even get an apology. As we were walking back to our car one of the officers said, I suppose you are one of the ones that are going to say we racially profiled you too. We just got back in the car and got out of there.

My husband drove right down to the substation to file a complaint. He told the supervisor that we don't appreciate this and my family was embarrassed, all these people were watching us and they just randomly picked us. My husband told the police supervisor at the substation that he wanted to see the stolen car report. They never did produce the report.

Sharla describes how embarrassing it was for her as a parole officer to be standing alongside of the road while police officers searched the car. Sharla said, "There were cars driving by and slowing down to get a look." She said, "We were all standing out on the side of the street at 12:30 a.m." Sharla attributes it all to being black and driving a nice looking car at 12:30 a.m. A few days after the interview I received a follow-up email communication from Sharla. She wrote that she forgot to mention that after the stop, "they did not receive a ticket." She also related that "they [the police] never knew I was a parole officer until they asked for my driver's license and saw my badge." Sharla writes verbatim in her email.

> They [the police] wanted to know what the badge was for and I told them I was a parole officer. One of the officers must have recognized me and he told me that he asked me to issue a warrant over the phone a while back and he told the officer—the one that had stopped us, that that he remembered me from the parole office.

DeMarcus, a black male in his late 20s, who is college educated with a master's degree, employed as a youth care worker, describes the embarrassment he felt when he and his wife (who is white) and their small child were stopped while driving on a highway in the midwestern United States. DeMarcus began the interview by telling me that even though he has never been in trouble or arrested, being stopped by the police is just "part of his world," he said, "I have just gotten used to it."

DeMarcus along with his wife and their daughter were returning from a long trip one afternoon driving to their home when they were stopped by a highway patrol trooper. DeMarcus describes the incident.

> We were on the highway just on our way home. I saw the police car pass us going the opposite direction. I noticed that he immediately made a U-turn and started to follow us. He really followed us for a while, maybe a mile or two, and then stopped us. He was a young White trooper. He told me the reason he was stopping me was because I was following a semitruck too close. I thought to myself what! He asked for my driver's license—and then with no explanation he asked me and my wife to get out the car. He separated us at opposite ends of the car. He started going back and forth between us asking us questions. It seemed like he was purposively trying to mix up our stories. He kept asking where we were coming from and where we were going and this and that. He kept asking the same questions over and over. My daughter was still in the back seat and she was scared.
>
> After a while he asked me if he could search my car. I told him well you're not going to find anything in the car except my bag of clothing. He

then said, where did you guys say you were coming from again, did you say you were from Texas? I was like no! I told you Albuquerque, and he was like are you sure you didn't say Texas. I said no I didn't tell you Texas. So he kept trying to use that line over and over again and he had us out there for a good 45 min. My wife started getting irritated. She told him this is against the law—you can't do this. He didn't say anything. Yeah, he searched and the first thing he went for was my bag. I have a big Nike duffle bag, big duffle bag for school and you know he's digging through clothes and shoes. You know he searched the car, let us go, and no ticket, not nothing...Even though you're like I don't want him to search my car because you're not going to find nothing...This whole thing made me feel bad, I was upset, it was just, you know, really embarrassing. I have learned not to argue with them [police] when I get stopped. If you do they make it hard on you. There is just not a dammed thing you can do about it.

DeMarcus believes the reason he was stopped was because the officer saw a black male and white female driving along the highway and probably thought that they were drug smugglers. DeMarcus concluded that the trooper kept trying to trip them up on their story by saying, "are you sure you didn't say you were from Texas." DeMarcus is convinced that his race prompted the suspiciousness on the part of the trooper coupled with the fact that he was just leaving a rural and predominantly white community. He said the officer used the pretext of following the semitruck too close as the reason to stop him even though, according to DeMarcus "he [trooper] could probably care less about that charge." He explains, "It was embarrassing to be stopped like this and standing along the highway with my wife and little girl while he searched our car and asking if I had any guns or drugs in the car."

Jada, a Hispanic woman in her early 30s described it this way:

I was embarrassed that someone who knows me would drive by and see me standing along the street with the police searching my car. You know there must have been four or five police cars. You know that you haven't done anything and it hurt so badly and you can't do anything about it. You know what, this all boils down to being a Latina driving a customized car in America. You learn to expect this.

Many described increased anxiety while driving and seeing the presence of a police car. For example, one participant remarked, "I started driving really conscientiously when I saw the police car." Another participant, Javier, a Latino from Dodge City in his early 20s described it this way, "I noticed the officer pull a U-turn and start to follow me. When I first saw him I really got nervous and in the back of my mind I knew he was going to start following me."

Rodney, a college educated African American male in his late 20s provides further context to what many minority citizens experience while driving.

> For many of us, especially African American males we laugh and joke about it, but this is a serious matter. Whenever I drive past the police, I find myself getting nervous even though I've done nothing wrong. We get a scary feeling when driving past the police, even when we've done nothing wrong. There's something about driving past the police that makes you scared and it turns you into the perfect driver. Whenever I'm driving and I spot the police, I'm aware of where they're at. I'm constantly checking my mirrors to keep an eye on them.

The sense of anxiety that citizens described while driving and spotting a police car, led to the "anticipation of being stopped." There is a subconscious feeling they could be stopped. Rita, a Hispanic woman in her late 20s describes the anticipation of being stopped this way: "As I was driving, I saw the police officer sitting in the parking lot and I was mindful of his next potential move." One citizen said this:

> I saw him [the police officer] sitting in the parking lot and he stared at me as I drove by. I knew there was a good chance he would start following me. I was about maybe a block away and I saw him pull out and come in my direction. He followed me for about two more blocks and I remember thinking, OK he is going to stop me any minute. That's just a fact when you are Black and driving late at night.

Citizens described feeling frustrated and angry when stopped by the police for what they believe to be racial profiling. The frustration and anger is usually controlled because they know if they openly exhibit emotion, it will make matters worse. Many described a sense of helplessness, or as one participant put it, "there is not a damn thing I can do about it." One young African American male in his mid-20s said:

> They [the police] always ask if they can search my car; they let me know that I have a choice. So I let them search because I know I had nothing to hide. I knew if said no, he would have called more officers and it would have been worse. You know there is nothing you can do, and you better not say anything or they will make it tough on you.

Theme 2: Symbolic Vehicle

The second theme that emerged from the interviews highlight the frustration and anger of being stopped for what they say is for stereotyping because of their race coupled with in some cases the type of car they drive. This was the case with Ana, a 34-year-old college-educated Hispanic female and former correctional officer now employed as an advocate for crime victims. Ana describes the anger and frustration she felt and how she questioned the officer's motive.

> I was driving a 1985 Cutlass Supreme low rider. It had gold plates. My family is in the business of customizing cars. My brother borrowed my car that day because he had a job out of town and my car got better gas mileage. My son had a doctor's appointment and I had to get him there. I asked my brother if I could use his car because my son needed medicine. He said, no sweat, take my Cutlass, we just painted it, but it's ready. My brother said to take his wife's tag and put it on the car. That tag had not been registered because they were restoring the car and they hadn't used it in forever.

Ana recalls that this was a onetime thing and that she just wanted "to get from point A to point B and back with no problems." She continues her story.

> The car had very expensive rims and sits low to the ground...I saw the sheriff's car traveling in front of me. I was a behind him a little ways. I made a turn onto [location purposively taken out] and noticed that the sheriff's car made a U-turn and got behind me and started following me. Now I am a very good driver and I was thinking to myself that this can't be happening. I know from my friends that they will stop you if you're driving a low rider because they think you are just gang banging Mexicans. He followed me for a while, maybe a mile or so and then stopped me. By this time I was pretty upset about what was happening... When he came up to the car I told him you better have a good reason to stop me. He told me he was randomly running tags and that he ran my tag and it was not assigned to the vehicle. I remember thinking he is stopping me because I'm driving a low rider which they associate with Mexican gang members. I got upset and yelled at him. I was yelling that this is not a serious thing and why did you turn around and follow me in the first place. He told me to get out of the car because I was being verbally aggressive. I kept on questioning him about why he turned around and started to follow me. He then grabbed me and forcibly pulled me from my car and handcuffed me. I remember that he searched me in front of his video camera. He searched my car and impounded it and he refused to let my brother pick it up. I think that he was maxing out his authority because I was so angry and not very cooperative with him. I asked if I could pull it into a parking lot and he said no. I know my actions might have made this worse, but I watched the whole thing play out and I knew what was going on. He turned around to follow me just because I am Hispanic driving a low rider. I was embarrassed that someone I know would see me standing alongside of the road in handcuffs. I lived in the area where I was stopped.

Ana believes she was profiled because of her Hispanic ethnicity coupled with the fact she was driving a customized Cutlass Supreme low rider. She said, "We were traveling westbound and there is no way he could get behind me unless he intentionally braked to do so. That's why I feel I was profiled."

Many racial minority citizens that were interviewed believe police authorities hold stereotypical beliefs about the type of vehicle that minority citizens drive as well as the appearance of their vehicles. For example, they believe if you are, for example, black, and driving an expensive car, this will attract increased police suspicion because of the belief that the vehicle is too expensive for a black citizen to drive. One black male said, "They stopped me because I was Black and driving a nice car. They probably think I am not supposed to drive a nice car. If I was driving my Kia I would have never been stopped." Another black male in his early 30s, is convinced he was stopped by police and peppered with interrogating questions for simply being black, and driving a newer model Mercedes. In another interview, Rick, a 28-year-old black male said, "You know, it was just the type of car I was driving." During the interview with Rick, it was revealed he was driving a 1995 Chevy Caprice with customized rims and tinted windows. Another participant, Angela, who is a black female in her early 50s, talked about being stopped by police authorities for driving a nice car.

> …It's like they think you are not supposed to driving this nice car. It's like we are still in slavery. They never issue me a ticket so I think it had to be because I was Black and driving that nice Jaguar. You know the thing is that I never got a ticket. They would just check me out and let me go.

Some racial minority citizens believe the make and model along with the appearance of their car will attract police attention because it is perceived as the type of car a minority would not drive. There is a belief that the police construct the "symbolic vehicle" based on stereotypes. The "symbolic vehicle" would include customized apparel such as wheel rims, nice paint job, sits low to the ground (low rider), window tint, gold around the tag, etc. Participants believe the police associate certain cars with black and Hispanic drivers.

An interview with Melvin, a black man in his early 20s reveals it was not necessarily a customized car that resulted in him being stopped, but rather for driving an expensive car. Melvin was stopped for a turn signal violation. Here is how Melvin describes it:

> When the police officer walked toward my 2005 Cadillac CTS, he says is this your car? The officer didn't ask for my driver's license, instead he wanted my insurance. I think the reason for this is because he thought a young African American male can't drive a nice car. After he looked at my

insurance, he then asked me for my driver's license. I thought it was fishy but being an African American sometimes you have to bite your tongue when it comes to certain situations.

Perhaps the story that most effectively illustrates the symbolic vehicle theme was one shared by a 62-year-old black male who is employed as a custodian. This story is especially important because the officer interjects the symbolic gesture of race and ethnicity along with the symbolic vehicle into the context of the stop.

I was driving my Ford F-50 two-toned extended cab pickup truck. I noticed the police officer driving in the opposite direction. As we passed each other, I noticed he looked directly at me and seemed to be surprised. It was kind of strange. I just had a feeling I would be stopped. I watched in my rear-view mirror and sure enough, he did a U-turn and turned on the red lights. I immediately pulled over and stopped...There were two White police officers in the police car. They approached on each side of the truck. He asked for my driver's license. I asked him why I was being stopped and he said for having tinted covers over my headlights. Now listen, you know this was at 10 o'clock in the morning...I received a ticket for driving with covers over my headlights. I didn't realize this was even a violation because they're sold in just about every automotive store. As he was giving me the ticket he kind of looked my truck up and down and said your truck kind of looks like the kind of truck a Mexican would drive.

Theme 3: Nature of the Violation

Another common theme was named "Nature of the Violation." In this theme, participants describe the pre-textual basis of their being stopped by police authorities. In other words, they believe the police routinely use, in their words, "petty" or "minor" traffic violations to stop and "harass them" because of their race.

The U.S. Supreme Court decided that pre-textual stops by police authorities are legally permissible. The Supreme Court in the 1996 decision *Whren v. United States* decided that the police can stop motorists and search their vehicles if probable cause exists that the occupants are, for example, trafficking illegal drugs or weapons. Under the Whren decision, police can stop motorists for a traffic violation even though the traffic violation may not be the underlying motive for the stop. Regardless of the legality of this police practice, participants feel that they are routinely stopped for "minor traffic offenses" and that the police often use these minor traffic offenses as a reason to profile them.

Many citizens reported that they did not receive a traffic citation after they were stopped. The irony here is many citizens may view this as a desirable outcome, but to minority citizens this seems to reinforce the racialized aspect of being stopped. For example, the absence of a traffic citation seems to signal to minority citizens that their suspicions of a racially motivated stop are supported. Professor Karen Glover (2009) made note of this in her research on racial profiling. According to Professor Glover (2009, p. 97), "The traffic stop, innocuous as it appears to some and especially when no citation is issued, is a micro-level occurrence that demonstrates the state's reach on a macro-level."

In 60 (65%) stops reported by participants, traffic citations were not issued. While on the other hand, 32 (35%) stops resulted in a traffic citation or a fix-it ticket being issued. In 30 (35%) stops reported were for what participants described as "being suspicious" and/or for "tinted windows."

Theme 4: Officer Demeanor

Citizens felt like they were treated like criminals after being stopped by the police. This is how Peter, a Hispanic male in his middle 30s, and a former U.S. Army demolition expert who holds a master's degree, describes his experience. As a preface to Peter's story, he was traveling in Wichita on a major thruway at about 5:00 p.m. His children, both Hispanic, were in the backseat. He was driving a black 1998 Dodge Neon with tinted rear windows. The car also had a clear plastic film cover over the license plate. The officer stopped Peter for the tinted windows.

Peter was in a hurry when he left his residence because he had to pick his wife up from work. In his haste to get his children out the door and into the car, Peter left his driver's license at home. During the stop, the officer confirmed that Peter had a valid driver's license. Here is how Peter describes his experience.

> I didn't feel like I was doing anything wrong and I really think this was a racially motivated stop. He [the officer] acted superior, talking down to me and his voice, his words, the way he talked and acted was aggressive. He treated me like I was inferior...I thought the way he treated me was awful and if they are getting away with this with me, what else are they getting away with?

As Peter continues to tell his story the emotionally laden context of the stop is revealed. I sensed that this incident was emotionally charged for Peter. He continues:

> My kids were frightened and they thought something was going to happen to me. You know, he didn't have to talk to me like that in front of my kids. They were afraid and saw law enforcement as bad people because of this situation. I mean, I was angry, but I didn't want my kids to see me that way, they [police] are not all bad, even if I think this one was wrong.

Peter believes his incident was racially motivated. For Peter, this was reinforced by the police officer's comments about what Peter believes is his Hispanic heritage. Peter explains further in the following passage.

> When he [police officer] came back up to the car, he said that he wasn't going to give me a ticket for the tint being too dark, but instead he was going to give me a ticket for you know those plastic film covers you can get to put over your license plate. He was still asking about my driver's license. I think I asked him why he still thought I didn't have a driver license even after he confirmed it in the computer. He told me that usually when he pulls people over like me they usually don't have a driver's license, or it's suspended and they start coming up with excuses as to why they don't have a license on them.

After the officer used the term "people like me," Peter recognizes that he may have just been profiled because of his Hispanic heritage. Peter is upset and questions the officer regarding the statement. He continues:

> I said, wait a minute! People like me! I asked him what he meant by people like me? He seemed surprised that I was questioning him, and then he really tried to explain himself. I think he knew I caught him. I really believe that he didn't think I was going to challenge him on that statement. He really started to change his tune after that.

Peter was greatly bothered by this stop. He believes the officer was pushing his weight around. Peter has never been in trouble with the police and spent many years in the military. After his discharge from the military, he enrolled in college and earned a master's degree. Peter said, "The officer kept repeating to me that not having your driver's license on your person is an 'arrestable offense.'" I asked Peter to explain why he felt that this incident was racial profiling. Peter believes that when the officer used the term "people like me," that the officer was making an association to undocumented Mexicans living in the United States. He said that the officer knew he got caught and did not expect me to challenge him. Peter believes that the officer used the threats of arrest to make it seem like he (the officer) was doing Peter a favor or cutting him a break. The motive, Peter believes, is so that he (Peter) would not make an issue out of the racialized remark. Peter said what really surprised him about this incident was that the officer was black.

During one group interview session of African Americans the discussion was centered on the officer demeanor theme. One male in his middle 20s suggested if the police were polite and improved their communication skills when dealing with minority citizens it would minimize many negative perceptions of the police. He said, "It's all in the way they talk to us." He admits he has a past arrest history along with several what he referred to as "run-ins with the police." He said the officer's communication during the initial contact can go a long way. The participant suggested in some of his encounters the officer's demeanor escalated his reaction which in some cases resulted in him arguing with and challenging the police. Here are a few remarks of one other focus group participant.

> In the academy, if they were to train them to be polite and then take action, it would kill a lot of problems. None of them know how to communicate. They don't even talk to us right. You are automatically a threat to them. I think a lot of Black men get offended because they [the police] make them feel like less than a man, especially in front of other people. If you run from them you get a case, if you say something smart to them, you get a case. You can't talk smart to them or question or challenge them about anything. There is nothing you can do. If you try to, it makes the situation worse.

Theme 5: Normative Experiences

Many citizens that were interviewed accept racial profiling a normative part of their lives. The interviews revealed a pervasive feeling that the chances of being stopped by police authorities for the most minor traffic infraction is very real for minority citizens. This was especially prevalent among black male participants. For example, during one group interview session with eight African Americans (six males and two females), one participant, a black male in his early 60s, when asked about what he things of when he hears the term racial profiling replied, "I think about Black men." Another participant underscored this sentiment and said, "I've really gotten used to being stopped, it's just a part of life for a Black man." Another participant replied, "Getting stopped by the police is a reality in our neighborhood. White communities don't understand because they don't face this like we do. It's a matter of fact to us." Recall Arnold, the African American minister who shared the many incidents of being stopped in eastern Kansas. Arnold said, "It's just a routine fact of life, at first I really had a lot of rage built up inside, but as I have matured in life, I learn to accept it as the norm."

Perhaps the most revealing statement that underscored the normative experience is the one volunteered by Cory, a black male participant in his late 20s. Here is what Cory said:

> It's almost like we are in slavery. Every time we are driving around we got to watch out because we might get stopped. You know I have become so used to the possibility of being stopped it's like an everyday thing. You get used to it after a while. When I see a police officer, I automatically begin to think that I may be stopped. It is always there in the back of your mind, it's automatic, you just think about it when you see the police car.

Cory's narrative is troubling. Here we have an African American male in his late 20s, a productive citizen raising a family, equating the experience of potentially being stopped by police authorities to slavery. He captures how a great many minority citizens feel. Participants constructed an almost normative expectation of being stopped by the police. The "normative experience" theme was strong throughout this study and was often intertwined with the other themes.

Theme 6: Race and Place

Many citizens that were interviewed believe there is a greater likelihood of being stopped in certain geographical areas of the communities in which they reside. They describe this in two parts. First, there is a sense that as racial minorities they are more likely to be stopped in what they described as predominately white and affluent neighborhoods. Second, there is an increased chance of being stopped in economically disadvantaged areas including areas targeted by the police.

Racial minority citizens say they consciously avoid driving through some affluent white neighborhoods for fear that they will attract police attention. This theme was discussed during one focus group. One black male who is employed as a house painter recalls driving through an affluent, predominately white neighborhood and being followed for several blocks by the police. He believes it was simply because he was black and "out of place." He explained he had a paint job that he was finishing in the neighborhood. He makes it a habit of not driving through some neighborhoods in order to avoid police scrutiny, even if it means driving several blocks out of his way. Many citizens that were interviewed described altering their routes in order to avoid police attention.

The race and place theme not only reveals a heightened awareness among participants of being stopped in predominately white affluent neighborhoods, but also neighborhoods disproportionally impacted by crime including those that are economically disadvantaged. Citizens reported being stopped by police authorities for driving, for example, in lower income areas, many of which have high crime rates.

☐ Solving a Complex Problem

Racial profiling is a phenomenon that many white citizens will most likely never experience in their lifetimes. Racial profiling may be witnessed by white citizens, but not experienced. Even the basic interaction between the police and citizens living in black communities is most likely "completely foreign to White citizens" (Barlow and Hickman-Barlow, 2000, p. 86). What was striking about the interviews reported previously in this chapter is that for many racial minority citizens, profiling by the police remains prevalent in many parts of their lives. So what are the solutions to begin to resolve the perception or reality of racial profiling? Moreover, what has to be done in order to restore the trust between the police and minority community? As a start, there are six prongs that are important in order to address this complex problem: (1) training; (2) fostering mutual trust and respect; (3) professional motorist contacts; (4) building and sustaining community coalitions; (5) communication, and (6) community-oriented policing strategies.

Training

Police officers should be trained in bias-based policing and the dire consequences of engaging in this practice. Corollary training should focus on cultural diversity.

Racial Profiling Training

Racial profiling training should include the purpose and scope of the agency's data collection strategies. This training should ensure that both recruit training and in-service training for veteran police officers provide information regarding racial profiling laws in the jurisdiction and data collection mandates (mandatory or voluntary) involving the department. If a police agency collects stop data, training should include the proper procedure to record information regarding police stops.

The most effective racial profiling training is training that is made as hands on as possible. Police officers may benefit from having active role-playing and problem-centered learning exercises. These include scenarios where, for example, racial minority citizens allege the police department engages in racial profiling. Police officers could then work in small learning groups to tailor strategies addressing the allegations. It may be beneficial to have members of the racial minority community participate in racial profiling training. This may result in an understanding from both the police and the citizens. In other words, the police and citizens learn from one another. This may heighten a mutual understanding of why the police do what they do in certain situations.

In racial profiling training, it is important to engage officers in reflection, an internal audit of sorts, of his or her practices in the field. This is reflective learning which has long been touted as an effective educational and training technique. Reflective learning techniques propose that learning does not necessarily result from the experience per se, but rather from effective reflection on that experience. Thus, reflective learning is the process where law enforcement officers internally examine and explore racial profiling from different worldviews, perhaps from the worldview of minority citizens who claim they have been racially profiled and from the worldview of police officers themselves. This can be accomplished in training sessions or other community friendly forums by problem posing and dialog.

The following three-step technique may be beneficial in creating a more interactive training environment, and by engaging officers in reflection on their stop practices.

1. First, have officers think about an experience they have had with being accused of racial profiling. Officers then write down in bullet point fashion thoughts and reflections about that experience. Officers who have not been accused of racial profiling can write down in bullet point fashion thoughts and reflections about the racial profiling controversy.

2. The next step is to have officers think about ways they can deal with accusations of racial profiling and consider if there was anything they may have done differently during the stop to resolve the perception of racial profiling on the part of the citizen.

3. In the final step officers would discuss long held beliefs, assumptions, and values about the racial profiling controversy.

Cultural Diversity Training

It is unknown if multicultural training for the police would result in fewer perceptions among the racial minority citizenry of racial profiling, or actual incidents of racial profiling. Likewise, it is unknown if it would make a prejudiced officer less prejudiced. However, diversity training is essential for police officers. It sends a positive message to the community. It has only been in the recent past that police agencies have begun to include diversity training as part of the pre- and post-service training requirements. Training that assists in familiarizing officers with ethnic and cultural groups in their community is important. Training in culture and diversity has a number of potential benefits.

...ted Policing

...find it beneficial to implement or expand exist-
...ted policing strategies as a way to enhance pub-
...tion through collaborative partnerships with the
... Community-oriented policing may also be ben-
...olice relations with racial minority communities.
...y-oriented policing strategies could result in resolv-
...staken perception of racial profiling.

...icing strategies call for an increased emphasis on
... policing as opposed strictly to crime reduction.
... committed to crime reduction strategies are more
...f racial profiling. On the other hand, agencies that
...reduction strategies pose a far greater potential for
... operating mentality to reduce crime by any means
...xtent of crime reduction strategies are carried out
...advantaged neighborhoods (often minority neigh-
...e numbers of stops are conducted. These practices
...he potential to lower trust in law enforcement and
...n of the minority community.

...not suggested that law enforcement desist from
...ategies in economically disadvantaged areas, but
...ented with a significant service orientation that is
...nal strategy. Community policing with its empha-
...itation actually includes proactive policing strate-
...under community policing the police would focus
... on small disorder problems that usually would
...for that matter, result in a police response under a
...del. Some examples of small disorder problems are
... public drinking, neighborhood blight, abandoned
...les, and the like. Focusing on small disorder prob-
...eighborhoods will bring the police into more fre-
...ith citizens in order to discuss and tailor solutions
...By addressing small disorder problems, more seri-
...roblems may be prevented. It should be underscored
...esolve small order problems should be done with
...ing in affected neighborhoods. Moreover, small dis-
...uld be addressed by a well-planned problem solving
...s not include aggressive and unequal enforcement
...ill further fracture the relationship between the
...ority community.

Multicultural training may potentially reduce the number of lawsuits. It may also reduce the possibility of civil disorder. Historically,
strategies employed by police in dealing with racial minority issues have
differed from other groups. While improvements in those strategies have
occurred in the recent past, further improvements are needed. Although
these improvements have often focused on African Americans, many
cultural diversity issues have similar implications for other racial and
ethnic groups. Coderoni (2002) writes:

> Cultural diversity training helps the police break free from their tradi-
> tional stance of being "apart from" the community to a more inclusive
> philosophy of being "a part of" the community. Realizing the difficulty
> of becoming a part of something that they do not understand causes a
> desperate need for an intense and ongoing educational process for devel-
> oping an understanding of cultural differences and how those differ-
> ences affect policing a free and culturally diverse society. (Coderoni,
> 2002, p. 14)

Fostering Mutual Respect and Trust

An important objective in both racial profiling training and cultural
diversity training is to provide police officers with information on the
issue of mutual respect. In fact, the Department of Justice's Office of
Community-Oriented Policing Services produced a training curriculum
for police officers on mutual respect. They suggest that an important outcome of this training is to increase police officers' awareness of respectful
police behavior. By doing so, their ability to work toward better community relationships will be strengthened. They further suggested interim
performance objectives of this training should be to:

1. Recognize that we are all influenced by past experiences and that
   treating people with dignity and respect is the foundation of good
   communication.

2. Recognize that a police officer's actions and demeanor shape the image
   of their agencies and of law enforcement in general.

3. Recognize that good law enforcement practices involve investigating
   patterns of criminal behavior and the use of race as a reason to stop
   someone is illegal.

4. Recognize that gaining community support and acceptance requires mutual trust and respect between the citizenry and the police.

5. Recognize that establishing positive community partnerships is an effective use of police authority (United States Department of Justice, 2001, p. 6).

Professional Motorist Contacts

Police officers should never understate the impression that a motorist stop can have on citizens. Weitzer and Tuch (2002) made an important point when they suggested the perceptions that citizens have of police stops may be considered just as important as the actual objective reality of the stop. This is salient in this research. The traffic stop is, in many cases, the only contact a citizen may have with the police. The manner in which the police officer communicates can leave lasting impressions. Many participants perceived that the police are demeaning, hostile, and talk down to them during a stop. Police officers should always act in a professional and courteous manner during a stop of an individual. In some cases the officer may have to be stern but being stern is very different from being demeaning and hostile.

Building and Sustaining Community Coalitions

It is beneficial for police authorities to establish and/or enhance their involvement with local community organizations such as the NAACP (National Association for the Advancement of Colored People), Urban League, Boy's and Girl's Clubs, Hispanic coalitions, and Asian or Indo-Chinese community centers and coalitions. Because the faith community provides a leadership role in many racial minority communities, increasing contact with them may be advantageous too. Coalitions should be formed to not only address issues centering on racial profiling but also to achieve better police community relations. When the police have good relations with the racial minority community it is much easier to tailor solutions to underlying causes of friction between the police and the community. It is critical that community input should be solicited during this review, including requests for public comment and discussion. Likewise, the police should inform the community of the various

---

options that a
and local level

Developi
will keep man
and concerns
tant issues. Ma
are not include
represented by
munity. They su
boards and coali

Communicat

Regular commu
dispel rumors an
the community b
ing. This can be
community forur
ing sessions, the
held only when h
Dialog between th

- Sessions with th
  members from
  for each commu

- Chaplain or faith

- Radio and TV sh

- Beat meetings th

- Facilitated discus
  increase police an
  upon actions

- Study circles, whi
  zation of the comr
  citizen concern; an
  and minority grou

Community-Orier

Police agencies may
ing community-orien
lic safety and interac
minority community
eficial in improving
Moreover, communit
ing the sometimes mi
Community po
the service aspect o
Police agencies solely
likely to be accused
are steeped in crime
officers to develop ar
necessary. A large e
in economically disa
borhoods) where lar
by themselves have
minimize cooperatic
It is certainly
crime reduction str
rather they be augn
built as an operatio
sis on service orier
gies. For example,
increased attentior
not be expected, or
crime reduction me
minor vandalisms,
property and vehic
lems inherent in r
quent interaction
to these problems.
ous crime-related
that working to r
affected citizens li
order problems sh
approach that do
activities which
police and the mi

☐ Conclusion

As the conclusion to this chapter was being written, another allegation of police abuse in Chicago was reported in the national news. A video recording, taken from a police cruiser's dash cam, was released to the public showing the October 2014 shooting death of Laquan McDonald, a 17-year African American male by a white Chicago police officer. The video depicts Laquan walking in the middle of street appearing to carrying a knife but presenting no threat to officers before he was shot. There were 16 rounds fired at the victim. The release of the video sparked large-scale protests in Chicago. Protesters contend that this is another example of racial bias in policing. Many are questioning why it took over a year to release the video. The Chicago police officer involved in the shooting has been charged with first-degree murder. African American leaders in Chicago have called for the resignation of police superintendent and a federal investigation into the practices of the Chicago Police Department.

The intersection of race and policing in the United States has a complex and troubled history. The troubled history impacts modern day police operations and presents a host of challenges for the police when addressing allegations of racial profiling, and in the mending of strained relations with racial minority communities. In short, there are no easy answers or solutions. Police agencies will increasingly be required to practice procedural justice of sorts. Procedural justice that includes transparency, fairness, and allowing citizens to have a voice. In order to mend strains in their relationship with the minority community, it will increasingly be important to allow minority citizens to collectively have the opportunity to explain their situation or tell their side of the story regarding their neighborhoods and/or communities. This includes having the opportunity to have their voices heard before the police make decisions about how their neighborhoods are policed.

☐ References

Barlow, D.E. and Hickman-Barlow, M. 2000. *Police in a Multicultural Society: An American Story*. Prospect Heights, Illinois: Waveland Press.

Birzer, M.L. 2013. *Racial Profiling: They Stopped Me Because I'm—*! Boca Raton, Florida: CRC Press.

Coderoni, G.R. 2002. The relationship between multicultural training for police and effective law enforcement. *FBI Law Enforcement Bulletin*, 71(11), 16–18.

Carlson, D.K. 2004. Racial profiling is seen as widespread, particularly among young Black men. Gallup. Retrieved from Gallup website: http://www.gallup.com/poll/12406/racial-profiling-seen-pervasive-unjust.aspx.

Christopher Commission. 1991. Report of the Independent Commission on the Los Angeles Police Department, Los Angeles.

Fridell, L., Lunney, R., Diamond, D. Kubu, B, Scott, M., and Laing, C. 2001. *Racially Biased Policing: A Principled Response*. Washington, DC: Police Executive Research Forum.

Genovese, E.D. 1976. *Roll Jordon Roll: The World of Slaves Made*. New York: Vintage Books.

Glover, K.S. 2009. *Racial Profiling: Research, Racism, and Resistance*. Lanham, Maryland: Rowman & Littlefield Publishers, Inc.

Hadden, S.E. 2001. *Slave Patrols: Law and Violence in Virginia and the Carolinas*. Cambridge, Massachusetts: Harvard University Press.

Hendrickson, P. 2003. *Sons of Mississippi: A Story of Race and its Legacy*. New York: Alfred A. Knopf.

Huie, W.B. 2000. *Three Lives for Mississippi*. Jackson, Mississippi: University Press of Mississippi.

Katz, W.L. 1995. *Eyewitness: A Living Documentary of the African American Contribution to American History*. New York: Touchstone.

King, R. 2012. *The Riot within: My Journey from Rebellion to Redemption*. New York: Harper.

Lynch, J.R. 1968. *Facts of Reconstruction*. New York: Arno Press.

Moss, E.Y. 1990. African Americans and the administration of justice. In W. L. Reed (Ed.), *Assessment of the Status of African Americans* (pp. 79–86). Boston: University of Massachusetts, William Monroe Trotter Institute.

Nunnelley, W.A. 1991. *Bull Connor*. Tuscaloosa: University of Alabama Press.

Patterson, O. 1998. *Rituals of Blood: The Consequences of Slavery in Two American Centuries*. New York: Basic Civitas Books.

Pitts Walter, M. 1992. *Mississippi Challenge*. New York: Bradbury Press.

Police Executive Research Forum. 2014. *Legitimacy and Procedural Justice: A New Element of Police Leadership*. Washington, DC: Police Executive Research Forum, U.S. Department of Justice, Bureau of Justice Assistance.

Ogletree, C.J., Prosser, M., Smith, A., and Talley, W. 1995. *Beyond the Rodney King Story: An Investigation of Police Conduct in Minority Communities*. Boston, Massachusetts: Northeastern University Press.

Quillian, L. and Pager, D. 2001. Black neighbors, higher crime? The role of racial stereotypes in the evaluation of neighborhood crime. *American Journal of Sociology*, 107, 117–167.

Quillian, L. and Pager, D. 2010. Estimating risk: Stereotype amplification and the perceived risk of criminal victimization. *Social Psychology Quarterly*, 73, 79–104.

United States Census Bureau. 2012. Law enforcement courts and prisons: Jail inmates by sex, race, and Hispanic origin. U.S. Census Bureau. Retrieved from: http://www.census.gov/compendia/statab/cats/law_enforcement_courts_prisons.html.

United States Department of Justice. 2015a. *Department of Justice Report Regarding the Criminal Investigation into the Shooting Death of Michael Brown by Ferguson, Missouri Police Officer Darren Wilson.* Washington, DC: U.S. Department of Justice. Retrieved on November 25, 2015 from: http://www.justice.gov/.

United States Department of Justice. 2015b. *Investigation of the Ferguson Police Department.* Washington, DC: U.S. Department of Justice. Retrieved on November 25, 2015 from: http://www.justice.gov.

U.S. Department of Justice. 2001. *Mutual Respect in Policing: Lesson Plan.* Washington, DC: Office of Community Oriented Policing Services.

Wadman, R.C. and Allison, W.T. 2004. *To Protect and Serve: A History of Police in America.* Upper Saddle, NJ: Prentice Hall.

Walker, S. 1980. *Popular Justice: A History of American Criminal Justice.* New York: Oxford University Press.

Walker, S. 1999. *The Police in America: An Introduction,* (2nd ed). Boston: McGraw Hill.

Williams, H. and Murphy, P.V. 1990. *The Evolving Strategies of Police: A Minority View.* Washington, DC: National Institute of Justice. Retrieved from https://www.ncjrs.gov/ pdffiles1/nij/121019.pdf.

Weitzer, R. and Tuch, S.A. 2005. Racially biased policing: Determinants of citizen perceptions. *Social Forces,* 83, 1009–1030.

Weitzer, R. and Tuch, S.A. 2002. Perceptions of racial profiling: Race, class, and personal experience. *Criminology,* 40(2), 435–456.

Whren v. United States. (1996). 517 U.S. 806.

Wyatt-Brown, B. 1982. *Southern Honor: Ethics and Behavior in the Old South.* New York: Oxford University Press.

Understanding the Law of Police Use of Force to Arrest

Alison Brown

☐ Introduction

The law is not emotional: it is analytical. To convict, the criminal law requires proof beyond a reasonable doubt of every component of a crime as that crime is written, not as the crime may be generally perceived. These basic truths of the criminal law often create a conflict between the public's perception of a fair and just outcome in a criminal case, and the actual outcome of a case based upon legal precedent that has developed over the last 1000 years. Nowhere is this conflict more apparent than in cases involving police use of force to arrest. While this conflict between the law and public perception has always existed, today it seems to be even more present in the endlessly increasing media reports from radio, television, newspapers, newsmagazines, and the internet streaming live 24/7 from computers, smart phones, tablets, and even watches. It is now almost impossible to escape the stories fighting for our attention.

Police using their authority to commit bad acts, or just over responding to a situation based on their emotions rather than their training, is not a new phenomenon. In 1963, a few horrific pictures filtered out of Selma, Alabama showing white police officers using the tools of their profession, including dogs, clubs, and other weapons, to suppress a civil-rights march. In 1991, a video of Rodney King being beaten by police with department issued clubs was played on the nightly news for months. With the advent of YouTube, every cell phone video capturing questionable police interaction with the public is available for instant replay by the media and the general public. Videos like the 2008 incident involving a Baltimore, Maryland officer screaming and ranting at young teens are likely to go viral, passed from person to person through social media until everyone in the country views it multiple times. Whether purposeful criminal acts, or just momentary loss of control, today it is likely the public will see the bad act and is not willing to tolerate it.

Following the 2014 shooting death of Michael Brown by a Ferguson, Missouri police officer trying to take Brown into custody, people from across the nation went to Ferguson to protest. Most of the protesters were marching to draw attention to concerns that police routinely use excessive force when arresting people of color. The protests were large enough, and garnered enough attention across the country, to cause politicians to promise to find answers to the protesters' questions. When the answers came, however, the public was not satisfied, just as they have not been satisfied with the answers provided by criminal justice professionals in most of the cases in which the police were investigated for use of excessive force, whether or not racial bias is perceived to be at issue. In many, although not all, of these types of events it is difficult to develop an understandable response to these questions because the answers are based upon the laws and rules concerning police use of force. This chapter will provide an explanation of the principal laws related to police use of force in connection with arrest. Specifically, this chapter will analyze the primary state and federal criminal law, as well as the federal civil law, which control an officer's criminal and civil liability for use of force during an arrest.

☐ Prosecuting Excessive Force under State Criminal Codes

Although every state independently determines which acts that it wishes to criminalize, most states have adopted laws prohibiting conduct outlawed by common law, including murder, manslaughter, battery, and assault. The common law is the body of law that began creation more than 1000 years ago in England, under the direction of William the Conqueror. It continued to evolve and expand over time to incorporate the changing needs of English society and was brought to America as part of the colonization process. When the United States broke away from England, however, both the new federal government, as well as the states, kept the common law and many of the customs and practices of English society so that citizens of the brand new nation would have some form of legal regulation that was both understandable and accepted.

Murder, rape, kidnapping, battery, and assault are generally understood within the United States to be terms for illegal acts. For example, every child in the United States learns at some point during their early childhood that taking a human life is murder and it is wrong. Similarly, while the criminal designations that the various states adopt to proscribe hitting, holding someone against their will, and forcible sexual contact may differ, every child knows that hitting another person, capturing another person, or improperly touching another person are bad acts. At the same time that children learn to identify bad acts, however, they also learn that sometimes bad acts are justified. So, children understand that taking a human life is bad but sometimes it is necessary to kill another person if one is acting to save their own life. In the same way, hitting another person is bad, but sometimes smacking a hand is the only way to teach a 3-year old not to touch a hot stove. This basic understanding that sometimes it is OK do bad things is written into every state criminal code under the general heading of "defenses to criminal acts." These defenses are some of the oldest parts of the criminal law, and versions fairly similar to those promulgated hundreds of years ago continue to be followed today.

Defenses can be categorized as: justification, excuse, alibi, and no crime. Except for the alibi defense, each of these types of defenses recognizes that the actor did the act. The "no crime" defense is used when the actor believes that the act is not an unlawful act under the law. The various excuse defenses are used when an actor admits he committed the act but asks to be excused from criminal responsibility by virtue of special circumstances which negate the actor's intent to act criminally. An accused using an excuse defense may claim to be legally insane or a juvenile. The final category of defenses are called justifications. Justification defenses are used when the actor admits to having committed a wrongful act, but claims the act was necessary to avoid a greater evil. Self-defense and defense of others are two types of justification defenses.

In common law "use of force to effect an arrest" was a justification defense available to anyone acting to stop and detain a felon. This defense recognized that an actor could use as much force as was necessary to effect the arrest, up to and including, deadly force. As common law evolved into statutory law, and designated law enforcement officers began to replace citizen vigilantes, most states accepted the legitimacy of the rationale behind the use of force doctrine and adopted legislation recognizing the common law defense of "use of force to effect an arrest."*

The public policy behind the use of force defense is clear. Policing is by definition a dangerous profession. Officers are sent to multiple calls for help during every shift. Citizens do not usually ask for help until the situation has arisen to a level where danger may occur, or has already occurred. If the police tried to do their jobs while fearing prosecution for carrying out an arrest, they may choose to walk away from individuals who refuse to cooperate with an arrest, rather than force the individual to submit. Additionally, officers have reason to believe that individuals will act dangerously during an arrest if given an opportunity. Although failing to cooperate with an arrest, and resisting arrest, are additional offenses in every state, an arresting officer must know that the law will back him up if he needs to enforce these, or any other, laws. Thus, because of the nature of the policing and the nature of arrests, both police and the community must understand that police are legally empowered to take control of a situation, and to remain in control of a situation until the situation no longer exists.

The common law rules regarding use of force to arrest have changed slightly over time, mostly as the result of judicial decisions. Cases dating back to the earliest state courts provide examples of police officers being prosecuted by the state or sued by an arrestee or their next of kin for using more force than was necessary to accomplish the arrest. Law enforcement officers have been able to defend their actions by relying upon the state's authorization to use that amount of force necessary to complete an arrest, and prevent the arrestee from defeating the arrest and escaping. A 1894 California case involving the prosecution of a law enforcement officer for homicide arising from an attempt to arrest provides a clear example of how state courts have applied the use of force defense to allegations of criminal conduct. In that case, the Supreme Court of California held that if an officer had probable cause to believe that a felony crime had occurred, and probable cause to believe that an individual had committed that felony crime, the law allowed the officer to take reasonable steps to stop the fleeing felon, even if it turned out that the individual was not the offender but "an innocent and respectable citizen."†

---

* *People v. Kilvington*, 104 Cal. 86, 37 P. 799, 1894.
† Ibid, at 93, 801, and 11.

A 1919 case heard by the Supreme Court of Washington was also asked to review a police officer's right to use the use of force defense. That court stated that Washington operated under the common law, and that under the common law a law enforcement officer making an arrest based upon probable cause could make an arrest. In making that arrest the officer was authorized by the law to use "that degree of force the circumstances of the case warrant; that is to say, if the crime is a misdemeanor he may use the force the law permits in making arrests for misdemeanors, and if it be a felony he may use the force the law permits in making arrests for felony."[*] If that officer is later prosecuted for assault, battery, or homicide he has the right to explain to the jury the circumstances surrounding the arrest, as well as his perception and understanding of those circumstances. Then, unless the jury finds that the officer was lying, or the response was too egregious to be justified, the jury must accept the officer's defense.[†] In short, this means that when a regular citizen is prosecuted for a crime, the state need only prove that the person committed the act with the requisite intent. When a law enforcement officer is prosecuted for a crime associated with having used force during an arrest, however, the prosecution must not only prove that the officer used that amount of force that rises to the level of a criminal act, but must also prove that the officer's use of that amount of force was not permitted by and justified by the use of force defense. This sets a very high standard for convicting an officer of a criminal act for having used force during an arrest.

States were largely unguided in their application and interpretation of the defense of "use of force to effect an arrest" until 1984, when the Supreme Court decided the case of *Tennessee v. Garner*.[‡] The facts underlying the Garner case involved a 1974 shooting death of a 15–year-old, unarmed teenager, Edward Eugene Garner, by a Memphis police officer. Garner's father filed a lawsuit, but the state defended the officer's actions under the provisions of that state's use of force defense. At that time the Tennessee law provided that "[if], after notice of the intention to arrest the defendant, he either flee or forcibly resist, the officer may use all the necessary means to effect the arrest.'"[§] Acting under the authority of this statute, a Memphis police officer shot and killed Edward Garner after Garner refused to comply with an order to halt, and attempted to flee over a fence at night in the backyard of

---

[*] *Coldeen v. Reid, Sheriff, et al.*, 107 Wash. 508, at 516, 182 P. 599, at 601, 1919 at 112.

[†] Ibid. See also, *Schumann v. McGinn*, 307 Minn., at 458, 240 N. W. 2d, at 533; *Holloway v. Moser, supra*, at 187, 136 S. E., at 376, 1927.

[‡] *Tennessee v. Garner et al.*, 471 U.S. 1, 105 S. Ct. 1694, 85 L. Ed. 2d 1, 1985.

[§] Ibid, at 4, 1698, and 5. Tenn. Code Ann. § 40–808, 1974.

a house he was suspected of burglarizing. The officer admitted that he used deadly force despite being reasonably sure the suspect was unarmed, and despite thinking that the suspect was a slightly built 17 or 18 year old.[*] The officer shot at Garner because he believed that the juvenile would be able to climb over the fence and outrun him, thereby escaping arrest. The officer believed that the only means to effect the arrest of Garner was to shoot to kill.[†]

The Federal District Court for the Western District of Tennessee reviewed the state's law permitting the police officer to use "all necessary means" to carry out an arrest, and found it to be constitutional based upon all legal precedent up to that time. The U.S. Court of Appeals for the Sixth Circuit upheld the District Court's decision, again based upon all legal precedent up to that time.[‡] Garner's father appealed that decision to the U.S. Supreme Court. The Supreme Court determined that the common law was superseded by the law of the U.S. Constitution. The Fourth Amendment encompassed the law regarding search and seizure. An arrest is, by definition, a seizure. Therefore, under the Fourth Amendment the Tennessee use of force rule was unconstitutional to that degree that it authorizes the use of deadly force to prevent the escape of an apparently unarmed suspected felon.[§]

The Garner decision restricts a state's ability to authorize law enforcement officers to use an unlimited amount of force to carry out an arrest, but it did not prevent states from protecting officers' use of *reasonable force* to carry out an arrest. So, the Garner case specifically held that using deadly force to shoot at an unarmed suspect to stop the suspect from fleeing is unconstitutional and therefore unreasonable. The majority of states, however, continue to maintain some form of statutory authority for police to use force to carry out an arrest (see Table 7.1). For example, Tennessee's current law uses the language provided within the Garner case.

> A law enforcement officer, after giving notice of the officer's identity as an officer, may use or threaten to use force that is reasonably necessary to accomplish the arrest of an individual suspected of a criminal act who resists or flees from the arrest.[¶]

---

[*] Ibid.

[†] Ibid.

[‡] *Garner v. Memphis Police Department, City of Memphis, Tennessee and Jay W. Hubbard and E.R. Hymon* in their official capacities, 6.

[§] *Tennessee v. Garner et al.*, 471 U.S. 1, 105 S. Ct. 1694, 85 L. Ed. 2d 1, 1985.

[¶] Tenn. Code Ann. 40-7-108(a), 2015. Resistance to officer.

TABLE 7.1 State Law Citations to Use of Force Regulations

State	State Code Abbreviations	Citation Authorization of Use of Force to Arrest	Citation Prohibition to Resist Arrest	Citation Tort Claim Protection for Use of Force	Citation Parameters for Use of Deadly Force
Alabama	Ala. Code	§ 13A-3-27(a)	§ 13A-3-28	§ 6-5-338	§ 13A-3-27(b)
Alaska	Alaska Stat.	§ 11.81.370	§ 11.81.400	*	§ 11.81.370
Arizona	Ariz. Rev. Stat. Ann.	§ 13-409	§ 13-2508	§ 13-413	§ 13-410
Arkansas	Ark. Code Ann.	§ 16-81-107	§ 5-6-612	*	§ 5-2-607
California	Cal. [Penal] Code	§ 835 and § 835a	§ 834a	Cal Gov. Code § 820.2	*
Colorado	Colo. Rev. Stat. Ann.	§ 18-1-707	§ 18-8-103	*	§ 18-1-707(2)
Connecticut	Conn. Gen. Stat.	§ 53a-22	§ 53a-23	*	§ 53a-22(c)
Delaware	11 Del. Code Ann.	§ 467	§ 1257	*	467(c)
Dist of Columbia	D.C. Code Ann.	§ 5-123.02	§ 22-405(b)	*	*
Florida	Fla. Stat.	§ 776.05	§ 776.051	§ 776.05	§ 776.05

(Continued)

TABLE 7.1 (*Continued*) State Law Citations to Use of Force Regulations

State	State Code Abbreviations	Citation Authorization of Use of Force to Arrest	Citation Prohibition to Resist Arrest	Citation Tort Claim Protection for Use of Force	Citation Parameters for Use of Deadly Force
Georgia	Ga. Code Ann.	16-3-20	§ 16-10-24	*	§ 17-4-20(b)
Hawaii	Haw. Rev. Stat.	§ 703-307	§ 803.7	*	§ 703-307(3)
Idaho	Idaho Code	§ 19-602	§ 19-610		§ 18-4011
Illinois	Ill. Comp. Stat.	§ 720 ILCS 5/7-5	§ 720 ILCS 5/7-7	*	§ 720 ILCS 5/7-5
Indiana	Ind. Code	§ 35-41-3-3(b)	§ 35-41-3-3	§ 34-13-3-3	§ 35-41-3-3(b)
Iowa	Iowa Code	§ 804.8	§ 804.12	§ 670.4 & 670.12	§ 704.1
Kansas	Kan. Stat. Ann.	§ 21-5227	§ 21-5229	§ 75-6101 et seq.	§ 21-5227
Kentucky	Ky. Rev. Stat. Ann.	§ 431.025 and § 503.090	§ 503.085 & 520.090	*	§ 503.090(3)
Louisiana	La. C.Cr.P.	Art. 220	Art. 220	*	La.R.S. § 14:20

(Continued)

TABLE 7.1 (*Continued*) State Law Citations to Use of Force Regulations

State	State Code Abbreviations	Citation Authorization of Use of Force to Arrest	Citation Prohibition to Resist Arrest	Citation Tort Claim Protection for Use of Force	Citation Parameters for Use of Deadly Force
Maine	Me. Rev. Stat. Ann.	17-A.M.R.S. § 107	*	15-A.M.R.S. § 704	17-A.M.R.S. § 107(2)
Maryland	Md. Crim. Law. Code Ann.	*	§ 9-408	*	*
Massachusetts	Mass. Gen. Laws	*	Ch. 268. § 32B.	*	*
Michigan	Mich. Comp. Laws	§330.1427A	§ 750.479 & § 750.81D	*	*
Minnesota	Minn. Stat.	§ 609.06	§ 609.06	*	*
Mississippi	Miss. Code Ann.	*.	§ 97-9-73	§ 11.46.9	*
Missouri	Mo. Rev. Stat.	§ 563.046	§ 575.150	*	*
Montana	Mont. Code Ann.	§ 46-6-104	§ 45-3-108	*	*

(*Continued*)

TABLE 7.1 (*Continued*) State Law Citations to Use of Force Regulations

State	State Code Abbreviations	Citation Authorization of Use of Force to Arrest	Citation Prohibition to Resist Arrest	Citation Tort Claim Protection for Use of Force	Citation Parameters for Use of Deadly Force
Nebraska	Neb. Rev. Stat.	§ 28-1412	§ 28-1409 & § 28-904	*	*
Nevada	Nev. Rev. Stat.	*	§ 28-1409	§ 41.032 et seq.	§ 171.1455
New Hampshire	N.H. Rev. Stat. Ann.	§ 633:7	§ 633:5	§ 633:6 and 633:7	§ 633:8
New Jersey	N.J. Stat. Ann.	§ 2C:3-7	§ 2C:29-2	*	*
New Mexico	N.M. Stat. Ann.	*	§ 30—22-1	§ 41-4-4	*
New York	NY CPL	§ 120.80. & § 140.15	§ 35.27	*	*
North Carolina	N.C. Gen. Stat.	§ 15A-401d	§ 14-223	*	*
North Dakota	N.D. Cent. Code	§ 12.1-05-07	§ 12.1-05.03	*	§ 12.1-05-07(2)

(*Continued*)

TABLE 7.1 (*Continued*) State Law Citations to Use of Force Regulations

State	State Code Abbreviations	Citation Authorization of Use of Force to Arrest	Citation Prohibition to Resist Arrest	Citation Tort Claim Protection for Use of Force	Citation Parameters for Use of Deadly Force
Ohio	Ohio Rev. Code Ann.	§ 2935.12 & § 2935.03	§ 2921.33	*	§ 2917.05
Oklahoma	Okla. Stat.	§ 21 Okl. St. 643	§ 21 Okl. St. 748	§ 21 Okl. St.748	§ 21 Okl. St. 732
Oregon	Or. Rev. Stat.	§ 161.235	§ 162.315	*	§ 161.239
Pennsylvania	Pa. Cons. Stat.	18 Pa.C.S. §	34 Pa.C.S. § 904	*	*
Rhode Island	R.I. Gen. Laws	§ 12-7-8	§ 12-7-10	*	§ 12-7-9
South Carolina	S.C. Code Ann.	*	§ 16-9-320	§ 15-78-70	*
South Dakota	S.D. Codified Laws	§ 22-18-3	§ 22-11-4	*	*
Tennessee	Tenn. Code Ann.	§ 40-7-108	§ 40-7-108	*	§ 39-11-620 & § 40-7-108

(Continued)

TABLE 7.1 (Continued)   State Law Citations to Use of Force Regulations

State	State Code Abbreviations	Citation Authorization of Use of Force to Arrest	Citation Prohibition to Resist Arrest	Citation Tort Claim Protection for Use of Force	Citation Parameters for Use of Deadly Force
Texas	Tex. Code Crim. Pro.	TCCP Art. 14.05 & Tex. Penal Code § 9.51	Tex. Penal Code § 9.52	*	Tex. Penal Code § 9.51(d)
Utah	Utah Code Ann.	§ 77-4-1	§ 76-8-305	*	§ 76-2-404
Vermont	Vt. Stat. Ann.	*	§ 13 VSA 1028	*	13 VSA § 2305
Virginia	Va. Code Ann.	*	§ 18.2-460	*	*
Washington	Wash. Rev. code	RCW § 10.31.050	RCW § 9A.76.020	*	*
West Virginia	W.Va. code	*	*	*	*
Wisconsin	Wis. Stat.	§ 939.45	*	*	*
Wyoming	Wyo. Stat. Ann.	*	§ 6-5-204	*	*

Note: The asterisk is used to denote no specific statute available in that state.

The Garner decision also impacted the "fleeing felon" rule. At common law a fleeing felon was by definition someone who was very dangerous. As the understanding of the term "felon" has evolved, though, it encompasses people who have committed nonviolent acts as well as violent acts. The Court in Garner recognized that the meaning of the word "felony" had changed, which meant that the rule which developed to prevent dangerous offenders from escaping capture had been expanded to include both dangerous and non-dangerous offenders. The Garner Court stated that

> It has been pointed out many times that the common law rule is best understood in light of the fact that it arose at a time when virtually all felonies were punishable by death. . . Neither of these justifications makes sense today. Almost all crimes formerly punishable by death no longer are or can be. And while in earlier times "the gulf between the felonies and the minor offences was broad and deep" today the distinction is minor and often arbitrary. Many crimes classified as misdemeanors, or nonexistent, at common law are now felonies. These changes have undermined the concept, which was questionable to begin with, that use of deadly force against a fleeing felon is merely a speedier execution of someone who has already forfeited his life. They have also made the assumption that a "felon" is more dangerous than a misdemeanant untenable.*

The Garner case forced states to reevaluate the authority that they granted to officers to use any amount of force in carrying out an arrest, but it is best known for limiting the legal right of officers to use deadly force. Today, in most states statutory authorization to use deadly force is addressed separately from non-deadly force (see Table 7.1). For example,

---

* *Tennessee v. Garner*, at 13–15, 1702–1703 and 11–12, citing "American Law Institute, Model Penal Code § 3.07, Comment 3, p. 56 (Tentative Draft No. 8, 1958) (hereinafter Model Penal Code Comment)." The full quote reads, "Neither of these justifications makes sense today. Almost all crimes formerly punishable by death no longer are or can be. See, e.g., *Enmund v. Florida*, 458 U.S. 782, 1982; *Coker* v. *Georgia*, 433 U.S. 584, 1977. And while in earlier times "the gulf between the felonies and the minor offences was broad and deep," 2 Pollock & Maitland 467, n. 3; *Carroll v. United States, supra*, at 158, today the distinction is minor and often arbitrary. Many crimes classified as misdemeanors, or nonexistent, at common law are now felonies. Wilgus, 22 Mich. L. Rev., pp. 572–573. These changes have undermined the concept, which was questionable to begin with, that use of deadly force against a fleeing felon is merely a speedier execution of someone who has already forfeited his life. They have also made the assumption that a "felon" is more dangerous than a misdemeanant untenable. Indeed, numerous misdemeanors involve conduct more dangerous than many felonies.

Tennessee adopted a separate law regarding use of deadly force following the Garner decision. The Tennessee law currently provides:

a. A law enforcement officer, after giving notice of the officer's identity as such, may use or threaten to use force that is reasonably necessary to accomplish the arrest of an individual suspected of a criminal act who resists or flees from the arrest.

b. Notwithstanding subsection a, the officer may use deadly force to effect an arrest only if all other reasonable means of apprehension have been exhausted or are unavailable, and where feasible, the officer has given notice of the officer's identity as such and given a warning that deadly force may be used unless resistance or flight ceases, and

  1. The officer has probable cause to believe the individual to be arrested has committed a felony involving the infliction or threatened infliction of serious bodily injury.

  2. The officer has probable cause to believe that the individual to be arrested poses a threat of serious bodily injury, either to the officer or to others unless immediately apprehended.*

The Tennessee law is very similar to the laws adopted by most other states, and has been found to be constitutional when reviewed.

While court decisions have brought about changes in state laws, no court decision has changed the basic precepts accepted since the advent of the common law: police officers are treated differently by the law. When prosecuting a nonpolice officer for a crime involving use of force, the prosecutor needs to show that the actor used force, because nonpolice are generally prohibited from using force against others. When prosecuting a police officer, however, there is no question that the officer used force, and maybe a lot of force. The prosecution must be able to prove that the amount of force used by the officer to complete the arrest was greater than permitted by law. "This rule takes into account the special situation of the police defendant."† Unlike private citizens, police officers

---

* Tenn. Code Ann. 39-11-620. Use of deadly force by a law enforcement officer.
† *Edson v. City of Anaheim*, 63 Cal. App. 4th 1269, 74 Cal. Rptr. 2d 614, 1998. (See also, *Graham v. Connor*, 490 U.S. 386, 109 S. Ct. 1865, 104 L. Ed. 2d 443, 1989).

act with the authority granted by the law to protect the public interest.* Law enforcement officers are directed to use force as part of their duties. No one seriously questions that "the right to make an arrest or investigatory stop necessarily carries with it the right to use some degree of physical coercion or threat thereof to effect it."† This means that police officers are not analogous to similarly situated ordinary battery defendants.‡ For these reasons, when a "defendant police officer is in the exercise of the privilege of protecting the public peace and order he is entitled to the even greater use of force than might be in the same circumstances required for self-defense."§ For all of these reasons, it is very difficult to prosecute a police officer for a state level crime arising out of an excessive use of force to arrest.

While it is difficult to meet the legal standards to bring state level criminal charges against police officers, it is certainly not impossible.¶ In 2015, a state prosecutor announced that her office would prosecute six Baltimore, Maryland, police officers who participated in the arrest of Freddy Gray. The state crimes filed against the officers included manslaughter, assault, misconduct in office, and false imprisonment. The State's Attorney for Baltimore City stated that after reviewing the evidence in the case, the officers acted outside the law by arresting Mr. Gray, as he had committed no crime, and therefore the officers had no probable cause to support his arrest. Charging an officer with a crime is just the first step, however. A jury will have to find that the officers committed the acts alleged and that the law of reasonable force to carry out an arrest did not act to shield the officers' actions from criminal liability.

☐ Prosecuting Excessive Force under Federal Law

In 1992 four police officers were charged by the Los Angeles District Attorney with the state crimes of assault with a deadly weapon and excessive use of force by a police officer. After a trial, a jury found all four

---

* Ibid.

† Ibid (citing *Graham v. Connor*, at 396, 1273, 616, 8).

‡ Ibid.

§ Ibid (at 1273, 616, 8).

¶ Alan Blinder and Richard Perez-Pena, 6 Baltimore Police Officers Charged in Freddie Gray Death. *New York Times* May 1, 2015. C., Doug. Many obstacles to prosecuting police. *The Baltimore Sun* July 12, 2015.

officers not guilty beyond reasonable doubt.* Because federal prosecutors perceived that the acts of the four officers as shown in the video violated federal criminal law, federal indictments were sought against the four officers. On August 4, 1992, a federal grand jury returned indictments against all four officers.†

The federal government's decision to prosecute the four officers was not double jeopardy. Under the legal concept of "dual sovereignty" every jurisdiction may prosecute an individual for crimes committed within its jurisdiction, even if the criminal acts are made criminal by another jurisdiction. Thus, for example, the U.S. Government could prosecute Terry Nichols for the federal crimes of conspiracy and use of a weapon of mass destruction, as well as other crimes arising out of his participation in bombing the Murrah Federal Building in Oklahoma City, Oklahoma in 1995, after which the State of Oklahoma prosecuted him for 161 counts of murder.

Federal criminal liability for excessive force used in an arrest typically arises under 18 U.S.C. § 242 ("§ 242").‡ This is a relatively old law, as the precursor of the modern day § 242 was adopted by Congress in the

---

* *Koon v. U.S.* and *Powell v. U.S.*, 518 U.S. 81, 88, 116 S. Ct. 2035, 2042, 135 L. Ed. 2d 392, 406, 1996. Koon, Powell, Briseno, and Wind were tried in state court on charges of assault with a deadly weapon and excessive use of force by a police officer. The officers were acquitted of all charges, with the exception of one assault charge [*88] against Powell that resulted in a hung jury. The verdicts touched off widespread rioting in Los Angeles. More than 40 people were killed in the riots, more [**2042] than 2,000 were injured, and nearly $ 1 billion in property was destroyed. New Initiatives for a New Los Angeles: Final Report and Recommendations, Senate Special Task Force on a New Los Angeles, December 9, 1992, pp. 10–11.

† Ibid.

‡ 18 USCS § 242, 2015. Based on title 18, U.S.C., 1940 ed., § 52, March 4, 1909, ch. 321, § 20, 35 Stat. 1092. Deprivation of rights under color of law. "Whoever, under color of any law, statute, ordinance, regulation, or custom, willfully subjects any person in any state, territory, commonwealth, possession, or district to the deprivation of any rights, privileges, or immunities secured or protected by the Constitution or laws of the United States, or to different punishments, pains, or penalties, on account of such person being an alien, or by reason of his color, or race, than are prescribed for the punishment of citizens, shall be fined under this title or imprisoned not more than one year, or both; and if bodily injury results from the acts committed in violation of this section or if such acts include the use, attempted use, or threatened use of a dangerous weapon, explosives, or fire, shall be fined under this title or imprisoned not more than ten years, or both; and if death results from the acts committed in violation of this section or if such acts include kidnapping or an attempt to kidnap, aggravated sexual abuse, or an attempt to commit aggravated sexual abuse, or an attempt to kill, shall be fined under this title, or imprisoned for any term of years or for life, or both, or may be sentenced to death."

years following the Civil War. Section 242 was passed to allow the federal government to prosecute a state official for using state authority to deny a citizen of the United States any right secured by the Constitution of the United States.* Section 242 reads in pertinent part:

> Whoever, under color of any law, statute, ordinance, regulation, or custom, willfully subjects any person in any State, Territory, or District to the deprivation of any rights, privileges, or immunities secured or protected by the Constitution or laws of the United States, or to different punishments, pains, or penalties, on account of such person being an alien, or by reason of his color, or race, than are prescribed for the punishment of citizens," shall be subject to specified criminal penalties.†

This law also provides penalties ranging in severity based upon the severity of harm suffered by the victim of the constitutional violation. If the harm is categorized as a kidnapping, sexual assault, or murder, the penalty may be as great as life imprisonment.‡ It was, in fact, § 242 under which the four officers in the Rodney King beating case were prosecuted by the federal government in 1992.

There are essential elements that the government must prove beyond reasonable doubt to secure a conviction under § 242 for police

---

* *Screws v. U.S.*, 325 U.S. 91, 98–100. 65 S. Ct. 1031, 1035, 89 L.Ed. 1495, 1501–1502, 1945. "Sec. 20 was enacted to enforce the Fourteenth Amendment. It derives from § 2 of the Civil Rights Act of April 9, 1866. 14 Stat. 27. Senator Trumbull, chairman of the Senate Judiciary Committee which reported the bill, stated that its purpose was "to protect all persons in the United States in their civil rights, and furnish the means of their vindication." *Congressional Globe, 39th Congress, 1st Session*, 211pp. In origin it was an antidiscrimination measure (as its language indicated), framed to protect Negroes in their newly won rights. See Flack, The Adoption of the Fourteenth Amendment, 1908, p. 21. It was amended by § 17 of the Act of May 31, 1870, 16 Stat. 144, and made applicable to "any inhabitant of any State or Territory." The prohibition against the "deprivation of any rights, privileges, or immunities, secured or protected by the Constitution and laws of the United States" was introduced by the revisers in 1874. R. S. § 5510. Those words were taken over from § 1 of the Act of April 20, 1871, 17 Stat. 13 (the so-called Ku-Klux Act) which provided civil suits for redress of such wrongs. See *Congressional Record, 43rd Congress, 1st Session*, 828pp. The 1874 revision was applicable to any person who under color of law, etc., "subjects, or causes to be subjected" any inhabitant to the deprivation of any rights, etc. The requirement for a "willful" violation was introduced by the draftsmen of the Criminal Code of 1909. Act of March 4, 1909, 35 Stat. 1092. And we are told "willfully" was added to § 20 in order to make the section "less severe." 43 Congressional Record, 60th Congress, 2nd Session, 3599pp.
† Ibid (18 USCS § 242, 2015).
‡ Ibid.

use of excessive force.* Typically, courts break the required elements of the crime of use of excessive force to arrest into four elements: (1) the defendant was acting under color of law when he committed the acts charged in the indictment; (2) the defendant deprived the arrestee of his right to be free of unreasonable seizures secured by the Fourth Amendment to the Constitution of the United States; (3) the defendant acted with a willful intent to deprive the arrestee of the constitutional right; and (4) the offense resulted in bodily injury to the arrestee or the offense included the use, attempted use, or threatened use of a dangerous weapon.†

The first of the four elements requires that the actor be "acting under color of law." This element recognizes that the authority to carry out the official duties of a governmental office, whether elected or appointed, is authority provided by the law. So, an individual acts under color of state law when exercising authority held by virtue of a state government office or position. Courts must evaluate evidence to determine whether the defendant was exercising power bestowed by state law or was acting only as a private individual.‡ The Supreme Court has clearly stated that § 242 excludes acts committed by persons carrying out their personal pursuits, even when that person is a law enforcement officer. Specifically, § 242 only encompasses overstepping or abusing the authority of a State office.§ Just because a police officer was rude, unpleasant, or mean while wearing a governmental uniform is not enough to support a § 242 contention that harm to a person arose out of an officer's legal authority. For example, in § 242 of a Florida sheriff, the court recognized that the sheriff, while wearing her uniform, used her handcuffs for the private ends of assaulting and scaring a young man she caught in a compromising situation with her daughter. The assault happened in the sheriff's home when she was returning from a duty shift. The court in that case stated:

> If the allegations are true, Collier's treatment of Butler was badder than old King Kong and meaner than a junkyard dog. She might even have acted like the meanest hunk of woman anybody had ever seen. Still, the fact that the mistreatment was mean does not mean that the mistreatment was under color of law.¶

---

* See *Tarver v. City of Edna*, 410 F.3d 745, 752, 5th Cir. 2005.
† *U.S. v. Rodella*, 2015 U.S. App. LEXIS 19275, November 4, 2015.
‡ *Screws v. United States*, 325 U.S. 91, 111, 65 S.Ct. 1031, 1040, 89 L. Ed. 1495, 1945.
§ *Butler v. Sheriff of Palm Beach County et al.*, 685 F.3d 1261, 1265 2012.
¶ *Butler v. Sheriff of Palm Beach County*, at 1269.

The second element of a § 242 charge arising out of excessive force to arrest is the "act" element. This element requires evidence that the defendant did some act(s) that deprived the arrestee of his right to be free of unreasonable seizures secured by the Fourth Amendment. Unreasonable seizures include the right to be free from unlawful arrests and the right to not be subjected to excessive force. Federal prosecutors use the facts of the interaction between the law enforcement officer and the arrestee to support the allegation that the arrestee was subjected to an unreasonable seizure. For example, Sheriff Thomas Rodella was alleged to have unreasonably seized an individual whom he arrested. However, it was not just the limited interaction of the arrest that supported the § 242 charge, it was the entire interaction between Rodella and the victim. Rodella began the interaction by aggressively following the victim's vehicle. Rodella was in an unmarked vehicle, and the victim was not alleged to have committed any traffic violations at this point. The victim was so frightened by Rodella's aggressive driving that he began to drive in excess of the speed limit to get away from Rodella's threatening driving behavior. Eventually, Rodella forced the victim off the road, leapt into the individual's passenger side seat, and displayed a firearm. Rodella's son pulled the victim from his vehicle, forced him to the pavement, after which Rodella picked the victim's head up by the hair and hit him in the face with his badge.* Rodella's actions were deemed to be carried out under color of law as he was "pursuing" the individual, and seized the individual under his authority as a law enforcement officer.

The third element of § 242 is the element that requires that the government prove that the amount of force was unreasonable and the officer knew it to be unreasonable. This element is the element of "willful intent" to deprive the arrestee of rights guaranteed by the Fourth Amendment. To be "willful" the government must be able to show that the accused either knew or should have known that the acts would be considered an unreasonable amount of force. In 2014, the Second Circuit Court of Appeals specifically analyzed this element in relation to police use of excessive force during an arrest. The accused officer in that case, Cossette, was charged with using force without provocation or need, specifically, with "assaulting a detainee who was already handcuffed in a holding cell and compliant with the police.† The court stated that Cossette could not truthfully argue that the state failed to prove this element. Every police officer in the country knows that "gratuitously assaulting a detainee, without provocation or need, constituted an unreasonable use

---

* *U.S. v. Rodella*, 2015 U.S. App. LEXIS 19275, November 4, 2015.
† *U.S. v. Cossette*, 593 Fed. Appx. 28, 30, 2014.

of force."* In another case out of Tennessee, a district court judge was prosecuted under § 242 for sexually assaulting women employees of the court. On appeal, the defendant judge claimed that although the federal court found that sexually assaulting women of the court was a violation of the due process rights of the victims, the defendant judge had no way of knowing that in advance as no court had ever before stated that standard. The sixth Circuit accepted this argument and overturned the judge's § 242 conviction. The U.S. Supreme Court, however, overturned the sixth Circuit.† That Court held that defendants are on notice of the wrongfulness of their action is either a preexisting case, or preexisting law has made the action illegal.‡

The fourth element of a § 242 alleging excessive force associated with an arrest is the "harm" element. This element requires that the government prove that the offense resulted in bodily injury to the arrestee or the offense included the use, attempted use, or threatened use of a dangerous weapon. The level of force alleged must result in an actual physical or emotional harm. The mere act of using some force to carry out an arrest does not rise to the level of harm necessary to support this element of a § 242 claim. Clearly, some level of force, usually minimal, is necessary to complete any arrest.§ Additionally, the seriousness of the injury is not necessarily equated to amount of force used by the officer.¶ While a greater injury provides stronger evidence that an arresting officer used an unlawful amount of force under the Fourth Amendment, smaller injuries may still convince the fact finder that excessive force was used to arrest.** In short, this standard requires that a harm be suffered, but cannot be read to permit injuries and harms that do not leave a mark upon the victim's body. Such a restrictive standard would encourage and approve the development of tortures that do not photograph well.

The federal government has effectively used § 242 to prosecute many officers for acts of unreasonable use of force to arrest. A well-known example is the 1992 case against the four officers who beat Rodney King during an arrest.†† Three of the officers, Powell, Briseno, and Wind, were charged with willful use of unreasonable force in

---

* Ibid.
† *U.S. v. Lanier*, 520 U.S. 259, 272, 117 S. Ct. 1219, 1228, 137 L. Ed. 2d 432, 446, 1997.
‡ Ibid.
§ *Cortez v. McCauley*, 478 F.3d 1108, 1112, 10th Cir. 2007.
¶ *Hudson v. McMillian*, 503 U.S. 1, 112 S. Ct. 995, 1000, 117 L. Ed. 2d 156, 166, 1992.
** *U.S. v. Rodella*, 2015 U.S. App. LEXIS 19275, ___, November 4, 2015.
†† *Koon v. U.S.* and *Powell v. U.S.*, 518 U.S. 81, 88, 116 S. Ct. 2035, 2042, 135 L. Ed. 2d 392, 406, 1996.

arresting King. The fourth officer who had been in charge that night, Stacey Koon, was charged with willfully permitting the other officers to use unreasonable force during the arrest. The federal jury convicted Koon and Powell but acquitted Wind and Briseno. During the sentencing hearing of Koon and Powell, the federal district judge provided a clear review of the criminal law as applied to the facts.* The judge stated that much of the officers' conduct that night was lawful, although at the end of the arrest their behavior crossed the law into unlawfulness. The court recognized that while the officers were found guilty of using the batons as weapons to violate King's constitutional rights, the fact that weapons were present or used was not in itself the unlawful act. The court stated that "police officers are always armed with 'dangerous weapons' and may legitimately employ those weapons to administer reasonable force." In the King case, King admitted that he had been driving while intoxicated, had tried to outrun the police, and had initially failed to obey officers' commands. In arresting someone for those acts police may need to use force, and in this case the officer's initial use of force was deemed to be "provoked and lawful." But, at some point the officers' conduct crossed the line from a legal use of force to arrest into an unlawful deprivation of civil rights.†

Unfortunately, media stories at the time depicted the decision by the federal court as proving that the jury in the state case was biased and wrong when, in fact, the two cases involved different laws with different legal standards. It is entirely possible that the state jury would have found Koon and Powell guilty beyond a reasonable doubt for violation of the federal crime of violating § 242, but the state jury was not asked that question. The state jury was asked whether the state had proven that the state law which permitted the use of force to arrest was violated beyond reasonable doubt. Applying the evidence presented in the case to the elements of the state crimes, the state jury found the officers not guilty beyond reasonable doubt. The federal jury was asked a different question: whether the amount of force used to arrest Rodney King was unreasonable under the Fourth Amendment to the Constitution beyond a reasonable doubt. That jury found two of the four officers guilty beyond a reasonable doubt of violating that legal standard. Regrettably, the consequences of asking two juries to review the same set of facts to make different legal decisions is poorly understood by noncriminal justice professionals. When juries make decisions that the public views as

---

* *Koon v. U.S.* and *Powell v. U.S.*, at 103, 2049, and 416.
† Ibid.

conflicting, the jurors themselves may be cast as acting out of bias rather than merely having reviewed and applied different laws.*

A more recent § 242 analysis was conducted by the U.S. Department of Justice when it investigated the facts of the 2014 shooting death of Michael Brown by a Ferguson, Missouri police officer.† In an 86-page report outlining all of the evidence, and reviewing the applicable legal standards, the report concludes that the "matter lacks prosecutive merit and should be closed."‡ In applying the § 242 legal standards, the Department of Justice concluded:

> Darren Wilson has stated his intent in shooting Michael Brown was in response to a perceived deadly threat. The only possible basis for prosecuting Wilson under Section 242 would therefore be if the government could prove that his account is not true—i.e., that Brown never assaulted Wilson at the SUV, never attempted to gain control of Wilson's gun, and thereafter clearly surrendered in a way that no reasonable officer could have failed to perceive. Given that Wilson's account is corroborated by physical evidence and that his perception of a threat posed by Brown is corroborated by other eyewitnesses, to include aspects of the testimony of Witness 101, there is no credible evidence that Wilson willfully shot Brown as he was attempting to surrender or was otherwise not posing a threat. Even if Wilson was mistaken in his interpretation of Brown's conduct, the fact that others interpreted that conduct the same way as Wilson precludes a determination that he acted with a bad purpose to disobey the law.

---

* See, for example, *State v. Simpson*, No. BA-097211 (Cal. Super. Ct., L.A. County June 17, 1994). Uelmen, Gerald F., Jury-Bashing and the OlJ. Simpson Verdict. 20 Harv.J.L.& Pub. Pol'y 475, 196.

Satterberg, William, Tales from the Interior: Voir Dire, 24 AK Bar Rag 18 (July/August, 2000). "The crowning touch is my O.J. Simpson trilogy. I ask the jurors whether or not they believe what they read in the newspaper, hear on the radio, or watch on television. By then, all hands are flying up quickly indicating that they do not believe any of those three news sources. I next ask the jurors to raise their hands if they can keep an open mind. Once again the hands fly up. By then, the trap is set. I then ask the jurors for a show of hands if they believe that "O.J. did it." Usually, but not always, a chuckle will arise in the courtroom. It is a valid technique, which goes to impress upon the jurors their need to keep an open mind, and judge a case only on the evidence presented, and not upon public opinion, sentiment, or press releases."

† Memorandum: Department of Justice Report Regarding the Criminal Investigation into the Shooting Death of Michael Brown By Ferguson, Missouri Police Officer Darren Wilson, U.S. Department of Justice. March 4, 2015. http://www.justice. gov/sites/default/files/opa/press-releases/ attachments/2015/03/04/doj_report_on _shooting_of_michael_brown_1.pdf

‡ Ibid, at 86.

While the findings of this investigation may not have resulted in the politically popular or emotionally satisfying outcome that was hoped for, this investigation did exactly what the law requires. The report clearly applies the law as it has developed over a long time, to the facts as they occurred on that day and time, to determine if the officer's actions constituted a federal crime under § 242.*

☐ Federal Civil Liability for Excessive Use of Force

Criminal prosecution is not the only remedy available to persons who believe that they have suffered harm. Victims themselves may sue the officer seeking damages in a civil court. Just as criminal wrongs are called "crimes," civil harms are known as "torts." The standard of proof to prove a tort is "preponderance of the evidence," which means "to be more sure than not." This standard of proof used in civil cases is much lower than the "beyond a reasonable doubt" standard of proof required to prove a crime, which means that it is easier to prove a civil wrong than it is to prove a crime. It is not unusual for someone to be found not guilty beyond a reasonable doubt in a criminal court, but then be found liable for the harms of the act in a civil court. A well-known example of this was seen in the O.J. Simpson cases.†

---

* Ibid. On March 4, 2015, the U.S. Department of Justice (U.S.D.O.J.) released its report ("U.S.D.O.J. Report") into the shooting death of 18-year-old Michael Brown by Officer Darren Wilson of the Ferguson, Mo. Police Department. The U.S.D.O.J. Report begins with an overview of the investigation into the shooting death of Michael Brown on August 9, 2014. The report provides an overview of the prosecutorial standard that federal prosecutors must meet before seeking an indictment against an individual. First, a federal prosecutor must be convinced that a federal crime occurred and that the accused committed that crime. Second, the prosecution must be in possession of that quantum of admissible evidence that could reasonably be expected to convince a jury beyond a reasonable doubt. After reviewing all of the available evidence the U.S.D.O.J. concluded that "Darren Wilson's actions do not constitute prosecutable violations under the applicable federal criminal civil rights statute, 18 U.S.C. § 242, which prohibits uses of deadly force that are "objectively unreasonable," as defined by the United States Supreme Court. The evidence, when viewed as a whole, does not support the conclusion that Wilson's uses of deadly force were "objectively unreasonable" under the Supreme Court's definition."

† *State v. Simpson*, No. BA-097211 (Cal. Super. Ct., L.A. County June 17, 1994). Uelmen, Gerald F., Jury-Bashing and the O.J. Simpson Verdict. 20 Harv.J.L.& Pub. Pol'y 475, 196.

While States recognize torts associated with excessive use of force, such as wrongful death, wrongful imprisonment, and assault, most civil lawsuits against officers are filed under the federal civil-rights statute codified at 42 U.S.C. § 1983. Whereas state torts are historically difficult to apply to police who are recognized to have a right to use force to carry out an arrest, the federal law creates a different form tort liability that seeks to address those specific harms suffered by persons who are deprived by state government officers of "'rights, privileges, or immunities secured' to them by the Constitution."[*] For the sake of brevity, litigation under 42 U.S.C. § 1983 is usually referred to as a "§ 1983" action.[†] While money damages are awarded to plaintiffs who win a § 1983 suit, the actual amount of damages is ordinarily determined according to principles derived from the common law of torts.[‡]

A § 1983 civil lawsuit, like a § 242 criminal action, requires evidence that an individual has acted under "color of law" granted by a state, territory, or the District of Columbia to cause a deprivation of a right guaranteed by the United States Constitution. But, the two laws are different, and dealt with very differently within the federal courts. A significant difference between the two laws is that § 242 extends to "any person" in any state, while § 1983 specifically protects "citizen[s]" of the United States.[§] A second major difference is that § 242 is a criminal action requiring proof beyond a reasonable doubt to convict, while § 1983 is a civil lawsuit. That means that proving a § 1983 allegation requires the much lower standard of proof of preponderance of the evidence, and the individual claiming the harm may file the lawsuit directly without involving a criminal prosecutor.

---

[*] *Memphis Community School Dist, et al. v. Stachura*, 477 U.S. 299, 306, 106 S.Ct. 2537, 2542, 91 L.Ed.2d 249, 258, 1986 (quoting, *Carey v. Piphus*, 435 U.S. 247, 253, 1978, quoting *Imbler v. Pachtman*, 424 U.S. 409, 417, 1976).

[†] 42 U.S.C. § 1983. Civil action for deprivation of rights. "Every person who, under color of any statute, ordinance, regulation, custom, or usage, of any State or Territory or the District of Columbia, subjects, or causes to be subjected, any citizen of the United States or other person within the jurisdiction thereof to the deprivation of any rights, privileges, or immunities secured by the Constitution and laws, shall be liable to the party injured in an action at law, suit in equity, or other proper proceeding for redress, except that in any action brought against a judicial officer for an act or omission taken in such officer's judicial capacity, injunctive relief shall not be granted unless a declaratory decree was violated or declaratory relief was unavailable. For the purposes of this section, any Act of Congress applicable exclusively to the District of Columbia shall be considered to be a statute of the District of Columbia."

[‡] Ibid. (See *Smith v. Wade*, 461 U.S. 30, 34, 1983; *Carey v. Piphus*, 435 U.S. 247, at 257-258, 1978; *Monroe v. Pape*, 365 U.S. 167, 196, and n. 5, 1961).

[§] Ibid.

42 U.S.C. § 1983 does not include officers acting under authority granted by the federal government. In 1971, however, the U.S. Supreme Court found that federal officials who violate the Fourth Amendment may be sued for damages.* This authority to seek legal redress against *federal law enforcement officers* has been subsequently expanded to include other constitutional rights, and is known as a "Bivens action."† The rules for proving a § 1983 violation and a Bivens violation are virtually identical. In both types of lawsuits a plaintiff may be awarded money damages from government officials who have violated constitutional or statutory rights.

To establish a cause of action under § 1983 or Bivens action, the individual claiming to have suffered harm, known as the plaintiff, must show that the defendant, an identified actual person acting under color of law, caused the plaintiff to suffer a violation of a clearly established constitutional right. The phrase "under color of law" has the same meaning in 18 U.S.C.S. § 242 as it does in 42 U.S.C.S. § 1983.‡ Any private citizen can commit an illegal act. By imposing the requirement that the actor has acted "under color of law" private conduct is excluded, and cases are limited to abuse of official powers.§

A § 1983 or Bivens requires that an identified "person" has acted to violate the citizen's rights. According to the Supreme Court based upon the clear language of the Eleventh Amendment granting states immunity from certain lawsuits, states are not "persons" subject to suit under § 1983.¶ The Court also determined that the Eleventh Amendment "bars suits not only against the State when it is the named party, but also when it is the party in fact."** "Its applicability is to be determined not by the

---

* *Bivens v. Six Unknown Fed. Narcotics Agents*, 403 U.S. 388, 91 S. Ct. 1999, 29 L. Ed. 2d 619, 1971.

† See, for example, *Carlson v. Green*, 446 U.S. 14, 100 S.Ct. 1468, 64 L.Ed.2d 15, 1980. (Eighth Amendment cruel and unusual punishment); *Davis v. Passman*, 442 U.S. 228, 99 S.Ct. 2264, 60 L.Ed.2d 846 (1979) (Fifth Amendment due process).

‡ *Butler v. Sheriff of Palm Beach County et al.*, 685 F.3d 1261, 1269, 2012.

§ Ibid.

¶ *Will v. Michigan Dept. of State Police*, 491 U.S. 58, 105 L. Ed. 2d 45, 109 S. Ct. 2304, 1989. USCS Const. Amend. 11. Suits against states—restriction of judicial power. The Judicial power of the United States shall not be construed to extend to any suit in law or equity, commenced or prosecuted against one of the United States by citizens of another state, or by citizens or subjects of any foreign state.

** *Scheuer v. Rhodes*, 416 U.S. 232, 237, 94 S. Ct. 1683, 1687, 40 L. Ed. 2d 90, 98. (Citing to: *Edelman v. Jordan*, 415 U.S. 651 1974); *Poindexter v. Greenhow*, 114 U.S. 270, 287 (1885); *Cunningham v. Macon & Brunswick R. Co.*, 109 U.S. 446, 1883).

mere names of the titular parties but by the essential nature and effect of the proceeding, as it appears from the entire record."*

A municipality does not have the same protections as a state government, which is notable as the majority of law enforcement officers are employees of municipal governments. In *Monell v. New York City Dept. of Social Services*, the Court held that municipalities are "persons" subject to damages liability under § 1 of the Ku Klux Act of 1871, 42 U.S.C. § 1983, for violations of that act visited by municipal officials.† The court narrowly defined municipal liability, however. It held "that municipal liability could not be premised on the mere fact that the municipality employed the offending official," but instead, "municipal liability could only be imposed for injuries inflicted pursuant to government 'policy or custom'."‡

To establish the liability of a municipality, the "causal" standard is understood as "deliberate indifference." " 'Deliberate indifference' is a stringent standard of fault, requiring proof that a municipal actor disregarded a known or obvious consequence of his action."§ The court clearly explained this standard in the 1989 case of Canton, *Ohio v. Harris*. The court held that a municipality can be found liable under 42 U.S.C.S. § 1983 only where the municipality itself causes the

---

* Ex parte New York, 256 U.S. 490, 500, 41 S. Ct. 588, 590, 65 L.Ed. 1057, 1062 (1921). See also, *Hafer v. Melo*, 502 U.S. 21, 25, 112 S.Ct. 358, 361-362, 116 L.Ed.2d 301, 309, 1991 "In *Kentucky v. Graham*, 473 U.S. 159, 87 L. Ed. 2d 114, 105 S. Ct. 3099, 1985, the Court sought to eliminate lingering confusion about the distinction between personal- and official-capacity suits. We emphasized that official-capacity suits "generally represent only another way of pleading an action against an entity of which an officer is an agent." *Kentucky v. Graham*, at 165 (quoting *Monell v. New York City Dept. of Social Services*, 436 U.S. 658, 690, n. 55, 56 L. Ed. 2d 611, 98 S. Ct. 2018, 1978). Suits against state officials in their official capacity therefore should be treated as suits against the State. 473 U.S. at 166. Indeed, when officials sued in this capacity in federal court die or leave office, their successors automatically assume their roles in the litigation. Because the real party in interest in an official-capacity suit is the governmental entity and not the named official, "the entity's "policy or custom" must have played a part in the violation of federal law." *Kentucky v. Graham*, at 166 (quoting Monell, at 694). For the same reason, the only immunities available to the defendant in an official-capacity action are those that the governmental entity possesses. *Kentucky v. Graham* at 167."

† *City of Oklahoma City v. Tuttle*, 471 U.S. 808, 105 S.Ct. 2427, 85 L Ed.2d 791 (1985) (quoting *Monell v. New York City Dept. of Social Services*, 436 U.S. 658, 1978).

‡ *City of Oklahoma City v. Tuttle*, 471 U.S. 808, 810, 105 S.Ct. 2427, 2429, 85 L Ed.2d 791, 796 (1985). See also, *Brd. Of County Commr's of Bryan County, OK v. Brown*, 520 U.S. 397, 117 S.Ct. 1382, 137 L.Ed.2d 626, 1997.

§ *Brd. of County Commr's of Bryan County, OK.v. Brown*, at 410, 1391, and 643.

constitutional violation at issue. Respondeat superior or vicarious liability will not attach under § 1983. It is only when "the execution of the government's policy or custom inflicts the injury that the municipality may be held liable under § 1983."[*] The Canton decision also clearly set forth the standard for holding a municipality liable under § 1983 for failure to train. That Court held that if certain employees are assigned specific duties that require those performing such duties to be provided more or different training in order to carry out those duties, and a municipality decides not to provide the employees such training, "the policymakers of the city can reasonably be said to have been deliberately indifferent to the need."[†]

Qualified immunity shields federal and state officials from money damages unless a plaintiff pleads facts showing (1) that the official violated a statutory or constitutional right and (2) that the right was "clearly established" at the time of the challenged conduct.[‡] Qualified immunity is only a defense in lawsuits against an official in their personal capacity.[§] The only immunities that can be claimed in an official-capacity action are forms of sovereign immunity, such as those immunities provided by the Eleventh Amendment.[¶]

The standard that actionable conduct involves violation of a clearly established statutory or constitutional right of which a reasonable person would have known protects officers from being required to know laws

---

[*] *City of Canton, Ohio v. Harris*, 489 U.S. 378, 385, 109 S.Ct. 1197, 1204, 103 L. Ed.2d 412, 424, 1989.

[†] *City of Canton, Ohio v. Harris*, 489 U.S. 378, 396, 109 S.Ct. 1197, 1208, 103 L. Ed.2d 412, 431 (1989).

[‡] *Ashcroft v. al-Kidd*, 563 U.S. 731, 131 S. Ct. 2074, 2080, 179 L. Ed. 2d 1149, 1155, 2011. *Pearson v. Callahan*, 555 U.S. 223, 231, 129 S. Ct. 808, 172 L. Ed. 2d 565, 2009. (Quoting *Harlow v. Fitzgerald*, 457 U.S. 800, 818, 102 S. Ct. 2727, 73 L. Ed. 2d 396, 1982).

[§] Ibid. (Citing to: *Owen v. City of Independence*, 445 U.S. 622, 1980; see also *Brandon v. Holt*, 469 U.S. 464, 1985).

[¶] Ibid. See also, *Hafer v. Melo*, 502 U.S. 21, 25, 112 S.Ct. 358, 362, 116 L.Ed.2d 301, 309–310, 1991. "Personal-capacity suits, on the other hand, seek to impose individual liability upon a government officer for actions taken under color of state law. Thus, "on the merits, to establish personal liability in a § 1983 action, it is enough to show that the official, acting under color of state law, caused the deprivation of a federal right." *Kentucky v. Graham*, p. 166. While the plaintiff in a personal-capacity suit need not establish a connection to governmental "policy or custom," officials sued in their personal capacities, unlike those sued in their official capacities, may assert personal immunity defenses such as objectively reasonable reliance on existing law. *Kentucky v. Graham*, pp. 166–167."

or judicial decisions before they occur.* "A clearly established right is one that is 'sufficiently clear that every reasonable official would have understood that what he is doing violates that right.'"† So, if an officer was acting in reasonable reliance upon an existing law or policy, the officer is granted qualified immunity from liability in the case.‡

Whether a method of arrest or detention, or the amount of force used to complete an arrest, is reasonable is an objective legal inquiry.§ Objective reasonableness is a legal standard. Objective reasonableness evaluates whether at the time of the challenged conduct any reasonable officer in the same situation would have known that his actions would be in violation of a constitutional right.¶ Understanding how objective reasonableness applies in any case depends upon the "facts and circumstances of each particular case."** "A court must make this determination from the perspective of a reasonable officer on the scene, including what the officer knew at the time, not with the 20/20 vision of hindsight."†† In an attempt to clarify this standard in the Kingsley case, the Court reviewed case law precedent to provide a nonexclusive list of considerations that may have applicability in a determination as to whether an officer's use of force was objectively reasonable.

> Considerations such as the following may bear on the reasonableness or unreasonableness of the force used: the relationship between the need for the use of force and the amount of force used; the extent of the plaintiff's

---

* *Camreta v. Greene,* 563 U.S. 692, 131 S. Ct. 2020, 2031, 179 L. Ed. 2d 1118, 1132, 2011. *Scott v. Harris,* 550 U.S.372, 377 127 S. Ct. 1769, 1774, 167 L. Ed. 2d 686, 692, 2007. In resolving questions of qualified immunity, courts are required to resolve a threshold question: taken in the light most favorable to the party asserting the injury, do the facts alleged show an officer's conduct violated a constitutional right? This must be the initial inquiry. If, and only if, the court finds a violation of a constitutional right, the next, sequential step is to ask whether the right was clearly established in light of the specific context of the case. Although this ordering contradicts the U.S. Supreme Court's policy of avoiding unnecessary adjudication of constitutional issues, such a departure from practice is necessary to set forth principles which will become the basis for a future holding that a right is clearly established.

† *Mullenix v. Luna,* 2015 U.S. Lexis 7160, November 9, 2015. (Quoting *Reichle v. Howards,* 566 U.S. ___, ___, 132 S. Ct. 2088, 182 L. Ed. 2d 985, 989, 2012).

‡ *Kentucky v. Graham,* 473 U.S. 159, 166–167, 105 S. Ct. 3099, 3105–3106, 87 L. Ed. 2d 114, 122, 1985. (Citing to: *Imbler v. Pachtman,* 424 U.S. 409, 1976 (absolute immunity); *Pierson v. Ray,* 386 U.S. 547, 1967 (same); *Harlow v. Fitzgerald,* 457 U.S. 800, 1982 (qualified immunity); *Wood v. Strickland,* 420 U.S. 308, 1975).

§ *Ashcroft v. al-Kidd,* 563 U.S. 731, 131 S. Ct. 2074, 179 L. Ed. 2d 1149, 2011.

¶ Ibid.

** *Graham v. Connor,* 490 U.S. 386, 396,109 S. Ct. 1865, 1872, 104 L. Ed. 2d 443, 455, 1989.

†† *Kingsley v. Hendrickson,* 135 S. Ct. 2466, 2473, 192 L. Ed. 2d 416, 426, 2015.

injury; any effort made by the officer to temper or to limit the amount of force; the severity of the security problem at issue; the threat reasonably perceived by the officer; and whether the plaintiff was actively resisting. We do not consider this list to be exclusive. We mention these factors only to illustrate the types of objective circumstances potentially relevant to a determination of excessive force.*

It is important to understand phrases such as "objectively reasonable" are legal terms of art, and cannot be understood to have the meaning they might have in ordinary conversation. For example, media stories covering prosecutorial investigatory reports in the shooting death of a 12-year-old boy by a Ohio police officer, seized on that phrase to suggest that the prosecutor found the shooting to be "reasonable."† Instead, the prosecutor was specifically required to use that phrase to describe the legal evaluation conducted.

While plaintiffs in § 1983 and Bivens cases may dislike the broad protections of the concept of the qualified immunity, the public policy justifications for it have long been accepted. Official immunity developed hundreds of years ago based upon two mutually dependent rationales: (1) the injustice, particularly in the absence of bad faith, of penalizing an officer for performing those acts of his job which require use of physical force and individual discretion; and (2) "the danger that the threat of such liability would deter his willingness to execute his office with the decisiveness and the judgment required by the public good."‡ In a society that expects the government to actively work to protect the individual's safety and individual's property rights against those who would wrongfully harm either, society's defenders, the police must be confident that if they carry out their duties in conformance with existing laws, rules, and policies, the government that employs them will protect them.

The media have reported that the family of Michael Brown has filed a § 1983 civil suit against the City of Ferguson, Missouri.§ If that case proceeds, a federal jury will eventually be asked to decide, if whether by a preponderance of the evidence, the City of Ferguson, Missouri was aware of, and deliberately indifferent to, obvious consequences of that city's policy or custom, which resulted in the shooting death of Michael

---

* *Kingsley v. Hendrickson*, 135 S. Ct. 2466, 2473, 192 L. Ed. 2d 416, 426, 2015.
† Graham, David, Yet Another Report Excuses Police in Tamir Rice's Death. The Atlantic. November 12, 2015. http://www.theatlantic.com/politics/archive/2015/11/report-vindicates-police-in-tamir-rices-death/415731/
‡ Ibid.
§ Robert Patrick, St. Louis federal judge dismisses several counts of Brown family lawsuit, *St. Louis Post-Dispatch*, July 14, 2015; Matt Pearce, Michael Brown's family sues Ferguson, Mo., for wrongful death. *Los Angeles Times*, April 23, 2015.

Brown. If the jury answers that question in the affirmative, the family of Michael Brown may be awarded money damages from the City of Ferguson. Just as importantly, the jury will have identified those specific acts which municipalities must recognize and change, effectively notifying all cities and police officers of those policies and procedures that must be changed to comply with the requirements of the constitution.

☐ Conclusion

If Michael Brown's family wins their § 1983 civil suit against the City of Ferguson, Missouri, many will be left with the impression that the Department of Justice report was wrong, and Darren Wilson escaped justice when prosecutors failed to prosecute him. The law is not that simple, however. Decisions by juries in civil suits are only a finding of financial liability, and cannot be compared to a legal determination of criminal guilt, whether under state law or § 242.

For both police officers, and those sitting in judgment of police officers, it can never be forgotten that the law is not emotional: it is analytical. An arrest should never devolve into an officer's irrational fear response, or a vengeful rage. At the same time, when reviewing an officer's conduct for criminal or civil liability, the standard cannot be emotional. The criminal law requires proof beyond a reasonable doubt of every component of a crime as that crime is written, not as the crime may be generally perceived. It is incumbent upon all citizens of the United States to do more than call the police for law enforcement service and judge the police for the manner of providing that law enforcement service. Americans should make an effort to understand the laws, as least generally, that dictate how an officer performs his duties and the protections accorded to him by the law for performing those duties within the permitted parameters. Real choices about changing the law require understanding it. Learning to differentiate between permitted and prohibited use of force is an important step in eliminating injustices perpetrated by law enforcement officers.

CHAPTER

Psychological and Social Factors in the Use of Force

Jodie Beeson

☐ Introduction

Psychologists have played a role in the selection of law enforcement recruits since the early 1900s. One of the first uses of psychology in police selection occurred in 1917 with the use of the Stanford-Binet Intelligence Scale in the pre-employment screening of potential candidates (Terman et al., 1917). Since that time, the use of psychological principles and police psychologists has steadily increased. Psychologists have addressed issues in the field of law enforcement and the health of law enforcement professionals from many directions.

By the 1960s, issues such as corruption, racial bias, coercion, and inappropriate use of force became key concerns in the field of psychology. In 1965, funding was made available by the Law Enforcement Assistance Administration to improve the services delivered by law enforcement professionals and to reduce corruption and abuse of power. By the 1970s, the use of pre-employment personality tests to assess the fitness of a candidate became a widespread practice. In 1973, the Police Task Force Report of the National Commission on Criminal Justice Standards and Goals recommended that all law enforcement agencies enlist help from those in the behavioral sciences to address issues in law enforcement (Bartol, 1996).

While the impact of excessive use of force by law enforcement professionals is great, the frequency of events where excessive use of force occurs are fortunately rare. Currently, psychologists approach the issue of excess use of force by law enforcement professionals from many angles. A law enforcement candidate's appropriateness for a law enforcement career is assessed with pre-employment screening for personality traits that may contribute to overly aggressive approaches to conflict and critical situations. In addition to pre-employment screening, various approaches to understanding excessive use of force by law enforcement professionals have been researched. Those areas include; the social learning process of officers during the career span, the impact of police culture on decision-making in critical instances, the cognitive decision-making process of officers in the line of duty, and the effects of intensity and stress on the behavior of law enforcement professionals in citizen interactions.

☐ Personality and Individual Characteristics

Understanding what officer characteristics are associated with instances of an excessive use of force is central to devising pre-employment screening protocols and post-employment policies to reduce the occurrence of inappropriate uses of force. In a study, police psychologists were asks to identify individual characteristics common among the officers they treated in association with an inappropriate use of force. The psychologists identified the following elements (Scrivner, 1994):

- Personality disorders including lack of empathy, narcissism, and antisocial disorders

- Individuals with early career issues such as impulsiveness, impressionability, low tolerance for frustration, and need for strong supervision

- Officers who utilized a more dominant policing style and were sensitive to challenges and provocation

- Individuals who were experiencing major life events such as divorce or a change in job situation or status

The use of pre-employment screening is the first step in reducing incidences of excessive use of force by law enforcement professionals. Pre-employment screening is used to identify individuals who may be at increased risk for aggressive or inappropriate behavior prior to employment. There is no widespread standardized process for the pre-employment screening of law enforcement officer candidates. Each agency constructs an independent screening process. While some agencies utilize an extensive battery of physical, cognitive, psychological tests, interviews, background checks, and polygraph tests prior to making hiring decisions, others make hiring decisions based on less information. Typically, larger agencies have more rigorous screening procedures. The following personality assessments are frequently used to make hiring decisions (Detrick and Chibnall, 2013; Surrette et al., 2003; Twersky-Glasner, 2005):

- Minnesota Multiphasic Personality Inventory 2—revised Form (MMPI-2-RF)

- Revised NEO Personality Inventory (NEO PI-R)

- California Personality Inventory (CPI)

- Edwards Personal Preference Schedule (EPPS)

- Big Five Inventory (BFI)

- Inwald Personality Inventory (IPI)

In an effort to evaluate the usefulness personality traits to predicted job performance in law enforcement officers, a study based on the big five personality traits as measured by the BFI as well as a measure of attitude and age, was conducted (Sanders, 2008) The BFI evaluates for the presence of five major personality traits. The five personality traits are the following:

- Extroversion

- Neuroticism

- Agreeableness

- Conscientiousness

- Openness

Generally, traits such as conscientiousness and extroversion are highly related to satisfactory job performance, while neuroticism may be associated with unsatisfactory job performance. For the study, satisfactory job performance was measured according to the following characteristics:

- Job knowledge

- Quality of work

- Cooperation

- Responsibility

- Initiative

- Quantity of work

- Dependability and

- Interaction with public

However, in the analysis of law enforcement officers, the association between these personality traits and satisfactory job performance was not a strong predictor of satisfactory performance. The age of the officer and his/her attitude toward the job were stronger predictors of performance quality.

One of the most commonly used assessments is the MMPI-2-RF. The MMPI-2-RF consists of scores on multiple personality scales. In a study of law enforcement officers that had passed pre-employment screening, the scales that related to personality traits associate with the excessive use of force are: thought dysfunction (disordered thinking), persecutory ideation (feeling misunderstood or blamed), and stress/worry (anxious apprehension or preoccupation with disappointment) (Ben-porath and Tellegen, 2011; Tarescavage et al., 2014; Tarescavage et al., 2015). Of those traits, thought dysfunction was the only trait that was significantly correlated with a higher risk for the use of excessive force. Thought dysfunction is characterized by disordered or unusual thought patterns. A person with thought dysfunction may not perceive or interpret events accurately (Alan et al., 2014). For example, an officer with thought dysfunction may perceive an interaction with a citizen as threatening, even if objective evidence would indicate otherwise.

In another study, a comparison of personality between candidates who were not recommended for hire, those who were considered to be "marginal" upon hire, and those who were recommended for hire (Fischler, 2004). The candidates who were not recommended for hire exhibited higher levels of unusual or disordered thinking, obsessive thinking, suspiciousness, impulsivity, aggressiveness, hostility, cynicism, alcoholism, and other traits indicating instability or psychological problems. When a comparison of candidates who were recommended for hire with candidates that were deemed marginal upon hire; the candidates that were recommended for hire experienced lower levels of sustained serious complaints. A factor analysis in the study identifies three basic groups of officer characteristics based on scores from their personality assessments:

- Well adjusted, agreeable, and possessing a high work ethic

- Antisocial, impulsiveness, and alcohol problems

- Disordered (unusual) thinking and suspiciousness

Individuals who scored higher in the disordered thinking factor had higher levels of sustained complaints. This can likely be attributed to an officer's inability to properly assess situations and respond accordingly as well as a tendency to assess a situation as more negative than objective reality would indicate.

☐ The Impact of Social Factors on Use of Force Decisions

Social Learning Theory

Social learning is a theory first proposed by Albert Bandura in 1971 that learning takes place through social modeling. In his experiment, he modeled aggressive behavior with a doll, Bobo, in front of children. He then allowed those children to play with the doll and observed their behavior. The children witnessing the aggressive behavior exhibited more violent behavior toward the doll than the children who had not witnessed this modeling (Bandura, 1971). In order for social learning to take place, following four conditions must be met:

- Attention: the learner must observe the behavior and the behavior must capture the learner's attention over all other stimuli

- Retention: the learner must distinctly remember the behavior and have the mental ability to rehearse the behavior

- Reproduction: the learner must be able to perform and practice the behavior

- Motivation: the learner must be motivated to perform the behavior

Differential Association Theory

Differential association theory is a social theory that suggests that deviant behaviors occur in social environments with close social groups. When individuals are exposed to groups that are exclusive and deviant behaviors are widely accepted and reinforced in a group where acceptance is highly desired, a motivation for social learning is created. In the case of police officers, the police subculture may create an environment where social learning paired with differential association may create the perfect stage for the development of behaviors that lead to an excessive use of force (Burgess and Akers, 2015; Chappell and Piquero, 2004; Maskaly and Donner, 2015).

Research indicates that attitudes toward deviant behavior in law enforcement are influenced by the subculture of the group and that it is necessary to "override" those behaviors with training to change the normative attitudes of the group (Chappell and Piquero, 2004). Law enforcement professionals may be particularly vulnerable to this type of social learning due to the awareness of the risk of death associated with working in law enforcement.

Terror Management Theory

Coping with the constant threat of mortality is referred to as terror management (Maxfield et al., 2014). In an individual with healthy psychological adaptive skills many strategies are utilized to address the anxiety associated with high-risk occupations. Those strategies may include cultural perspectives, social attachments, religion, cognitive reappraisal, and humor. Cognitive reappraisal is the regulation of thought processes to reduce anxiety by restructuring one's appraisal of a threat situation. For example, an officer may recognize the threat of mortality, but decide that he or she is extremely unlikely to face that event due to high levels of professional proficiency. One coping mechanism that persons associated with law enforcement professionals often recognize is the use of humor and even black humor to address stressful working environments. The use of humor to deal with stressful conditions allows for individuals to reframe conditions in order to relieve the tension created by an emotional closeness to the situation. The use of humor is also associated with social bonding (Long and Greenwood, 2013; Rowe and Regehr, 2010; Wilkins, 2014).

In the absence of effective strategies to cope with the threat of mortality, law enforcement officers may resort to maladaptive strategies, experience increased anxiety, and potentially develop a psychological dysfunction that would increase the risk for using excessive force (Maxfield et al., 2014). In a condition where the salience of the presence of the threat of mortality is particularly high, individuals are more likely to respond in a more punitive and more defensive manner.

Integrating Social Theories

Maskaly and Donner propose the integration of terror management theory and social learning theory to understand instances where officers use deadly force against unarmed individuals. This integration of theories is used to explain cases such as the shooting of Tamir Rice on November 22, 2014 in Cleveland, Ohio. Six days prior to that event an officer was killed in the line of duty in Akron, Ohio. The death of the officer in close geographic proximity may have increased the officer's awareness of the threat of mortality. If the subculture in the department was favorable toward authoritarian and aggressive reactions to threats, the officers may be more likely to utilize a more aggressive approach to ambiguous situations than at other times (Maskaly and Donner, 2015).

☐ Cognitive Decision-Making Factors

In a perfect world, law enforcement officers would make decisions regarding the level of force that should be used in any given situation according to a clear set of objective criteria. Officers are instructed to use deadly force only in situations where there is not another reasonable option. Many officers receive extensive training in tactical decision making. Yet, in practice, the decision to use force is not always made in an objective manner. There are many factors that influence the cognitive decision-making processes of an officer in the line of duty. In a meta-analysis of 44 analyses regarding event characteristics and factors where a use of force decision was made, specific characteristics fell into four categories: encounter characteristics, suspect characteristics, officer characteristics, and community characteristics (Bolger, 2014).

Encounter Characteristics

Encounter characteristics are factors that relate to the interchange between the officer and/or officers at the time when a decision was made on the level of force to be used. Of the four sets of characteristics, the characteristics of the encounter had the highest effect on the level of force used. The significant factors associated with an increased level of force were the following:

- Offense seriousness

- Suspect resistance during the course of an arrest of suspect

- Level of conflict at scene

- Number of officers at scene

Of those factors, the level of resistance of the suspect had the greatest impact on the level of force decision, followed by whether or not the encounter occurred during the course of an arrest. Interestingly, the presence of a weapon was not a significant factor.

Suspect Characteristics

Suspect characteristics are characteristics of the suspect that were evident at the time of the encounter. The following factors had a significant effect on the level of force used:

- Suspect race

- Suspect sex

- Suspect demeanor

- Suspect social class

- Suspect intoxication

Of the above listed factors, the demeanor of a suspect was by far the factor that had the greatest impact on the level of force used. This is logical, as there would be a greater need to use force in a situation where the suspect was uncooperative or out of control. The sex and the race of the suspect were significant factors in most studies.

Officer Characteristics

Officer characteristics relate to the officer most directly related to the suspect in the encounter. The only factor associated with a direction in the level of force used in an encounter was sex. Female officers were less likely to use force.

Community Characteristics

The factors related to community characteristics included in the study were: economy, racial makeup of community, and the crime rate in the community. None of these characteristics had a significant influence on the decision regarding the level of force used.

The Impact of Emotional Factors and Anxiety

In a society where television shows and YouTube videos about law enforcement officers are so prevalent, there is a tendency for citizens to overestimate their understanding of the emotional and cognitively demanding situations law enforcements officers are in while making decisions regarding the use of force. While watching videos taken by bystanders during a police encounter, it would seem that all of the pertinent information is available right there on the monitor. However, there are several factors that would impact the officer's ability to make a clear decision that are not apparent from a video. Decisions are made through cognitive processes in the frontal lobe of the brain. This is a process that occurs throughout one's waking hours without much awareness of the process. However, when an individual has other processes running at the same time, decision-making processes have to share the available cognitive resources. Other processes can include distractions, emotions, anxiety, or any other process that would use cognitive resources.

In a study, designed to evaluate the effect of anxiety on performance while shooting a gun during a simulation exercise (Nieuwenhuys et al., 2012), participants were exposed to situations where either a suspect with a gun would appear or a suspect without a gun would appear. If the suspect had a gun, the participant was to shoot at the suspect. If the suspect did not have a gun, the participant was to shoot at a black square. The participants were also presented with a high-anxiety situation and a low-anxiety situation. In the high-anxiety situation, a "blow-back" gun would shoot plastic pellets at the participant's feet if they did not shoot an armed suspect on time. In the low-anxiety situation the suspect would shoot back on the video, but the participant would receive no physical punishment.

The results of the study clearly indicated that the correct decision on whether or not to shoot a subject based on whether they were armed or not, the time to make a decision, and accuracy of shooting were all effected by the high-anxiety condition. Participants were more likely to shoot an unarmed suspect and take less time to decide whether to shoot or not in the high-anxiety condition. The accuracy was slightly lower in the high-anxiety condition.

In a phenomenological study of police academy cadets, cadets were placed in a variety of reality-based training scenarios that were both physically and emotionally taxing. The cadets were then asked to report on their experiences (Broomé, 2011). The results indicated that, while the scenarios were simulated, they each experienced physiological, emotional, and cognitive reactions to the simulated events. In more stressful events, participants experienced "flight, fight, posture, and freeze" reactions to the events in the simulation. These are typical parasympathetic nervous system responses humans and animals exhibit when exposed to perceived or actual danger. Their responses became more automated and less complex when exposed to high-intensity situations. The study indicates that officers involved in an actual encounter most likely experience the same symptoms and that their responses may be more automatic and less capable of distinguishing nuances in situations.

Working memory is also a factor in officers' decision-making processes regarding the decision to shoot or not to shoot, based on whether a suspect has a weapon or a nonthreatening object such as a cell phone. One study found that participants with lower working memory capacities tended to make more wrong decisions in both conditions. This effect was enhanced when either negative emotions or heightened arousal was factored into the equation (Kleider et al., 2010).

The aforementioned studies illustrate the limitations of the cognitive processes necessary for decision making under intense, ambiguous situations. This presents definite implications for training officers. While most officers receive tactical training and training regarding the ethics and policies of training, these studies indicate that this approach would not change an officer's ability to respond appropriately in a high-intensity situation. Practice and rehearsal can improve the ability to function in high-intensity situations. While practice and rehearsal are not practical solutions for such high-impact low-frequency events, simulation trainings may offer an answer. In Canada, researchers studied the effects of using simulated exercises to recreate the physical and emotional intensity of real-world use of force incidents (Armstrong et al., 2014). Research also supports situational awareness (SA) training as an effective approach to improving an officer's ability to make decisions in high-intensity situations. SA training utilizes the technology of virtual reality to create and manipulate simulated environments and situations that would be similar to the environment an officer would face in the line of duty. The benefit of virtual reality is that the simulation can be stopped and restarted on demand to allow for reflection and input by trainers (Saus et al., 2006). With the chance to break the scenarios into different parts, participants become more aware of how different responses change the entire scenario. Benefits of this training include increased awareness of the factors leading up to a use of force incident and the ability to practice reacting under stressful circumstances.

□ Conclusion

The issues relating to the use of force by law enforcement professionals are complicated and require input from many disciplines. Personality psychology offers insights to the selection of police officer candidates with the intellectual and psychological stability and the qualities that are best suited for the work required of a law enforcement professional. Social psychology and the theories of social learning, differential association, and terror management offer insights into the socialization and learning of law enforcement officers after employment and initial training that may influence an individual officer's ability to make appropriate decisions regarding the use of force. Cognitive psychology offers insight to the decision-making processes and the limits of officers in making decisions in high-intensity situations, as well as training approaches to improve the cognitive performance of officers. Together, these insights offer pieces to the puzzle of addressing issues related to the problem of excessive use of force by law enforcement professionals, while understanding the absolute necessity for an officer to act in a manner that reduces risk for officers while on duty.

☐ References

Alan F. F., Bolinskey, P. K., Levak, R. W., and David, S. N. 2014. *Psychological Assessment with the MMPI-2/MMPI-2-RF* (Third Edition). Abingdon: Routledge.

Armstrong, J., Clare, J., and Plecas, D. 2014. Monitoring the impact of scenario-based use-of-force simulations on police heart rate. *Evaluating the Royal Canadian Mounted Police Skills Refresher Program*, 15(1), 51–59.

Bandura, A. 1971. *Social Learning Theory*. Englewood Cliffs, New Jersey: Prentice-Hall. Doi:10.1111/j.1460-2466.1978.tb01621.x.

Bartol, C. R. 1996. Police psychology: Then, now and beyond. *Criminal Justice and Behavior*, 23(1), 70–89.

Ben-Porath, Y. S. and Tellegen, A. 2011. *Manual for Administration, Scoring, and Interpretation*. Minneapolis: University of Minnesota Press.

Bolger, P. C. 2014. Just following orders: A meta-analysis of the correlates of American police officer use of force decisions. *American Journal of Criminal Justice*, 40, 466–492. Doi:10.1007/s12103-014-9278-y

Broomé, R. E. 2011. An empathetic psychological perspective of police deadly force training. *Journal of Phenomenological Psychology*, 42(2), 137–156. Doi:10.1163/156916211X599735.

Burgess, R. L. and Akers, R. L. 2015. A differential association-reinforcement theory of criminal behavior. *Social Problems*, 14(2), 128–147.

Chappell, A. T. and Piquero, A. R. 2004. Applying social learning theory to police misconduct. *Deviant Behavior*, 25(December 2013), 89–108. Doi:10.1080/01639620490251642.

Detrick, P. and Chibnall, J. T. 2013. Revised NEO personality inventory normative data for police officer selection. *Psychological Services*, 10(4), 372–377. Doi:10.1037/a0031800.

Fischler, G. L. 2004. Identifying psychological predictors of police officer integrity problems. Community Oriented Policing Services (COPS) Office of the United States Department of Justice (US DOJ) CFDA No. 16.710, "Creating a Culture of Integrity."

Kleider, H. M., Parrot, D. J., and King, T. Z. 2010. Shooting behaviour: How working memory and negative emotionality influence police officer shoot decisions. *Applied Cognitive Psychology*, 24(5), 707–717. Doi:10.1002/acp.

Long, C. R. and Greenwood, D. N. 2013. Joking in the face of death: A terror management approach to humor production. *Humor*, 26(4), 493–509. Doi:10.1515/humor-2013-0012.

Maskaly, J. and Donner, C. M. 2015. A theoretical integration of social learning theory with terror management theory: Towards an explanation of police shootings of unarmed suspects. *American Journal of Criminal Justice*, 40(2), 205–224. Doi:10.1007/s12103-015-9293-7.

Maxfield, M., John, S., and Pyszczynski, T. 2014. A terror management perspective on the role of death-related anxiety in psychological dysfunction. *The Humanistic Psychologist*, 42(1), 35–53. Doi:10.1080/08873267.2012.732155.

Nieuwenhuys, A., Savelsbergh, G. J. P., and Oudejans, R. R. D. 2012. Shoot or don't shoot? Why police officers are more inclined to shoot when they are anxious. *Emotion*, 12(4), 827–833. Doi:10.1037/a0025699.

Rowe, A. and Regehr, C. 2010. Whatever gets you through today: An examination of cynical humor among emergency service professionals. *Journal of Loss and Trauma*, 15(5), 448–464. Doi:10.1080/15325024.2010.507661.

Sanders, B. A. 2008. Using personality traits to predict police officer performance. *Policing: An International Journal of Police Strategies and Management*, 31(1), 129–147.

Saus, E.-R., Johnsen, B. H., Eid, J., Riisem, P. K., Andersen, R., and Thayer, J. F. 2006. The effect of brief situational awareness training in a police shooting simulator: An experimental study. *Military Psychology*, 18(sup3), S3–S21. Doi:10.1207/s15327876mp1803s_2.

Scrivner, E. M. 1994. The role of police psychology in controlling excessive force, 1, 30. Retrieved from https://books.google.com/books?hl=en&lr=&id=_VJF9QyA5SsC&pgis=1.

Surrette, M. A., Ebert, J. M., Willis, M. A., and Smallidge, T. M. 2003. Personality of law enforcement officials: A comparison of law enforcement officials' personality profiles based on size of community. *Public Personnel Management*, 32(2), 279–286.

Tarescavage, A. M., Corey, D. M., and Ben-Porath, Y. S. 2014. Minnesota multiphasic personality inventory-2-restructured form (MMPI-2-RF) predictors of police officer problem behavior. *Assessment*, 22(1), 116–132. Doi:10.1177/1073191114534885.

Tarescavage, A. M., Corey, D. M., Gupton, H. M., and Ben-Porath, Y. S. 2015. Criterion validity and practical utility of the Minnesota multiphasic personality inventory-2-restructured form (MMPI–2–RF) in assessments of police officer candidates. *Journal of Personality Assessment*, 97(4), 382–394. Doi:10.1080/00223891.2014.995800.

Terman, L. M., Otis, A. S., Dickson, V., Hubbard, O. S., Norton, J. K., Howard, L., and Cassingham, C. C. 1917. A trial of mental and pedagogical tests in a civil service examination for policemen and firemen. *Journal of Applied Psychology*, 1(1), 17–29.

Twersky-Glasner, A. 2005. Police personality: What is it and why are they like that? *Journal of Police and Criminal Psychology*, 20(1), 56–67. Doi:10.1007/BF02806707.

Wilkins, J. 2014. The use of cognitive reappraisal and humour as coping strategies for bullied nurses. *International Journal of Nursing Practice*, 20, 283–292. Doi:10.1111/ijn.12146.

Police Violence, Public Response
The Public Gets What It Tolerates

Carolyn Speer Schmidt

☐ **Police Violence, Public Response:
The Public Gets What it Tolerates**

The United States is a representative democracy where the will of the people indirectly but eventually finds its voice in public policy. This tie between what "the people" want and what they get is real and is supported by what scholars call a "living constitution" along with a dynamic legal landscape. In the years since the Industrial Revolution in the United States, the subsequent growth of urban areas, and the establishment of a professional police force, public opinion has grown in importance. In the last several decades, and in particular recently in light of the events flowing from the Ferguson unrest of 2014, it has become clear that the public and political response to police violence are intimately linked. Ultimately, it comes down to how police violence, and any public violence that might happen as a result, is perceived by the middle and upper classes in the United States, especially as represented by older, better-educated, white voters. In fact, it is this group, and not necessarily the groups most directly impacted by police violence, that has the most political power to effect change in the country. When the larger society views police violence as justified, the political response is muted or nonexistent. But when the violence offends established middle class social norms, politicians are more likely to respond with public statements, policy initiatives, or other responses that will bring real change to communities.

The issue of police violence is one that has been with the United States for well over 100 years. Called alternatively "police brutality," "police violence," and "use of force," the general concept has remained the same throughout the years:

> The relationship between police perpetrators and their victims has remained roughly the same. Like criminal suspects generally, victims of police brutality were mainly poor and working class, often immigrants or newcomers to the city. Jews and other southeastern Europeans were common complainants at the turn of the century, while African Americans and Latinos gradually replaced them by the mid-twentieth century. The overrepresentation of these groups was not just a result of economic and demographic trends; it was also aggravated by racial tensions and bias ... Such conflicts were usually between police and lower class immigrants or African Americans, but on occasion—as in the clashes between police and antiwar demonstrators in the 1960s—they also flowed upward (Johnson, 2003: pp. 3–4).

The excessive use of police violence has been an important research area in the United States for many decades. Writing in 1970, Gamson and McEvoy called police violence an accepted norm in the United States where for many, "there is apparently a thin blue line between order and chaos. Breach it and untold furies lie beyond. The police require unconditional support when they are in combat; sins are understandable and forgivable when they occur in the stress of battle" (Gamson and McEvoy, 1970: p. 98). Three decades later, Ross found that while people do not condone "excessive" police violence, what actually constitutes excessive varies by person, and in fact most people do not tend to see any police violence as being excessive (Ross, 2000).

The issue of police treatment of civilians is more complicated than the specific instance of police violence. According to the Pew Research Center, few Americans now believe the police treat different racial and ethnic groups equally, with most Americans believing that racial minorities are treated less well by the police. Only 30% of Americans believe that officers are held accountable when police exhibit misconduct, and 70% of African Americans believe that police departments do a poor job of punishing police misconduct. This issue becomes particularly stark with regard to the treatment of Americans by race/ethnic group. Overall, 32% of Americans believe the police do an "excellent" or "good" job at treating all Americans equally. Only 10% of African Americans hold that opinion. The issue of the use of force makes a particularly striking example of how these two group of Americans differ: 41% of whites believe the police use the "right amount" of force for each situation whereas only 6% of African American hold the same view (Pew Research Center, 2014a, b).

On every measure, there is a stark difference between how African Americans view the police and how whites do. Even in the case of local policing, where most Americans express "at least a fair amount of confidence ... [that] forces avoid using excessive force and treats blacks and whites equally," there remains significant racial divides in opinion (Pew Research Center 2014a, b, para. 2). Overall, whites are twice more likely to believe the police treat different racial groups equally than are African Americans, and the number of African Americans who have "very little" confidence in the police has increased from 34% in 2009 to 46% in 2014. Police departments' use of military style equipment is of particular concern to African Americans, with 68% having very little or no confidence in the police's ability to use these resources appropriately; 60% of whites have a great deal or "fair" amount of confidence that these resources are being used appropriately by the police (Pew Research Center, 2014a, b).

These stark differences in opinion are likely due to the very different experiences subgroups of Americans have when coming into contact with the police. Taking a historical view of police violence, Johnson finds that excessive use of police force and police brutality has consistently impacted racial and ethnic minorities and the working class disproportionately (Johnson, 2003). Gabrielson et al. point out the problem has become markedly more noticeable in recent years, and today, "[y]oung black males ... [are] at a far greater risk of being shot dead by police than their white counterparts" (Gabrielson et al., 2014, para. 1). The federal data are shocking: between 2010 and 2012 there were 1217 deadly police shootings in the United States, with black males being 21 times more likely to be killed at the hands of the police than are white men. For blacks between the ages of 15 and 19 the rate of death was 31.17 per million. Whites died at the rate of 1.47 per million in that same time frame. To put it in perspective, ProPublica calculated how many whites would be killed if they were the victims of police violence at the same rate: 185 additional deaths over the 2-year period would make the rates equal (Gabrielson et al., 2014).

Unfortunately, the nature of recordkeeping makes getting complete data for deaths by police action impossible in the United States. The FBI (Federal Bureau of Investigation) statistics provide the minimum count for these deaths, because reporting is voluntary. There are 17,000 police departments in the country, and several of them have never filed reports regarding police shootings and other uses of force. Other departments have filed reports for some years and not for others. Departments in the state of Florida, for example, have not filed reports since 1997. Yet even with the incomplete data available to researchers, "the disparity between black and white teenage boys'" chances of being killed at the hands of the police is so significant that it the rates are clearly not an artifact of the poor recordkeeping (Gabrielson et al. (2014, para. 11). Regardless of the age of the victim, the vast majority of police officers involved in violence of this kind are white officers, although slightly more than 10% of this violence is committed by African American officers. Many of those who were killed by police between 2010 and 2012 were fleeing or resisting arrest, and a disproportionate number of these killed for this reason were African American. There is no wonder that the data between the views held by African Americans and whites is so vastly different. Their experiences are very different as well.

Clearly, then, most of those killed by police are engaged in formal interactions with law enforcement. Those people who live in high-crime neighborhoods or who are otherwise exposed to crime at a rate that is higher than that for the larger society tend to have more negative views of the police, and those people who come into formal contact with law enforcement in any capacity are significantly more likely to have negative views of the police than do those whose contact remains informal. Those with no actual contact with the police have the most positive view of them. Being the victim of a crime is especially likely to lead to a negative view of the police, regardless of race or ethnicity (U.S. Department of Justice, 2003). Given these data, it comes as no particular surprise that 76% of African Americans see problems with the United States justice system with regard to racial issues and law enforcement while only 33% of whites hold the same view (Pew Research Center, 2015a, b). Disturbingly, Pew polling indicates that a majority of African Americans anticipate relations between the police and minorities to worsen in the future.

These statistics may not seem particularly surprising post Ferguson. Statistics such as these have been regularly discussed on the media, but what remains a question is why such strong opinions on the part of African Americans appear to have had so little impact on public policy. To understand this problem, it is important to understand voting rates in the United States. The "voting rate" is the measure of the number of voters as a proportion of the overall number of people in a particular population or subpopulation in a community. Historically, voting rates in the United States are well below those in other countries with free and fair elections. While many reasons for this trend in the United States have been posited, generally political scientists agree that the nature of the two-party system combined with relative social stability combine to give the United States such low voting rates. For example, in 1978, only 48.9% of eligible voters participated in the national election, and while the statistics bounced around slightly over the years, the general trend was toward lower participation over time. In 2014, only 41.9% of the eligible voting population participated in the election (File, 2015).

The full impact of American voting rates does not come into focus until the numbers are broken down by race and ethnicity. Since voting was expanded to include African American men after the Civil War and then to include women in the early twentieth century, whites have voted at higher rates than any other racial or ethnic category in almost every national election. In the last 30 years, only the 2008 and 2012 presidential elections, both of which had Barack Obama on the ballot, saw blacks vote at a higher rate than whites, and even in those years, the rates were very close with about 70% of the eligible African American voting population voting in each year. But in previous presidential election years whites outvoted African Americans by approximately 10 percentage points, and outvoted Hispanics and other racial minorities at rates that ranged between 15 and 20 percentage points (United States Elections Project, 2015). Other measures of social status and class are also significant in this discussion. Across all federal elections in the last 30 years, eligible voters over age 60 are significantly more likely to vote than any other age category, and vote at rates that are 30 percentage points higher than eligible voters 18–29 years of age. Similarly, voters with a postgraduate education outvote those with less than a high school education by 25 percentage points (United States Elections Project, 2015).

Taken together, then, we find that whites are almost always more likely to vote than are African Americans in the United States, but further, those people who are younger, less well educated, and a member of a minority are significantly less likely to vote than are those who are older, better educated, and white (United States Elections Project, 2015). That is, precisely the same people who have higher rates of formal interactions with law enforcement, more negative views of law enforcement, and higher rates of death at the hands of law enforcement are those who are statistically least likely to vote and therefore least likely to have the ability to impact public policy in the direction of their views. And while voting is technically within the grasp of most non-felon American citizens, in reality such things as distrust of government and a feeling of nonrepresentation means that minorities in general, and poorer members of minority communities specifically are least likely to connect voting behavior with public policy results.

As a consequence, police violence has historically been met with occasional acts of public violence such as rioting. As Conyers argued in 1981, "[t]he evidence shows that unequal treatment in the criminal justice system and political powerlessness add to the anger of those who riot. The evidence shows that a pattern of police violence makes a city prone to a riot. And clearly, undeniably, and unequivocally, the evidence shows that police brutality precipitates riots" (Conyers, 1981: p. 5). In fact, while the current social climate links racial and ethnic minorities with these public acts of discontent, historically speaking, the link between police violence and public rioting is more a function of groups feeling powerless than it is about race specifically. It may seem surprising, but:

> Large-scale disorder and riots were commonplace in the American cities of the mid-1800s. The business elites and middle class of American cities increasingly feared for the stability of society .... Elites' fear of riots and civil disorder, combined with their interest in protecting property, prompted the desire for a mechanism to control those seen as threats to the stability of society. Their fear of the dangerous classes was the major factor motivating the establishment of city police departments (Holmes and Smith, 2008: pp. 21–2).

Labor unrest in the late nineteenth and early twentieth centuries tended to be bloody conflicts between first the Pinkertons who broke 77 strikes between 1869 and 1892 (as in the Battle of the Monongahela in 1892) and later the police and even the military as in the Pullman strike in 1894 (Ladd and Rickman, 1998; Websdale, 2001). The political response to these conflicts tended to rest solely on the middle and upper classes' perception of the reasonableness of the violence overall, and the police violence specifically. When the strikers were seen as being in the right, society tended to side with them, and when they were seen as being in the wrong, society sided with the police, regardless the amount of violence used to quell riots or break strikes. Police violence surrounding labor unrest was not the only concern at this time; "[m]iddle class, native-born whites became increasingly incensed by frequent corruption scandals and accounts of brutality, motivating a political movement to reform the police" (Holmes and Smith, 2008: p. 23).

Similarly, with the 1968 Chicago riots, the nation was "horrified" to watch the violence unfold each night on the news, and as with the labor unrest from decades before, the anger and feelings of disaffectedness came not from racial minorities (Grossman, 2012). Instead, the 1968 Chicago riots involved discontented young people of a variety of social, racial, and ethnic backgrounds. Yet, in retrospect, it is striking to look at the language of the officers who were engaged in the Chicago police violence: Len Colsky, a former Chicago police officer recalls, "Things became very confusing. I remember well in 1968 where it was hard to distinguish the hippies from the criminals; they all looked the same. And the ones who were causing trouble and promising to do damage looked and dressed like hippies" (as quoted in Kusch, 2004). That is, the very act of political protest served to signal to police that all discontented young people they encountered protesting were potential physical threats and should legitimately be treated with a violent response. Certainly, similar arguments were made about the enraged crowds protesting in Ferguson, Missouri in 2014, and because the crowds were disproportionately African American, the visual signaling of "otherness" from the police was equally as clear.

Of course what links riots such as the ones in Chicago in 1968 and in Ferguson in 2014 was the extensive media coverage of the events. In contrast, the Stonewall riots of 1969, which were important enough to have sparked the gay rights movement, were treated at the time as a local issue and were covered only on the local news in New York City (Rothman, 2015). Clearly, not all acts of police or public violence are treated equally by the media. Yet there is absolutely no question that media coverage of these events is a critically important element in their political impact. On the one hand, when media accounts emphasize social violence and the risk that police officers face in the line of duty, regular media reporting of these events can "promote public and official tolerance for police violence" (Hirschfield, 2010). Ross (2000) argues there is no clear reason why some acts of police violence excite media attention while others do not. In fact,

> The majority of incidents of police violence receive little media attention. Unless the case is "sensational," articles about police abuse are often relegated to the "metro" or back portion of the newspaper and/or given little space, becoming almost lost among other, well-covered "news events" (e.g., entertainment and sports). On the other hand, those events that receive considerable media attention do raise people's concerns regarding controversial police practices which, in turn, may lead to public unrest (Ross, 2000: p. 120).

But when the media does cover acts of police violence, and when it does so in a critical manner, it can directly impact both public opinion of the events and public policy changes that can flow from them.

The 2014 Ferguson unrest illustrates this point very well. Images of police in military gear excited the public imagination across the country, not only in the small Missouri town where the violence was taking place. As the unrest continued throughout the late summer, and national media attention grew, local and national politicians, and even the President of the United States spoke out against racial injustices in Ferguson. Without the media attention, it is difficult to believe there would have been a Justice Department investigation and a finding that the protestors' free speech rights had been violated by the local police (Bora, 2015). But what is notable from the perspective of the political impact of and response to police violence in Ferguson is that prior to the 2014 unrest, "the uneasy relationship between its growing black population and its mostly white police force barely registered in local headlines" (Breitbart, 2015). It certainly never broke into the national consciousness before the police donned military gear and the population protested in the streets.

Over a year after the initial Ferguson unrest, Breitbart (2015) reported that the political landscape for the town changed. The city has a new police chief, city manager, and municipal judge, and they are all African Americans. The city council has three African American members as well. And even though a U.S. Justice Department report found no grounds to prosecute the officer involved in the shooting of Michael Brown, it was so critical of Ferguson's municipal government and police department that most of the top leaders resigned as a result. The police department is now wearing body cameras as well, and it is initiating a community policing effort to get the police out of their patrol cars and onto the city streets. These are real changes, both in policy and in action, and they came as a direct result of the events surrounding the unrest and the police violence that precipitated it. But again, none of these outcomes would have been likely had the media coverage been lacking.

It is also important to note that while there have been some positive changes in Ferguson, the racial divide regarding the events is still stark. For example, 23% of whites thought the decision not to charge Darren Wilson, the officer who shot Michael Brown, was the wrong decision, and 80% of African Americans thought so. African Americans were also more likely to believe that race was a factor in that decision (Pew Research Center, 2014a, b). Yet public opinion is changing in ways that might be surprising. Today, 59% of Americans overall believe that the United States needs to continue to make changes in order to achieve racial equality between African Americans and whites. And while there is a racial divide on the issue, with 86% of African Americans having that view and 53% of whites agreeing, in 2014 only 39% of whites held that view (Pew Research Center, 2015a, b). This is a likely consequence of the Ferguson unrest and the media coverage that accompanied it.

Within the current political realities of the United States, what whites, and particularly older and better educated whites believe about issues has real policy implications for the country. Because whites vote at higher rates and more regularly than any other racial or ethnic group in the United States, changing their opinion is more likely to impact public policy than even the strengthening of opinions in the African American and other racial minority communities. As Ross argued, "Although it is difficult to determine whether police violence will increase in the future, unless we break the pattern of apathy, obedience/deference to authority, and sublimated frustration, which is periodically vented through protest only after a sufficient number of events have taken place, we cannot realistically lessen and control police violence. If the public, government, and law enforcement officials remain complacent, it may well be business as usual for police departments, the government, and citizens alike" (Ross, 2000: p. 126).

Public opinion has the power to influence political policies that go well beyond police violence as well and reach into many other aspects of the criminal justice system. For example, in Ferguson attention is now being paid to municipal fines and the crippling cost they bring on the poor community in the city. Across the country, public opinion has driven crime policies in many arenas and in the last few decades these policies have contributed to a huge growth in the prison population (Hetey and Eberhardt, 2014). Today, the United States has the highest incarceration rates in the world with a rate of 500 prisoners per 100,000 residents (Tsai and Scommenga, 2012). This explosion in the prison population has had a particular impact on young (20–34) African American men, 11.4% of whom are incarcerated (Tsai and Scommenga, 2012).

Clearly, many issues surrounding police violence and other aspects of the criminal justice system are not "fair." But in a representative democracy like the one that functions in the United States, "fairness" is measured largely by those who make policies, and those people are chosen by those who vote. The dangerous irony is that when groups of people become, or feel that they have become, socially disenfranchised and marginalized, they are less likely to vote, and are left with avenues of political self-expression that are likely to be less effective and more violent. At this point, those groups lose much of the ability to control their own message and are left with the whims of a media that sometimes covers police violence and a community's response to it, and sometimes does not. Even when these issues break onto the national agenda through sufficient media coverage, the nature of the coverage itself has an outsized impact on how the larger society will judge the event. When, as happened in the last few decades, the middle and upper classes perceive these events are threatening the peace and safety of the community, these voters respond by supporting increasingly oppressive policies that have the ultimate impact of making matters worse for those communities that have resorted to nonstandard modes of political expression. It is possible, in the wake of the Ferguson unrest, however, that media coverage has changed enough to impact the consciousness of the larger community. It has long been clear that African Americans and other racial minorities have seen significant social problems that whites have not. But the most recent data indicate the opinion gap between the races may be closing in the United States.

☐ References

Bora, K. June 30, 2015. Ferguson riots: Justice department says police response violated citizens' rights. *International Business Times*. Retrieved from http://www.ibtimes.com

Breitbart N. August 8, 2015. Ferguson still recovering from riots one year after Michael Brown's death. *Breitbart News*. Retrieved from http://www.breitbart.com/

Conyers, J. 1981. Police violence and riots. *The Black Scholar*, 12(1), 2–5. Retrieved from http://www.jstor.org/stable/41067960

File, T. 2015. Who votes? Congressional Elections and the American Electorate: 1978–2014. U.S. Department of Commerce Economics and Statistics Administration, U.S. Census Bureau.

Gabrielson, R., Jones, R. and Sagara, E. October 10, 2014. *Deadly Force, in Black and White*. ProPublica. Retrieved from http://www.propublica.org/

Gamson, W. and McEvoy, J. 1970. Police violence and its public support. *The Annals of the American Academy of Political and Social Science*, 391, 97–110. Retrieved from http://www.jstor.org/stable/1040028

Grossman, R. April 29, 2012. For five days and nights in August 1968, Chicago was a war zone. *Chicago Tribune*. Retrieved from http://articles.chicagotribune.com

Hetey, R. and Eberhardt, J. August 5, 2014. Racial disparities in incarceration increase acceptance of punitive policies. *Psychological Science*. Retrieved from http://pss.sagepub.com

Hirschfield, P. May 2010. Legitimating police violence: Newspaper narratives of deadly force. *Theoretical Criminology*, 14(2), 155–182.

Holmes, M. and Smith, B. 2008. *Race and Police Brutality: Roots of an Urban Dilemma*. New York: State University of New York Press.

Johnson, M. 2003. *Street Justice: A History of Police Violence in New York City*. Boston: Beacon Press.

Ladd, K. and Rickman, G. 1998. The Pullman Strike: Chicago 1894. *Kansas Heritage*. Retrieved from http://www.kansasheritage.org/pullman/

Kusch, F. 2004. *Battleground Chicago: The Police and the 1968 Democratic National Convention*. Retrieved from http://www.press.uchicago.edu/Misc/Chicago/465036.html

Ross, J. I. 2000. *Making News of Police Violence: A Comparative Study of Toronto and New York City.* Westport, Connecticut: Praeger.

Rothman, L. September 25, 2015. How TIME covered the Stonewall riots. Retrieved from http://time.com/4042859/stonewall-inn-history-time/

Pew Research Center. August 25, 2014a. Few say police forces nationally do well in treating races equally. Retrieved from http://www.people-press.org/

Pew Research Center. December 8, 2014b. Sharp racial divisions in reactions to Brown, Garner decisions. Retrieved from http://www.people-press.org/

Pew Research Center. April 28, 2015a. Divide eetween blacks and whites on police runs deep. Retrieved from http://www.people-press.org/

Pew Research Center. August 5, 2015b. Across racial lines, more say nation needs to make changes to achieve racial equality. Retrieved from http://www.people-press.org/

Tsai, T. and Scommenga, P. 2012. U.S. has world's highest incarceration rate. *Population Reference Bureau.* Retrieved from http://www.prb.org/

United States Elections Project. 2015. Voter turnout demographics. Retrieved from http://www.electproject.org/home/voter-turnout/demographics

U.S. Department of Justice. 2003. Factors that influence public opinion of the police. Research for Practice. NCJ 197925.

Websdale, N. 2001. *Policing the Poor: From Slave Plantation to Public Housing.* Boston: Northeastern University Press.

Prevention and Training

Vladimir A. Sergevnin and Darrell L. Ross

Incidents where excess force is used are preventable. There are many preventative measures that reduce the risks of excessive force, such as preemployment screening, education/training, appropriate psychological and social support services, and organizational structure. This chapter will discuss the various approaches used in law enforcement to reduce the excess use of force.

☐ Introduction

Law enforcement personnel are constantly striving to promote and preserve a positive, moral image of their departments to the public they are sworn to serve and protect in democratic society. However, the community's perception is influenced by multiple variables and use of force has one of the strongest impacts on it. Continuously honorable and conscientious police work of hundreds of thousands of law enforcement officers across the nation can be discredited by one story of excessive force.

Due to several recent controversial use of force incidents, use of force phenomena has moved into the public, academic, and even political spotlight. A sharp rise in rulings nationwide that law enforcement officers violated departmental policies and procedures in using deadly force has prompted a review of use of force prevention and training concepts. The training concept has to be reassessed in a broader scale from recruitment and hiring to discretion and ethical dimensions. Nationwide efforts have been undertaken by law enforcement institutions to confront and reevaluate the use of force paradigm. While the scope of existing publications addresses many use of force prevention and training issues, a comprehensive law enforcement approach has not been available. The importance of a comprehensive and coordinated use of force prevention and training approach for law enforcement officers, along with other proactive and reactive measures such as recruitment, hiring, and enhanced policies and protocols, are emphasized in this chapter. This chapter is an exploratory assessment and an overview of the nature and extent of the law enforcement prevention and training response to use of force issues.

☐ Challenges of Use of Force Training

To clearly understand the role of use of force training in today's world and to ensure that basic recruit training and in-service training use of force realistic programs are the rule rather than the exception, training planners and administrators should start from comprehensive job task analysis efforts to define exactly what use of force training is in place and how much of it is needed. For many peace officer standards and training (POST) units, this has proved to be a very challenging task.

For decades, professional and research associations, such as the International Association of Chiefs of Police (IACP), the Police Executive Research Forum (PERF), the Police Officers Safety Association (POSA), have tried to provide standards and guidelines for use of force training. Despite these efforts police practitioners and academicians believe that use of force training is inadequate or insufficient (IACP, 2012; PERF, 2015).

The traditional model of use of force training for decades has been focused on perfecting technical skills and their speedy application. The majority of training materials and certification tests are focused predominantly on these two parameters. On the other hand, developing a knowledge base and skills in the rational, emotional, and psychological dimensions of use of force was not a priority for agencies and training institutions. When law enforcement trainers are dealing with police tools and weapons, a paramilitary training philosophy seems applicable and valid. Unsatisfactory training or an absence of training is considered by the courts to be organizational negligence and deliberate indifference (Birzer, 2003; Martinelli, 2015). In response, majority of law enforcement agencies and well-recognized training institutions have developed a variety of approaches.

☐ Recruiting, Selecting, and Evaluating

Use of force by law enforcement officers is not an isolated issue in law enforcement actions. It is connected to all dimensions of police work, management, and organization. When law enforcement administrators have concerns about the use of force practices in the agency it is imperative to approach this critical issue as a whole phenomenon and start with recruitment, selection, and retaining personnel who will use powers and force appropriately and will minimize any potential problems with community on these grounds. The new era of policing requires appropriate strategies and methods of recruitment and selection.

For several decades' personnel practices emphasized enforcement capabilities of the candidates, recruiting and selecting futures warriors on the American streets. The recent trend toward a general community policing approach has transformed the focus to service-related profiles of the recruits. This remarkable change initiated the slow movement toward recruiting and selecting to law enforcement agencies individuals predisposed to solving social and psychological problems among members of the community applying intellectual and emotional skills rather than crime fighters armed with the traditional technical skills of police work. Because of that according to PERF's recent discussion on use of force training, it is imperative for the police agency to provide potential applicants with a sense of how the department sees its mission ("warriors vs. guardians"). Articulating respect to human life and rights, concern to democratic ideals and liberties, partnership, collaboration, and commitment to communities provides a proactive message and clear expectations of the desired qualities to potential candidates.

Some researchers have concluded that a relatively small number of officers are responsible for the majority of complaints about excessive force (Lersch and Mieczowski, 1996; Brandl et al., 2001). Multiple studies have tried to identify some personal characteristics of individuals predisposed to use excessive force and use them as a basis for selection decisions. There are several factors that should be taken into account in developing recruitment and selection strategies which have some proven indications in possible prevention of excessive use of force.

Increased educational standards are viewed as one of the factors which can contribute to diminish potential problems with excessive use of force. Law enforcement and correctional institutions across the nation through selection standards are searching for college-educated candidates under the assumption that college-educated officers will not use force extensively. Early research on the relationship between education and use of excessive force in particular, has produced inconsistent and conflicting findings (Brandl et al., 2001). Current research indicates that only officers receiving the benefit of a 4-year degree were significantly less likely to rely on physical forms of force in their daily encounters with the public but simply attending college is not enough when it comes to less reliance on physical force. In this respect, actually completing a 4-year program is most beneficial (Paoline and Terrill, 2007; McElvain and Kposova, 2008; Rydberg and Terrill, 2010, Paoline et al., 2015).

Research has shown that female officers are less likely to use physical force and are more effective communicators. Additionally, female officers are better in de-escalating and defusing potential use of force confrontations before those encounters turn deadly. A 2002 study by the National Center for Women and Policing illuminates the differences in the way that men and women perform their policing duties and found that the male officer is several times more likely than his female counterpart to have an allegation of excessive force or to be named in a complaint of excessive force (Longsway, 2002) These findings highlight the importance of hiring women as a strategy for reducing problems of excessive force.

It is beneficial for a law enforcement agency to conduct a self-assessment and determine the agency's recruitment, selection, and retention goals in the use of force area. The essential step in designing an effective recruitment and selection process is to determine whether the agency has incorporated any specific tools to select individuals which are conservative in application of force and generate fewer complaints from the public. The purpose is to identify competencies during selection such as problem solving and judgment, stress reaction, integrity, self-control, visual acuity, perception, and emotional health which assist in selecting satisfactory candidates. Law enforcement recruits need to display a strong service orientation that fosters goodwill within their communities (Stanard and Associates, 2015). In addition, an agency should conduct a community assessment to determine citizens' view, criticism, or support toward use of force practices. It is important to determine the "degree" of community satisfaction with use of force policies and practices.

A proactive system of personnel reviews and follow-up can address individual problems in use of force practices and can reduce the need for a law enforcement agency to deal with excessive use of force investigations. Evaluations enable supervisors to meet with an officer, discuss his or her use of force practice, and formally record frequency, strengths, weaknesses, complaints, and community expectations. Early identification of unacceptable behavior in use of force application should be communicated to the officer along with offering assistance, additional training, and thorough explanation of agency and community expectations. Citizen complaints on officers' use of lethal and LTL (less than lethal) forces is a critical problem. Citizen complaint reports is one of several ways researchers can obtain data on the use of force issue (Ross, 2005). According to Hickman, during 2002 large state and local law enforcement agencies, representing 5% of agencies and 59% of officers, received a total of 26,556 citizen complaints about police use of force: about a third of all force complaints were not sustained (34%), 25% were unfounded, 23% resulted in officers being exonerated, and 8% were sustained; and using sustained force complaints as an indicator of excessive force resulted in an estimate of about 2000 incident of police use of excessive force among large agencies in 2002 (Hickman, 2006).

Early intervention systems (EISs) (also known as early warning programs) have been used by many agencies for more than two decades, and the recent evolution of EIS is having increased success in addressing and preventing various personnel issues, including excessive use of force. According to Alpert and Walker (2000), the three main elements of an early warning system are: identification of officers with problematic behavior; intervention to correct the problem; and follow-up with those who have received assistance. The early intervention system (EIS) is a key element in the strategy to address at-risk behavior. Once an officer exceeds an established number of risk factors (such as reaching the top percentage of officers who have used force or received a complaint within a certain time period, officer-involved shooting, preset number of complaints, etc.), an early intervention assessment will be conducted. This kind of assessment may also be conducted at the discretion of a supervisor. The rationale behind EIS is to intervene and provide assistance by identifying possible problematic behaviors before they result in actions that are contrary to the use of force policy and protocol, and ethical standards. Identification of problematic officers leads to the development of various types of assistance or mentoring programs focused on the critical area. The Miami-Dade police department has established one of the earliest EIS in the United States, and demonstrated some success. Its approach clearly indicates that since 1981 the number of officers identified for excessive use of force has substantially diminished (Rothlein, 2015). While the CALEA (The Commission on Accreditation for Law Enforcement Agencies) guidelines provide a basic outline of what an EIS or early warning system should entail, at this time, there are no consistent standards for identifying problem officers.

☐ Training Framework and Limitations

Failing to provide ongoing training to officers commensurate with their duties can increase the agency's exposure to civil liability. In *City of Canton v. Harris* (1989) the U.S. Supreme Court ruled that a local government can be held liable under § 1983 when it fails to provide training to agency personnel. Failure to train may serve as a basis for § 1983 liability when the failure amounts to "deliberate indifference" to the rights of persons with whom the police may come into contact. The degree of fault is fundamentally related to the policy requirement noted in *Monell v. New York Department of Social Services* (1978). Moreover, *Monell* will not be satisfied by a mere allegation that a training program represents a policy for which the city is responsible. The Supreme Court stated that "in light of the duties assigned to specific officers or employees, the need for more or different training is so obvious, and the inadequacy so likely to result in the violation of constitutional rights, the policy makers of the city can reasonably be said to have been deliberately indifferent to the need." Addressing the need for use of force training in light of these cases on a regular basis places an agency in compliance with the *Canton* decision. In addition the Court's decision in *Graham v. Connor* (1989) should be reviewed with officers and supervisors in order for agency personnel to understand what criteria the court establishes and uses to examine a claim of excessive force and further explain how the decision integrates into the agency's force policy. To protect an agency from potential claims of a failure to train its use-of-force training system, and to increase officer safety and survival in the field, a pattern of providing documented training needs to be developed. Annually, a total of 32–40 h of training is recommended which can be presented in 8–10 h blocks each quarter, or a 16- to 18-h block semiannually. This assists in maintaining officer certification, competency, and proficiency. Additionally the *Canton* decision outlines that officers should "receive ongoing 'realistic training' commensurate to their job tasks." Thus training that is designed to replicate field stressor variables and environmental conditions confirms the court's admonition to provide realistic training. Providing realistic training on a frequent basis will place the agency in compliance with the *Canton* decision and assures the best method of developing and retaining skills that improves officer safety. Police administrators confirmed that training needed to be focused on situations based in reality as opposed to training that simply provides certification (IACP, 2012).

Some court cases stress the necessity for dynamic scenario-based training to provide imitation of a level of threat and improve use of force decision making. For example, in *Zuchel v. City and County of Denver, Colorado (1993)*, the court ruled that simply watching a film regarding lethal force decision making did not meet realistic training objectives and held the agency liable for failing to train (Sergevnin and Ross, 2012). At the same time many police administrators questioned if training had become ineffective because it was based on what an officer could not do rather than a positive format focused on what an officer could do or in fact must do with respect to the use of force (IACP, 2012).

Present day use of force training utilizes adult learning principles as well as problem-based training, role-play, lectures, and demonstrations to provide the recruits and officers with the skills needed to be successful in critical situations. The use of force training was traditionally developed, directed but also limited by the POST boards, agency administrators, the financial abilities of an agency, and various state statutes. POST agencies update basic training curriculum infrequently, agency administrators are not interested in increasing training hours thus the amount of training does not match the need, and state statues are not "catching up" with new technological realities and law enforcement practices (Sergevnin and Ross, 2012).

Use of force training traditionally has been rather disjointed and technical skills oriented rather than decision-making focused. Officers learn the use of firearms, the Taser, baton, pepper spray, handcuffing, and others as isolated skills (Arnspiger and Bowers, 1996). Training focuses on the efficiency of an isolated element in the force spectrum gradually increasing general military-like aggressiveness of total use of force tools application.

Law enforcement trainers use the military-like methods to condition their personnel to overcome natural reluctance to use deadly force (Williams, 1999). Traditional training techniques are used to dehumanize "suspects." Instructors refer to suspects in various derogatory terms conditioning officers to think of suspects as less than human and who deserve the application of force (Williams, 1999; Wittie, 2011). This type of conditioning contradicts humanity ideals expressed in mission statements and helps to develop dangerous stereotypes which can lead officers to unnecessary force.

Computerized technological advances in scenario-based training present other new challenges: some smaller law enforcement agencies do not have funds to purchase rather expensive equipment. Those departments which got the machinery face other limitations such as the fact that officers are trained without real life stressors. Also various use of force training equipment does not allow enhancing communicating and de-escalating skills.

Recently many law enforcement administrators felt that due to negative public perception and fear of lawsuits, some officers were inadvertently being trained to return fire only when fired upon rather than using that force reasonably necessary to prevent injury or death (IACP, 2012).

☐ Training Models and Needs

Generally, law enforcement agencies around the nation are utilizing three types of use of force training: (a) basic training which focuses on common minimum standards of use of force and basic skills; (b) in-service training which is oriented on knowledge and skills updates, and (c) specialized training as a channel to develop and provide unique skills. Law enforcement administrators have noted that use of force recruit training is not sufficient and in-service training has not been validated in the same rigorous fashion as academy training, and that the level of accountability is far different for officers when approaching in-service training—as they do not fear failure or loss of job based on poor performance during these exercises (IACP, 2012).

Traditional models of use of force training rely on static repetitions of standard defensive tactics and techniques which can prepare officers to some degree to deal with resistance on the street (Ashley, 2003). According to Newstrom (1993), 40% of skills learned in training are transferred immediately; 25% remain after 6 months; and only 15% remain 1 year later. Roughly 20% of the critical skills needed to do a job are provided by training programs; 80% are learned on the job.

In the past, training was mainly focused on the development of isolated technical skills (such as firearms target practices and defensive tactics), rather than decision-making practice. This traditional approach generally dominates the use of force training realm in recruit training. According to a recent PERF national survey of 280 law enforcement agencies on current recruit training practices, the major segments are still firearms training (58 h) and defensive tactics (49 h), while use of force scenario-based training is only 24 h, communication skills—10 h, de-escalation—8 h, and crisis intervention—8 h. Similar distribution of training effort can be found in in-service training: firearms training 18% of training time, defensive tactics 13%, while use of force scenario-based training is only 9%, communication skills—5%, de-escalation—5%, and crisis intervention—9% (PERF, 2015). Traditional use of force model has substantial setbacks: focus on one of the element(s) of the possible situation, unrealistic "slow motion" or light impact techniques, no imitation of physical resistance, and unrealistic environment.

Since 2000, law enforcement agencies have started an active search for new training models. In 1999, the COPS office provided funding to PERF and the Reno (Nevada) police department to develop an alternative national model for training new officers that would incorporate community policing and problem-based learning techniques. The resulting police training officer (PTO) program addresses the traditional duties of policing in the context of specific neighborhood problems and includes several segments on the use of force. Many agencies are using the outlines of the PTO program to develop their own in-house programs adapted to their particular needs.

Recent demands in professionalizing law enforcement activities enlarged simulation training that utilizes the environment reconstruction approach to closely approximate actual confrontations, by creating model situations and allowing the trainee the use of near true intensity force. This method of training can enhance officers' behavior and develop realistic expectations regarding specific methods of use of force effectiveness, while enhancing officer abilities in actual physical confrontation. Many law enforcement administrators suggest that video and audio recordings should be used more routinely as tools to manage and train officers. Use of audio–video will allow first-line supervisors to critique use of tactics or communication meant to manage conflict (IACP, 2012).

Use of force training should reflect the needs of law enforcement agencies and individual police officers in pursuing the functional balance between institutional goals, the agency's current position, and personal expectations. The training needs has to be identified in such a way that it demonstrates the officer's comprehension and confidence level in the skill required, using the authorized techniques and equipment in accordance with agency policy. There are three major levels at which training needs should be identified: (a) at the state level; (b) at the agency level; and (c) at the individual level.

At the state level, use of force training needs analysis involving the POST boards acting as a sponsor in cooperation with the state law enforcement associations, and other stakeholders (such as basic training academies) to carry out training needs analysis. Training needs analysis often occurs as a result of political and mass media attention to certain downfalls (e.g., excessive use of force), new legislation, enhanced technology, and changes in law enforcement practices. Police training boards and police academies should be becoming increasingly proactive in recognizing the training needs through intensifying research efforts, organizing, updating, and evaluating use of force curriculum.

At the agency level, some police departments have strategies, which can be instrumental in the development of training needs. Clear objectives should be identified at this level. Outside consultants should be hired because most law enforcement administrators do not have the skills to identify training needs. The absence of an accurate system to update training needs often results in wasted resources by repeated training.

To ensure effective use of force policy implementation, training must address force decision-making review; proper application of physical control techniques; competency in using force tools, including all restraints, impact weapons, aerosols, conducted energy devices (CEDs), and all firearms; knowledge of medical assessment requirements and summoning emergency medical personnel; summoning back-up; summoning supervisory personnel; transportation protocols; report writing requirements, and conducting use of force investigations. Providing training on agency policy should be done on many levels: FTO (field training officer) program, roll call, firearms training, subject control training, and any use-of-force equipment training (i.e., handcuffs and other restraints, aerosols, CEDs, impact weapons, and other authorized equipment) (Sergevnin and Ross, 2012). Use of force training should also include frequent review of agency policy, state statutes, and federal guidelines concerning its application. According to Schlosser and Gahan (2015) the implications of the research findings suggest that officer training should emphasize ground control/ground fighting as a larger part of the training than the use of the baton. The use of the baton seems to be diminishing, and it could be conceivable that one day officers will no longer carry them. The use of OC (oleoresin capsicum) spray and the advent of Tasers could be what are affecting the minimal use of batons. Also, it is possible that the use of batons, even when appropriate, appears to be more aggressive, and officers are concerned about public opinion. Also, they suggest that the display of Tasers should be addressed through scenario-based training at a greater level at the same time some police administrators are concerned that too much technology and too many choices in weapons systems degraded an officer's operational awareness and slowed reaction times (IACP, 2012).

Addressing the individual level of training needs is crucial for the development of use of force training. Identification of individual training needs performance evaluation, current levels of skills measured against required levels of individual performance, changes of functions brought about as a result of in service training, individual plans of filling the gaps in skills, knowledge, and experience. Some law enforcement administrators are concerned that more training needed to be focused on communication and command presence. Often later in their careers, officers did not look prepared, while younger officers relied too much on physicality as opposed to using verbal tactics to de-escalate and mitigate confrontational situations (IACP, 2012).

According to Schlosser and Gahan (2015) officers who work for smaller departments should be provided more training with single officer arrest situations as they are less likely than larger departments to have back-up. Also, they stress that the importance of verbal tactics should continue to be emphasized as one of the most important training skills for law enforcement officers. Recent media headlines have been filled with upsetting stories of minorities allegedly suffering injuries, and even death at the hands of police officers. As a result, there has been a reactive trend to avoid using deadly force by officers and on training focused on how to de-escalate the use of deadly force. To prevent possible excessive use of force incidents and to provide better services to the communities the recruits will be serving, law enforcement agencies and training facilities are incorporating human relations training specifically focused on understanding the cultural patterns and characteristics of the respective communities. Wrong perceptions and biases can contribute to excessive force applications toward minority and immigrant representatives. Including members of the community in the training process could have beneficial results.

Police officers interact with very diverse populations under unlimited variations of circumstances. These present strong challenges for use of force training. Therefore, officers need to be trained and practice rapid adjustment to accommodate a variety of different members of the public in a wide spectrum of circumstances. Communication skills training has to focus on balancing between gaining control (and compliance) and expressing empathy and maintaining public trust. Language problems may also represent an important training need. Communication skills should be an integral component of a comprehensive use-of-force training program.

To train law enforcement officers to make a decision to use lethal force is one of the most critical areas of police training. That is why firearms training is prevalent in the block of the use of force segment of basic training. According to the PERF survey the median number of hours for firearms training is 58 h nationwide in basic training, 93% of agencies provide in-service firearms training, and from all in-service training hours 18% go to firearm training (PERF, 2015). Most police departments only have firearms training about two times a year, averaging less than 15 h annually (Grossi, 2011). As a rule use of lethal training consist of classroom instruction of deadly force policy and procedures and other legal topics, shooting range practices, and scenario and simulator exercises. The courts continually indicated that firearms training needs to be relevant, realistic, and regular.

Shooting range exercises vary greatly among academies and agencies. Most state legislatures enacted acts requiring all law enforcement officers annually to complete a handgun qualification course from curricula based upon model standards established by the state POST. Recruits and officers usually practice target shooting with and without taking cover at a distance of 3, 7, 15, 25 yards, etc. Shooting range course are limited in scope. This course evaluates an officer's ability to perform basic shooting skills in a controlled setting and in a low-stress environment. Generally such exercises do not indicate whether officers have received recent, relevant, and realistic training necessary to perform their job. Police academy students qualify using a law enforcement handgun, duty belt, and holster as typically worn by patrol officers and issued or approved by their academy. Students must successfully qualify to pass the firearms unit exam. Academies maintain a record of the qualification attempt(s) of recruits.

There is a national consensus that the key to improving police-recruit training is to move from traditional classroom and static target shooting to more hands-on instruction by increasing the use of scenario-based training hours. Scenario based firearms training is going beyond the static and often limited range training models. Scenario-based training is giving an officer experience and exposure to real-life experience without facing the risk of deadly situations or serious injury. Use of force simulators provide an important training tool which allows transferring trained judgment and firearms skills from the classroom and the firing range to actual field encounters. Simulator training should not replace range training but is designed for stress intensity training, that can assist officers in improving their assessment/perception abilities and actions (Ross et al., 2012a).

Use of force training programs succeed if the law enforcement officers can demonstrate that they have mastered the skills taught. They should be able to apply the skills learned in the training facility or at an agency, and their performance must improve in a way that benefits the police department. Training evaluation is a systematic analysis of data that helps law enforcement administrators make an informed decision. The current practice is limited to evaluation of the single training event.

☐ Conclusion

Use of force prevention and training is the only panacea that leads to professionalism in this critical area of policing. Such an emphasis requires a change to the system that currently exists, with police administrators at all levels taking a greater responsibility for specific use of force prevention and training development according to modern standards. The focus for law enforcement administrators in use of force training should be promoting a need for all officers to receive training on the agency's use of force policy and procedures on a regular basis. Police departments are responsible to make sure that use of force training is consistent with policies and protocols. Law enforcement agencies should become learning institutions, capable of developing use of force training programs suited to their departmental and individual demands, continuously assessing training challenges and approaches.

☐ Cases cited

City of Canton, Ohio v. Harris, 1989. 489 U.S. 378, 109 S. Ct. 1197.
Graham v. Connor, 1989. 490 U.S. 386, 109 S. Ct. 18651989.
Monell v. New York Department of Social Services, 1978. 436 U.S. 658.
Zuchel v. City and County of Denver, Colorado, 1993. 997 F. 2d 730, 7th Cir.

☐ References

Alpert, G.P. and Walker, S. 2000. Police accountability and early warning systems: Developing policies and programs. *Justice Research and Policy*, 2(2), 59–72.

Arnspiger, B. and Bowers, G.A. 1996. Integrated use-of-force training program. Available online: https://www2.fbi.gov/publications/leb/1996/nov961.txt. Retrieved: November 26, 2015.

Ashley, S. 2003. Use of force simulation training: The key to risk reduction. Available online: http://www.sashley.com/SimulationTraining.htm. Retrieved: February 6, 2003.

Birzer, M. 2003. Learning theory as it applies to police training. In: M. Palmiotto and M. Dantzker (Eds.), *Policing and Training Issues* (pp. 89–114). Upper Saddle River, New Jersey: Prentice-Hall.

Brandl, S., Stroshine, M.S. and Frank, J. 2001. Who are the complaint-prone officers? An examination of the relationship between police officers' attributes, arrest activity, assignment, and citizens' complaints about excessive force. *Journal of Criminal Justice*, 29(6), 521–529.

IACP. 2012. Emerging use of force issues. Balancing public and officer safety. *Report from the International Association of Chiefs of Police/COPS Office Use of Force Symposium*. Office of Community Oriented Policing Services, U.S. Department of Justice. Washington, DC. Online: http://www.theiacp.org/portals/0/pdfs/emerginguseofforceissues041612.pdf.

Grossi, D. 2011. Police firearms training: How often should you be shooting? Available online: https://www.policeone.com/training/articles/3738401-Police-firearms-training-How-often-should-you-be-shooting/. Retrieved: November 5, 2015.

Hickman, M. 2006. Citizen complaints about police use of force. Bureau of Justice Statistics (BJS), US Department of Justice, Office of Justice Programs, USA. Available online: http://www.ncjrs.gov/App/publications/abstract.aspx?ID=210296.

Lersch, K.M. and Mieczowski, T. 1996. Who are the problem-prone officers? An analysis of citizen complaints. *American Journal of Police*, 15, 23–44.

Longsway, K. 2002. Men, women, and police excessive force: A tale of two genders. National Center for Women and Policing, April 2002.

Martinelli, T. 2015. Unconstitutional policing: Part 3—a failure to train is compensable liability. *Police Chief*, November 2015. http://www.policechiefmagazine.org/magazine/index.cfm?fuseaction=display&article_id=3947&issue_id=112015

McElvain, J. and Kposova, A. 2008. Police officer characteristics and the likelihood of using deadly force. *Criminal Justice and Behavior*, 35(4), pp. 505–521.

Newstrom, J. October 1993. Transfer of training. In: P.L. Caravaglia (Ed.). *How to Ensure Transfer of Training. Training and Development* (pp. 63–68). From http://arl.cni.org/training/ilcso/transfer.html. Retrieved November 26, 2002.

PERF. 2015. Re-engineering training on police use of force (August 2015). *Critical Issues in Policing Series*. Washington, DC: Police Executive Research Forum.

Paoline III, E. and Terrill, W. 2007. Police education, experience, and the use of force. *Criminal Justice and Behavior*, 34(2), 179–196.

Paoline III, E. A., Terrill, W. and Rossler M. T. 2015. Higher education, college degree major, and police occupational attitudes. *Journal of Criminal Justice Education*, 26(1), 49–73.

Rydberg, J. and W. Terrill. 2010. The effect of higher education on police behavior. *Police Quarterly*, 13(1), 92–120.

Ross, D., Murphy, R. and Hazlett, M. 2012a. Analyzing perceptions and misperceptions of police officers in lethal force virtual simulator scenarios. *Law Enforcement Executive Forum*, 12(3), 53–73.

Ross, D.L. 2005. A content analysis of the emerging trends in the use of nonlethal force research in policing. *Law Enforcement Executive Forum*, 5(1), 121–148.

Rothlein, S. 2015. Early intervention systems for law enforcement. *Public Agency Training Council*. Online: http://patc.com/weeklyarticles/intervention.shtml

Schlosser, M. and Gahan, M. 2015. Police use of force: A descriptive analysis of illinois police officers. *Law Enforcement Executive Forum*, 15(2), 1–12.

Sergevnin, V. and Ross, D. 2012. Police use-of-force policy and force training model: Best practice. *Law Enforcement Executive Forum*, 12(1), 139–146.

Stanard and Associates. 2015. *Public Safety Testing Products and Services Catalog*. Chicago, p. 3.

Walker, S. Milligan, S.O. and Berke, A. 2007. *Early Intervention Systems: A Guide for Law Enforcement Chief Executives*. Washington, DC: Police Executive Research Forum, U.S. Department of Justice, Office of Community Oriented Policing Services.

Williams, G.T. 1999. Reluctance to use deadly force. *FBI Law Enforcement Bulletin*, 68(10), 1.

Wittie, M. 2011. Police use of force. *PB & J*, 2(2). Online: http://www.wtamu.edu/webres/File/Academics/College%20of%20Education%20and%20Social%20Sciences/Department%20of%20Political%20Science%20and%20Criminal%20Justice/PBJ/2011/2n2_03Wittie.pdf.

dly force. The firearms evolution is traced from 1791, the era
econd Amendment to the present day. The third section con-
e civilian's military-authority and status. French considers that
esting outcome of the militarization of law enforcement is the
nding rank-status phenomenon. Larry French concludes with a
n of various recommendations from U.S. Supreme Court deci-
esidential Blue Ribbon Commissions, and legislation. The con-
lso reviews psychological factors and the mental suitability of
rcement personnel.

pter 6 "Racial Profiling: The Intersection of Race and Policing"
by Dr. Michael L. Birzer takes a critical look at racial profil-
chapter is divided into five categories: the introduction covers
ured history, the underpinning of race, and the second section
ly deals with racial profiling which is further subdivided into
l and affective, symbolic vehicle, nature of violation, norma-
rience, and race and place. The third section discusses solving a
problem with subsections on training, fostering mutual respect,
al motorist contacts, building and sustaining community coali-
mmunication and community oriented policing.

essor Birzer provides an excellent background on racism in
and the profiling of blacks and Hispanics in America. He pro-
iled cases of minorities receiving rude and abusive treatment
police. Dr. Birzer suggests that courtesy and a respectful treat-
inorities during police stops would go a long way in improving
des of blacks and Hispanics towards the police. There is ample
t racial profiling does occur and stopping someone based on
or ethical heritage is prejudicial. The police could solve many
oblems with minorities if they had legitimate reasons for stop-
providing an explanation on why people have been stopped.
seventh chapter "Understanding the Law of Police Uses of
rrest," was authored by Professor Alison Brown. This chapter
what law is in layman terms, so that a non-lawyer can compre-
t law is all about. A discussion of prosecuting excessive force
e criminal codes is thoroughly discussed. This section explains
mon-law is and how it led to statutory law. Also reviewed is the
e defense. The landmark case of *Tennessee v. Gardner* pertaining
of deadly force is carefully reviewed.

ssor Brown reviews the prosecution of excessive force under
v. This section discusses federal criminality for excessive force
arrest that arises from federal statutory law. The elements per-
federal law are explained. The 1983 federal statutory pertains
v enforcement officers while the Bivens cases refers to federal
ement officers. Both the 1983 law and Bivens are laws that

Conclusion

Michael J. Palmiotto

Use of force can be traced back to ancient times. Those in authority
whether formal or informal have used force to control the behavior of
their subjects. Formal governments or those not so formal governments
maintained control of the people through the use of force. History is
full of examples where either the military or some semi-military group
was authorized to subject the people of the state to fall in line to the
establishment.

Chapter 1 "Use of Force throughout History" has as a basis that
throughout most of history formal law enforcement agencies did not
exist. Even though formal law enforcement was nonexistent, order was
necessary to have a functioning state. Governments, whether sophisti-
cated or unsophisticated, maintain social control which may be associated with physical or coercive powers of those in authority.

Similar to today, early forms of policing in ancient times emphasized social and criminal control which can be traced to the family, tribe
or clan which assumed responsibility for the safety of their members.
The concept of "kin police" developed with the concept that an attack on

one member of the group was an attack on the entire group. The members of the group enforced the law which was often inhumane and retaliatory. This could be considered an early example of excessive use of force.

Policing traced to ancient Egypt had responsibilities similar to modern day. The major empires of the ancient world—Babylonians, Assyrians, Egyptians, Greeks, and Romans all had systems to maintain order, a major responsibility of policing to this day. The acts of violence can be traced to ancient times as well as to the early decades of the twenty-first century. Information on the maintaining of order during ancient times is somewhat sketchy and informal. Throughout history those in authority have used force against those below them in status, power, and authority.

Chapter 2 "Police Use of Force" reviews the controversial issues connected with the legitimate and illegitimate authority of the police to use force. The illegal or unacceptable or excessive use of force has often been referred to as police brutality. The use of force by the police can be defined as occurring "any time the police attempt to have citizens act in a certain way." Incidents of police use of excessive force have included beating civil rights protestors, deliberating kicking and choking someone while making arrests, and unprovoked use of deadly force when attempting to control riots and disturbances. There are situations in which individual officers, a group of officers, or a large number of officers within the police department, thus pervading the culture of an entire police department, may carry out acts of excessive force.

Incidents of the "use of excessive force" by police officers, or "police brutality" can be traced to early times in police history. Some forms of "police brutality" have also been referred to as the "third degree," a term that came into vogue during the early decades of the twentieth century and refers to excessive force during the questioning of suspects. Apparently, the term "first degree" means the arrest, the "second degree" the transportation to a place of confinement, and the "third degree" the interrogation, which frequently meant brutality.

The third degree does not occur to the extent as it did in the early decades of the twentieth century but it does occasionally occur. Excessive force occurs not only in poorly managed departments but also in well managed departments. Although use of force occurs in police–citizen contacts, it rarely occurs. The use of force or threat of force takes place in only one percent of police encounters.

Chapter 3 "Use of Deadly Force" explains and defines deadly force, described as force capable of causing serious bodily injury or death. The police can only use deadly force to save their lives or another person's life. The concept of deadly force can be traced to the middle ages in England when all felony crimes were punishable by death. Under this concept

---

it was not considered a serious offense fo who committed a felony. Under the Americ offense is first degree murder, the only fel penalty. When a police officer uses deadly citizen he is using power greater than a juc

The use of force and specifically deadl the police began arming themselves. It be ond decade of the twentieth century and is decades of the twenty-first century. Mo deadly force and stating when deadly forc use of deadly force when perceived by the tions and riots.

Chapter 4 "Nonlethal Weapons and Szde Yu reveals how nonlethal weapons a in use of police use of force against citiz gerous criminals daily, and when under attacker by any means possible. The use the police even if the criminal does not threat is imminent. The police need non discretion the officers may feel that nonl duing the offender without causing him police officer's life is not being threatene should be available as an alternative to ons means weapons that are not mean that nonlethal weapons cannot inflict f

The chapter "Militarization of th Armand French reveals how militariz by the police. French writes that part the type of equipment available to lav cally the increased firepower of mod undercurrent of racial/ethnic, sectariar ent in a complex multi-cultural envirc leads to the problem. Add the prolifer and assault weapons within the gene worsens. Although the United States h law enforcement, there exists a long h between the military and police enforc

Dr. French provides a brief hi connection from colonial days to our provides information on the role of tl ment. He also discusses the roles th cies, such as the F.B.I. and U.S. Marsh next section discussed by Professor F

cover cases when law is used by law enforcement officers to violate the rights of citizens. Law enforcement officers can be prosecuted for violating the civil rights of citizens.

Chapter 8 "Psychological and Social Factors in the Use of Force" was written by Dr. Jodie Beeson, a psychologist. She traces the role psychologists play in dealing with the police and the use of force back to the early 1900s. She reviews the 1960s, a period of turmoil when the role of the psychologist substantially increased. Federal governmental agencies were interested in professionalization of the police. Eventually, pre-employment tests to assess fitness of candidates became an acceptable practice. Dr. Beeson reviews personality and individual characteristics which could lead to excessive force. The impact of social factors on use of force decisions are discussed along with cognitive decision-making factors. This chapter provides a good overview as to why some police officers may be prone to use excessive force.

Dr. Carolyn Speer Schmidt authored Chapter 9 "Police Violence, Public Response: The Public Gets What It Tolerates." She advocates that the political impact of police violence can be proportioned to the larger societal view of violent acts being either reasonable or unreasonable. Public perception can be divided with whites tending to view police violence as justified and racial and ethnic minorities, especially African-Americans, viewing such acts as injustices. Since older, better educated whites have a higher rate of voting than younger less well-educated minorities, the impact of whites is greater on public policy in the United States.

The last chapter of this book "Prevention and Training," was written by Drs. Vladimir A. Sergevnin and Darrell L. Ross. The authors initiate their chapter with the idea that law enforcement personnel are constantly striving to promote and preserve a positive, moral image of their department. Due to controversial use of force incidents, the use of force phenomenon has moved into the public, academic, and even political spotlight. Nationwide efforts have been undertaken by law enforcement agencies to confront and reevaluate the use of force paradigm. Sergevin and Ross divide their chapter into several sections which they review. The sections include challenges of use of force training, recruiting, selecting, and evaluating training framework and limitations and training models and needs. The authors indicate that training should take place on three levels: the state level; the agency level; and at the individual level. These three levels are carefully explained.

The authors in their conclusion claim that use of force prevention and training may be the only approach to police professionalism. Further, all officers should be trained in their department's use of force policy and procedures. Police departments should become learning institutions in developing use of force training and prevention.

INDEX